**Keep It Short & Simple:
How to Give a Great Presentation**

By Aaron D. Anderson and David S. Leong

**Book design and illustrations by Glynn Brannan
Edited by Tara Courtland
Cover design by Marin Leong**

ISBN 978-0-9967998-1-2

ACKNOWLEDGEMENTS

We want to express our gratitude to Glynn Brannan and Tara Courtland for their tireless work and incredible professionalism in helping to pull this book together under a tight deadline.

Special thanks go to Marisa Guida for her outstanding contributions to an earlier version of this material and for her leadership in the Winning Presentations classes. Special thanks also to Marin Leong for her outstanding book cover design.

Thanks also to Darren LaCroix, Patricia Fripp, Craig Valentine, and Ed Tate, who inspire us through their teaching and coaching excellence.

We will also always be grateful to our students (both at the university and in countless businesses) who provide us with the opportunity to hone our craft and challenge us to reach beyond what we already know.

Last and most importantly – thank you Jennifer, Koa, Kai, and Zoey; Patti, Jesse, and Marin. You are our whole world.

CONTENTS

INTRODUCTION

ABOUT THIS BOOK

"Simple can be harder than complex.
You have to work hard to get your thinking clean to make it simple."
- Steve Jobs, Apple founder

This is a book about presentations. It shows you how to prepare, design, and deliver a great presentation. It also shows you how to create a speech but you'll make far more presentations in your life than you ever will speeches.

Presentation vs. Speech

What's the difference between a presentation and a speech? Some people use those words interchangeably but the difference is important. A speech is a presentation, but not all presentations are speeches.

A presentation is an activity in which someone shows, describes, or explains something to an audience. A presentation often uses visual aids and usually requires interaction on the part of an audience.

In the business world, you'll give presentations almost every day.

At work you'll constantly be making presentations to update your boss, lead a meeting, pitch an idea to management, or persuade your coworkers to invest time in a new idea. At many companies, presentations are how business gets done.

You'll give dozens of presentations every week and thousands every year in your personal and professional life.

You will give far fewer speeches (if any).

A speech is a formal address or discourse delivered to an audience. Examples of speeches include a keynote address, a coach addressing the team before a game, a commencement address, a eulogy, or a wedding toast. A speech is when you stand in front of an audience and speak to a group of people who listen but usually don't interact with you. A good speech can shape how people think and feel about a subject and perhaps even change their behavior. So can a good presentation.

This book shows you how to create and deliver both great presentations and great speeches. We focus on presentations first and speeches second because that's the order in which you will use both in your professional life. In the end, does it really matter if you use the word "presentation" or "speech?"

Let's put it this way: would you prefer it if your boss said "At today's meeting I want you to present some ideas about how we can save money" or "At today's meeting I want you to give you a speech about strategies for saving money?" Neither sounds like fun, but the word "speech" carries with it a level of formality and separation from your audience that is out of synch with today's fast paced and interactive work environment.

Regardless of whether you need to make a presentation or a speech, this book will give you the tools to do it well. The truth is, when you develop your presentation skills, your speaking skills improve as well.

Why Theatre?

A presentation is like a play: whether rehearsed or impromptu, it's an interaction between you and a live audience in real time.

Theatre is the only field that focuses on conveying stories and ideas by a live person in real time. Whether you're informally talking to a single person or formally presenting to a room full of thousands, knowing a few basic theatre skills will help you do better. These skills can help you present anything to anyone, anywhere.

We began our careers as (and continue to be) professional theatre artists. We have over 60 years of combined experience creating and presenting all kinds of stories to tens of thousands of people around the world in many different settings. Through years of additional experience working in business and healthcare and coaching from some of the most recognizable innovators in the field, we learned how to translate what we knew from theatre into simple exercises that anyone could do: how to outline any type of presentation; how to explain complex ideas to any audience; and how to design visuals or other aids so that the presentation fits into a clear and persuasive package.

It's a myth that some people are "natural" presenters and others are not. The art of giving a winning presentation or conducting an inspiring meeting is a discipline you have to learn.

Once you learn them, the skills are transferable to everything you do in your personal and professional life.

How to Use This Book

This is a practical guide. The easiest way to learn how to put together, rehearse, and deliver a winning presentation is to actually DO it. You can learn a lot about presenting just by reading through this book and thinking to yourself "Wow, yeah, I never thought about it like that" or "of course, that makes perfect sense!" But the best way to get the most out of this book is to work through creating, rehearsing, and delivering an actual presentation.

Each section will ask you specific questions about your next presentation. You can write in the book as you answer the questions or do each exercise, but we suggest putting your answers on sticky notes and sticking them in the relevant sections. This will allow you to change you answers, rephrase the wording, and move whole sections around whenever you want to. It will also allow you to put together as many presentations as you want whenever you want.

Why Short and Simple?

Look around you. In today's world, most communication is short and simple.

Traffic signs say simply: "Stop," "Do Not Enter," and "No Left Turn." In fact, many signs don't even have words: they have simple iconic images or symbols that convey the message universally.

Check your phone: it displays everything in a short and simple way. If you receive a text message that says "Brunch @12! CU there?" you understand with one quick glance.

Time and clarity are becoming more and more important in today's fast paced world. If you are asked to give a presentation at work, your boss might say something like: "Keep it short; just give me the 30-second version."

Decades ago in the not-too-distant past, the world moved at a slower pace. In the "good old days" your grandparents talked about, stores were closed on Sundays and families sat around the radio or television listening to or watching their favorite program together. It was normal for everyone to be away from their phones or otherwise out of touch for hours - even days - at a time. Can you imagine?

The world isn't like that anymore. Things now move at lightning speed - literally. The Internet keeps us closely connected (sometimes more than we'd like) and the new norm is that everyone is doing the work of many people. Your time is valuable, your coworkers' time is valuable, and your bosses want you to produce more and more. You might even communicate with your coworkers in the next room via email or text just to save time!

Nowadays, constant communication is so routine that you have to make special arrangements to be out of touch. Unless you block time off to spend an evening with friends, read a book, or watch a movie, odds are you're "on" all the time. This would have made your grandparents crazy. But guess what? The odds are you are totally comfortable with this pace. The world has changed! You are good at processing information in small bites while filling in the blanks.

So, if we're all used to living at this pace, why are we continually subjected to long and tedious reports and presentations that take valuable time away from our workday and make us want to throw darts at the presenter?

Why, if we're asked to give a presentation, is our default setting to open up a computer and start typing words onto slides and then, when presenting, to project those words on a screen and read them out loud?

What's happening is we're stuck with the notion that presentations are chunks of information delivered in an old-fashioned style of public address.

The worst advice about public speaking is also the most common: begin by telling them what you're going to tell them, tell it to them, and then end by telling them what you told them. Because why bore them with information once when you can bore them with it three times?

Great presentations are like a good book or movie. Even if you know what's going to happen (because you read the book jacket or review), you don't know HOW it's going to unfold. Just like a great movie, a great presentation keeps your audience on the edge of their seats. In order to keep your audience interested and engaged, you need to continue to surprise them.

The Solution: Short and Simple

One of the most important steps in preparing any presentation is being **CLEAR** about what you need to say. The easiest way to do this is to **distill your message down to its shortest, simplest form.**

For instance, before PhD candidates are allowed to begin writing their dissertations, most advisors make sure they can explain why their ideas are important to people outside their field. The purpose of this exercise is not to dumb down the science but simply to force them to make sure their ideas are clear before trying to write an entire book.

Another benefit to distilling an idea down to its shortest, simplest form is that **it's easier to add to a short presentation than it is to take away from a long one.** Designing a presentation that's short and simple (and then adding onto that) gives you the freedom to condense the longer version if something goes wrong and you find yourself running short on time.

And speaking of things going wrong, **short and simple presentations are much easier to remember** than long, complex ones. Crafting a short, clear message will simply make it easier for you to remember the main points of what you need to say.

HOW do you do that?
That's what this book is all about.

**A TRUE STORY OF THINGS GONE BAD TURNED GOOD
A CASE STUDY**

The CEO of a multinational corporation stood up to give her presentation. There was a lot on the line. An industrial accident had caused the government to propose new regulations that could potentially disrupt the whole company and everyone in the audience knew it.

Professional designers had spent weeks putting together a PowerPoint slide show to demonstrate the problem and lay out a new vision for the future of the company.

Then, just as the CEO rose to speak . . . someone tripped over a cord and unplugged the projector. It blinked off and then came back on after a moment but . . . where the slide show should have been there was now only a blue screen and the following message:

"Warming up . . . 20 minutes remaining . . . 19 minutes remaining . . ."

Panicked technicians rushed to the stage. The audience became restless. Should everyone just wait until the projector rebooted?

Some people began to grumble. Was this just another sign of a deeper failure of leadership? The entire meeting seemed on the verge of falling apart.

Luckily the CEO had worked to craft her message so she could overcome any problem quickly while still projecting personal presence and authenticity.

She knew what her goal was (to calm anxiety); what details were MOST important for her audience (that the company had a plan); and she had rehearsed how to instantly adjust to any mistake.

"It's okay everyone," she said calmly. "We tripped . . . but this company will not fall down."

The audience - a room full of bankers, lawyers and accountants - applauded. Her calm control of the situation subconsciously made everyone feel better about her leadership.

She continued with confidence, "I can talk to you with or without a projector, and we will thrive with or without new regulations. Here are the three most important things you need to know right now . . ."

She continued as if there had never been a problem. The projector started working again in the middle of her talk - and without missing a beat she skipped forward in the slide show to her current point.

By the end she had delivered her message so clearly and so successfully that few people could tell you exactly when the projector came back on. It didn't matter. Her presentation did everything she wanted it to do - and then some!

She turned a potentially disastrous moment into an inspirational one. In fact, it was so memorable, we kind of wish we had told her to unplug the projector deliberately.

She had the same presentation tools you are holding now. These tools helped her identify exactly what she needed to say and exactly how she needed to say it, and allowed her to instantly adjust to the unexpected, and to deliver her message clearly and concisely, with authenticity and passion.

PART 1
THE FIVE FUNDAMENTAL SKILLS

PART 1   SECTION 1

CLARIFY IT
THE IMPORTANCE OF PLANNING

BAD PLANS WASTE TIME

You read the assignment again hoping you misread it but . . . nope. Next week you have to present in class. So of course you get started right away. Just kidding! You put off working on it as long as you can . . . but eventually - days later - you get to work.

You open up PowerPoint on your computer and stare at the screen. How do you start? There is a lot of information to cover. How long do you have again? Wow! There's no way you'll be able to get to all that in. What facts should you cut? No time to worry about that now. You're behind schedule. Just crank it out!

You start filling slides with data. What order should it go in? How many slides can you use? Just to be safe, you make the font size smaller so you can add more facts on each slide.

Before you know it, presentation day is here. You know you have too many slides and you didn't have time to see how long it would take to say all that. But you figure you can just read a little faster if you have to. There is way is too much information for you to have memorized anything, but you plan to just read directly off the slides anyway, so no big deal. Of course that's boring, but everyone does it, right? At least soon it will all soon be over!

You volunteer to go last in the hope that if the class runs out of time the teacher might let you wait until next time! Or maybe you won't have to go at all!

As usual, everyone ahead of you takes longer than they were supposed to. By the time your turn comes around the whole class has been sitting and listening to boring presentations nonstop for nearly three hours. Everyone in class would rather kill themselves than listen to another presentation . . . and the class ends in a couple minutes. Surely the teacher will let you wait until next time.

But no! Your teacher turns to the class and says, "I know we've been here a long time and we're all very tired, but we only have one more presentation to go. We really need to finish these so we can move on to the next class topic. Let's all just stay a few extra minutes so we can hear Shannon's presentation."

Everyone groans but most people stay - grudgingly. This day was already long, and now it's even longer. Everyone looks at you. Every minute you talk is time away from their life outside class and they know it.

You swallow, click on your first slide and begin to read as fast as you can. Your presentation is too long and poorly organized. It's clear that no one is actually listening to you. You try not to think about how much you hate it when people waste your time as much as the look in their eyes says you are wasting theirs. But what else could you do?

YOU KNOW THAT NEXT TIME, YOU NEED A BETTER PLAN.

THE IMPORTANCE OF PLANNING

"To achieve great things, two things are needed; a plan, and not quite enough time."
- Leonard Bernstein, 20th century composer and conductor

Even though no one would ever tell their audience: "Here's big pile of facts. Figure it out for yourself," that's exactly how a lot of presentations are put together.

Lack of organization is most obvious when a presentation has to be shortened at the last minute. Ever heard a presenter say, "I just found out that I have less time than I thought so I'm going to have to talk faster?" How did that presentation go? The person might as well have said: "I'm disorganized and I have no idea what the most important part of my talk is to you but I'm going to plow forward anyway because I'm more concerned with my own panic than about wasting your time."

If you think you have to talk fast to get in all your information, it means you didn't filter your information well enough - you don't know what you can leave out. All facts are the same to a presenter who doesn't take time to figure out what facts are the most important for their audience.

The trick to having enough time is knowing what details are important and which ones can be left out if you need to.

What you need are some organizing principles: some ways of figuring out how to prioritize what you have to say. Once you do that, you can expand or contract your presentation to fit any time frame or audience expectation.

A good presenter can deliver memorable and effective presentations no matter how much - or how little - time they have.

Time Spent Now Saves Time Later

Whether you have been researching your topic for years or merely hours, there are always more facts than presentation time. This creates a problem: how do you get in all the facts you need in the little bit of time you have to present? And how do you know what facts you need in the first place? It may seem counterintuitive, but the more time you spend planning your presentation before you start, the more time you'll save in the end!

Too many people think of their presentation as a thing that can live on its own - as a document that is equally valid no matter who the audience is. This is a huge mistake. The most important part of planning any presentation is to start by giving some thought to your audience. The good news is that there is a quick and simple way to do this that will save you lots of time and effort in the end.

CHAPTER 1
KNOW YOUR AUDIENCE

"You simply cannot begin structuring your speech until you intimately understand the needs of your audience."
- Craig Valentine, 1999 Toastmasters World Champion of Public Speaking

Facts + Audience = Presentation
Facts may be facts, but a presentation is ALWAYS facts + an audience.

For example, what if you were asked to give a presentation about this fact:

Fact: Company A has been sold to new investors.

First, imagine you are an employee of that company: There are rumors that your job may be terminated or moved overseas in the transition.

At the beginning of that presentation, what will you be thinking?

What questions will you be likely to ask?

Next, imagine that you are one of the new investors. The acquisition of this company will give you access to markets you've been trying to develop and will let you provide more work opportunities for your employees.

At the beginning of that presentation, what will you be thinking?

What questions will you be likely to ask?

The same presentation will NOT work the same for both audiences.

The workers will hate it if you try to give them a presentation about how much money the investors will make, and the investors will hate it if you try to give them a presentation about how the sale negatively impacts current workers. **Same facts, but RADICALLY different presentation needs.**

Your physical environment can also drastically alter the impact of your words.

For instance, imagine that you and your spouse are having problems and you decide to talk about how to improve your relationship.

First, imagine that conversation taking place on a romantic beach on vacation.

Next, imagine that same conversation in a car parked next to Walmart because you had to pull over during a fight.

Even if you use the same words in both settings, does one scenario have a better chance of success?

Before you can design your presentation, you first need to know some fundamental things about your audience.

Your presentation isn't about you or whether or not you feel nervous.

It's about your audience and how they feel about your subject.

Make It About Them

The first things you need to know about your audience are the same things a journalist would ask about any subject:

Who? What? When? Where? Why? How?

Journalists know that they shouldn't put together a report until they know the answers to these basic questions. You too need to know some basic things about your audience before trying to put together your presentation.

In the theatre, all actors begin by trying to understand the point of view of the character they are going to portray. **Similarly, you should plan your presentation by first trying to understand the point of view of the people you are going to talk to.** The questions on the following page will help you do that.

But first, because this is a textbook for a class, it is necessary to make a VERY important distinction here:

Over the course of your education, you'll be asked to give many "presentations" with no particular audience in mind. Teachers often assign presentations for three main reasons:

- It forces you to research, read and filter a certain amount of information. Therefore, asking you to give a "presentation" is also a way for them to check that you have done the work.

- If you are asked to "present" on information covered in your textbook, it allows others in the class to hear that information in a variety of ways, thus reinforcing the overall learning for the class as a whole.

- It gives you the opportunity to practice a very important life skill - speaking in public.

Note that we put the word "presentation" in quotes here. This is because when you are given an assignment like this, you are not really being asked to give a **PRESENTATION**, you are being asked to give a **REPORT**. In essence, you are being asked to provide a list of information to your teacher that your teacher already knows.

Unfortunately, it is very difficult to put together reports like this.

After all, if your goal is to show your teacher that you have digested a lot of information, is there any information that you shouldn't include? There is no limit! You have no real filtering ability or guiding principles to help you put that report together.

Next time you are assigned a "presentation" that is really a report, do yourself a favor and **create another audience for your talk besides your teacher! Imagine a person or group who could BENEFIT from knowing the information on which you have been asked to report!** This will let you filter your information and prioritize what you need to say - which will in turn make it much easier for you to put together your presentation!

Before you begin, **tell your teacher that you would like to present as if for a real audience. Ask them to suggest a person or group.** All teachers will recognize the instructional benefit of this (we know - we've asked every teacher in the world and they all said yes). If for some reason your teacher doesn't immediately agree that presenting to someone besides them is a **GREAT** idea, show them this page and ask them their advice for an alternate strategy for organizing your information. Your time, your classmates, and your teacher will thank you for it.

Now on to the questions you need to ask before putting together any presentation. The next few pages contain some worksheets that will help you organize your information. Use the pages on the right hand side for your next presentation. The pages on the left show examples of the types of things you might write.

WHO, WHAT, WHEN, WHERE, WHY, HOW?
Remember - It's about THEM

EXAMPLE: Using a scenario we talked about earlier, if you had to give a presentation to group of employees of a company that is about to be sold to new investors, your answers might look something like these.

WHO ARE THEY?

How many will there be?
Age, sex, education, experience?
Are there different groups or factions?

Current factory employees. 64 of them. Age 18-57. High school education, some with college degrees. Most have experience only in manufacturing. There is possible tension between older union members and younger people who didn't join the union.

WHERE ARE THEY?

(and could this influence the conversation?)
Big room or a small room?
Are there other presenters?
In person or over the phone?

The only spaces that will hold that many people are on the factory floor or a large conference hall. But presenting on the factory floor would make this meeting look like a scene out a movie - the conference room is probably better.

WHY ARE THEY THERE?

Do they have a personal interest or are they required to be there?

It is a voluntary information meeting (no one required to attend), but interest is so high I wouldn't be surprised if all 64 people showed up.

WHO, WHAT, WHEN, WHERE, WHY, HOW?
Remember - It's about THEM

YOUR TURN: Answer these questions about the audience for your next presentation.

You don't need to go into too much detail.

The amount that will fit on a sticky note is enough.

WHO ARE THEY?

How many will there be?
Age, sex, education, experience?
Are there different groups or factions?

WHERE ARE THEY?

(and could this influence the conversation?
Big room or a small room?
Are there other presenters?
In person or over the phone?

WHY ARE THEY THERE?

Do they have a personal interest
or are they required to be there?

WHO, WHAT, WHEN, WHERE, WHY, HOW?
Remember - It's about THEM

EXAMPLE: Using a scenario we talked about earlier, if you had to give a presentation to group of employees of a company that is about to be sold to new investors your answers might look something like these.

WHAT DO THEY WANT?

What is their DESIRE or PROBLEM?

They don't know the details of the sale. They will want to know how the sale will affect their department and their job in particular. There have been numerous false rumors about the role corporate mismanagement played in current fiscal problems.

WHEN DO THEY WANT IT?

How immediate is their need for your information?

Now. With every passing day, more rumors start. Also because some people will be laid off, it is important that they be given as much time as possible to look for new jobs.

HOW FAMILIAR ARE THEY WITH YOUR TOPIC?

How much background do you need to provide?

They will be very familiar, but because of the false rumors about mismanagement, it will probably be useful to briefly touch on the real underlying reason for the sale (cheaper overseas manufacturing costs).

WHO, WHAT, WHEN, WHERE, WHY, HOW?
Remember - It's about THEM

YOUR TURN: Answer these questions about the audience for your next presentation.

You don't need to go into too much detail.
The amount that will fit on a sticky note is enough.

WHAT DO THEY WANT?

What is their DESIRE or PROBLEM?

WHEN DO THEY WANT IT?

How immediate is their need for your information?

HOW FAMILIAR ARE THEY WITH YOUR TOPIC?

How much background do you need to provide?

What Else You'll Learn

Actors and journalists use these questions because you can learn a lot by answering them.

Sometimes when answering, you'll discover that you don't know all the things about your audience that you should. For instance, perhaps you don't know how many people will be in the room or whether or not they are already familiar with your topic.

If there are gaps in your answers, those are some of the things you need to find out. Do a little digging before putting your presentation together. It can make a big difference.

Sometimes by answering the questions, you'll even begin to discover the best way to deliver your talk.

For instance, in our example we discovered that we might have a choice about WHERE it would be best to give this presentation. You'll not always be able to choose the location of your presentation, but you might be able to make some adjustments to the space you've been assigned.

How would you even know to think about that possibility without answering those basic questions?

By answering questions about **who, what, when, where, why, and how** you might also discover that a certain person in your group is best suited to deliver the presentation. For instance in our example, it's clear that a low level manager would not be the best person to give this presentation. Someone higher up in the company would be much better.

Again, you might not have the luxury of deciding on the best person to give a presentation - but then again you might. Knowing this will come in handy if you ever have to give a group presentation.

Answering basic questions about your audience gives you valuable insight about how best to structure what you need to say, who would be best to say it, and where it would be best to present.

Dig Deeper

The next thing you need to know about your audience is what emotions are involved.

Research shows that emotions play a much more important role in decision-making than most people realize. In fact, recent research suggests that before anyone makes any "rational" decisions, they have already begun to filter the information pre-cognitively based on an emotional response.

Scientists used to think of the rational mind as being kind of like a judge dispassionately weighting all the evidence before thinking, but recent neurological studies suggest that "rational" thought actually operates more like a lawyer arguing one side of a case: your mind gives added weight to evidence that supports things you already believe and looks for ways to dismiss things that don't agree with the emotions that are already happening.

Our emotions drive us in one of two basic directions: towards something or away from something.

Before beginning to put together your presentation, you need to know what aspects of your presentation might predispose your audience to agree with what you are saying and which aspects might make them disagree with the way your facts are presented.

In other words, what will they like about what you are saying and what will they not like about what you are saying?

Since none of us are mind-readers, we need to brainstorm a little bit and take a moment to write down as many ideas as we can before deciding which ones will be most helpful to keep in mind when organizing our presentation.
Answer the questions on the next two worksheets on pages 27 and 29. You don't need to go into too much detail.

Don't edit your thoughts at first. The goal is to write down as many things as occur to you.

SEGMENT YOUR AUDIENCE
A STORY OF LESSONS LEARNED THE HARD WAY

The sample presentation in this chapter is based on a real event. A few years ago, we worked with a client who had a terrible presentation experience and was determined to never make the same mistake again.

He had worked for weeks preparing to give a presentation about the closing of a factory. His job was to inform the workers about the transition and about what the closing meant for the company as a whole. The factory was one piece of a larger system and many of the workers owned stock in the company even as they worked for it.

The presenter's first (huge) mistake was assuming that because the workers were vested in the company, they would see the obvious benefits for them as stockholders. When he began putting together data for his presentation, he recognized that nearly everyone in the factory would come out ahead in the long run; and so as a result, his presentation focused only on the good things the factory closing would accomplish. He assumed that if he could just overwhelm his audience with the positive facts, he would overcome any possible resistance before the end of his presentation. As you can probably guess, this did not work out well for him.

Because his presentation preparation focused almost exclusively on the positive aspects of the sale, he was woefully unprepared for the tidal wave of negative reaction that hit him the moment he began to talk. In particular, he had failed to recognize that there was an entire group of people who were against the closing. During his presentation, this group challenged every fact he tried to present. In the end, they literally booed him off the stage.

The presenter's second (huge) mistake was thinking of his audience as a unified whole. In any group of people there will almost always be subgroups or individuals who will react differently than the majority. The next time you have to present to a large group, give some thought to the different SEGMENTS of people within the larger group.

In retrospect (and with a little coaching), the presenter realized that if he had done just two things differently - not assumed that good news is enough in times of uncertainty, and not assumed that everyone would react the same – his presentation would have been much better received.

The next time you have to give a presentation to a large group of people, do yourself a favor and pay attention to both the positive AND negative reactions your audience is likely to have. Also pay attention to the possible reaction of different groups within the larger gathering.

WHAT WILL THEY **LIKE** ABOUT YOUR INFORMATION?

Pick one part of your audience: What will they LIKE about your idea?
Or what might they HOPE would happen as a result? (Brainstorm: don't edit your ideas yet)

EXAMPLE: Using a scenario we talked about earlier, if you had to give a presentation to group of employees of a company that is about to be sold to new investors, your answers might look something like these.

WHAT WILL THEY LIKE?

They hope that things will turn out okay for them.

Most people will be happy to find out that their job is secure.

The company will be more financially stable so there will be more job security in the long run.

WHAT WILL THEY LIKE?

The severance package is generous.

Job training provisions will be provided for almost everyone.

WHAT WILL THEY LIKE?

That's all I can think of right now . . .
negative aspects are
imagine . . .

WHAT WILL THEY LIKE?

They don't have a choice.

The deal is done. This isn't a discussion about whether or not the sale will go through, but rather what it means for them.

What's the MOST COMPELLING reason
for them to agree with your point of view?
(Does anything make this a no-brainer?)

WHAT WILL THEY **LIKE** ABOUT YOUR INFORMATION?

Pick one part of your audience: What will they LIKE about your idea?
Or what might they HOPE would happen as a result? (Brainstorm: don't edit your ideas yet)

YOUR TURN: Answer these questions about the audience for your next presentation.
You don't need to go into too much detail. The amount that will fit on a sticky note is enough.

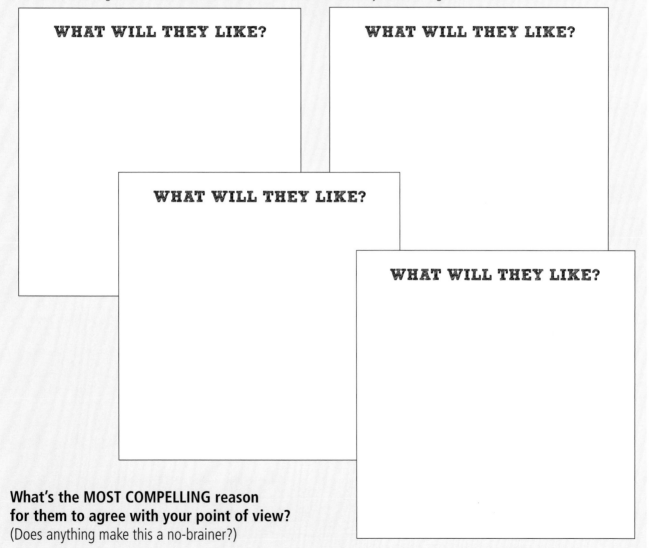

WHAT WILL THEY LIKE?

WHAT WILL THEY LIKE?

WHAT WILL THEY LIKE?

WHAT WILL THEY LIKE?

What's the MOST COMPELLING reason
for them to agree with your point of view?
(Does anything make this a no-brainer?)

WHAT WILL THEY **NOT LIKE** ABOUT YOUR INFORMATION?

Pick one part of your audience: What will they NOT LIKE about your idea?
Or what might they FEAR would happen as a result? (Brainstorm: don't edit your ideas yet)

EXAMPLE: Using a scenario we talked about earlier, if you had to give a presentation to group of employees of a company that is about to be sold to new investors your answers might look something like these.

WHAT WILL THEY NOT LIKE?

Everything.

There is so much emotion wrapped up in this, I'm worried that it might just turn into a shouting match.

Many people in the room will keep their job, but some of them won't; for those people, their worst fears are becoming a reality.

WHAT WILL THEY NOT LIKE?

Everyone is going to ask about THEIR job! But there are 64 different answers to that question!

Everyone is going to want to second guess the decision to sell but that discussion won't help anyone.

Some people will be angry about the way this announcement is being handled.

(IS there a better way?)

WHAT WILL THEY NOT LIKE?

Man, I don't want to do this! ... But that's MY fear, not theirs.

Is there any way to make this not about fear?

Probably not. People will be coming into this meeting already afraid.

I will have to deal with that one way or the other – right away would probably be best.

WHAT WILL THEY NOT LIKE?

Some of them won't want to listen to me because they wish this decision had gone a different way. But it didn't.

I need to find a way to emphasize the good parts of this deal without downplaying the reality that some people are going to lose their jobs.

What's the MOST COMPELLING reason
for them to agree with your point of view?
(Does anything make this an obvious sticking point?)

WHAT WILL THEY **NOT LIKE** ABOUT YOUR INFORMATION?

Pick one part of your audience: What will they NOT LIKE about your idea?

Or what might they FEAR would happen as a result? (Brainstorm: don't edit your ideas yet)

YOUR TURN: Answer these questions about the audience for your next presentation. You don't need to go into too much detail. The amount that will fit on a sticky note is enough.

WHAT WILL THEY NOT LIKE?

WHAT WILL THEY NOT LIKE?

WHAT WILL THEY NOT LIKE?

WHAT WILL THEY NOT LIKE?

What's the MOST COMPELLING reason for them to agree with your point of view?
(Does anything make this an obvious sticking point?)

Always Work Toward Understanding Their Emotions

As you can see, just by answering a few basic questions, you have already learned a great deal about how to structure your presentation.

For instance, in our example we became aware that many in the audience will not like what we have to say.

Thinking about THEIR emotional response is a great way begin thinking about the best way to structure your presentation.

For instance in our example, if we were to begin by going into detail about the financial facts of the sale, some people might not even listen to us - in fact we might get shouted down by people clamoring to know things about rumors they've heard.

This knowledge gives us a way to begin prioritizing the information we need to present. In this case, we need to find a way to address our audience's fears right away. In **Chapter 19: "How to Give a Persuasive Presentation,"** we will address the need to **INOCULATE** the audience against fears in more detail. But for now, it's simply enough to recognize that you need to focus on your audience before putting together any presentation.

One of the first steps in putting together any presentation is understanding your audience.

And the main thing you need to know about your audience is what **type of emotional predisposition they might have about your information.**

Now, once you have that information, what do you do with it?

The next step is to KNOW YOUR PURPOSE.

KEY TAKEAWAYS - KNOW YOUR AUDIENCE

■ The same facts mean different things to different people.

■ Before you begin, you need to do some research about your audience.

■ Who are they?

■ What do they want from you?

■ When do they want what you are offering?

■ Where are they?

■ Why are they listening to your presentation?

■ How familiar are they with what you are talking about?

■ What will they like about your idea or information?

■ What will they not like about your idea or information?

CHAPTER 2
KNOW YOUR PURPOSE

"Whether you are going to a breakfast meeting with a potential investor, making a sales talk,
or delivering a product presentation, you need to first come up with the key message
you want to leave with your audience."
- James C. Humes, author and former presidential speechwriter

You've just reached an important pivot point. You have a topic to present and some idea about how your audience might react to it. This means you can now begin to shape HOW best to tell your story.

Actors call this idea knowing your **OBJECTIVE**, and it is one of the most important ways that all performances are shaped.

The best way to craft an effective presentation is to start with the end result in mind.

By the end of your presentation, what do you want your audience to **FEEL** that they are not already feeling? What do you want them to **DO** that they are not already doing? What do you want them to **THINK** that they are not already thinking?

Have you ever listened to a presentation that didn't really seem to have any purpose? Bad presentations don't end; they just stop. The last words of many bad presentations are "uh . . . that's all I've got."

The best presentations do something more than simply inform or educate an audience.

There is an entire chapter in the second part of this book that will help you put together an informative presentation in ways that engage your audience (page 228). But for now just know that before you can put one together, you need to filter some of your information.

You need to know what DOESN'T need to go in any presentation. If your goal is to educate your audience about your topic, how does that tell you what parts are more important than others? All facts are educational and informative.

You need a more specific way to think about your purpose to help you focus on the facts that matter most.

Know Your Purpose: FEEL

Because emotion plays such a central role in how information is received, one of the simplest filters is just planning how you would like to engage your audience emotionally.

For instance if you want to **INSPIRE** an audience to do even better than they're already doing, you'll create a very different presentation than one meant to **WARN** an audience that they are failing and need to do better.

INSPIRE A FEELING

None of the famous speeches you've ever read or heard were about the INFORMATION in them. They were about inspiring a FEELING in the audience. For instance, look at the way the Rev. Dr. Martin Luther King Jr. structured his iconic 1963 speech. Any information in it was used simply to paint a picture:

> I have a dream that one day down in Alabama, with its vicious racists, with its governor having his lips dripping with the words of interposition and nullification – one day right there in Alabama little black boys and black girls will be able to join hands with little white boys and white girls as sisters and brothers.

> I have a dream today.

> I have a dream that one day every valley shall be exalted, and every hill and mountain shall be made low, the rough places will be made plain, and the crooked places will be made straight, and the glory of the Lord shall be revealed and all flesh shall see it together.

> This is our hope. This is the faith that I go back to the South with. With this faith we will be able to hew out of the mountain of despair a stone of hope. With this faith we will be able to transform the jangling discords of our nation into a beautiful symphony of brotherhood. With this faith we will be able to work together, to pray together, to struggle together, to go to jail together, to stand up for freedom together, knowing that we will be free one day.

> This will be the day, this will be the day when all of God's children will be able to sing with new meaning "My country 'tis of thee, sweet land of liberty, of thee I sing. Land where my fathers died, land of the Pilgrims' pride, from every mountainside, let freedom ring!"

Not only will your tone be different for each, but the illustrative examples you choose might also be different. The call to action at the end might be the same ("Let's do better!"), but the **FEELING** of journey you craft will be very different.

On the following page is a list of **ACTION VERBS** that will help you craft the best overall emotional impact for your presentation. Remember, at this point you're still just brainstorming ideas for the actual presentation you'll eventually craft. Don't worry about finding the right words; simply pick a few to help guide you as you take the next steps.

Pick three or four things that you would like your audience to **FEEL** at the end of your presentation (Choose words from the list or feel free to make up your own words).

For Example

If you were putting together a presentation for workers in the scenario we talked about earlier (a company sold to new management), you would want to circle words about reassurance and support. Because you know your audience will come to the meeting with a lot of fear, you will need to try to lower their fear without discounting it.

In the best of all possible worlds, you would want your audience to leave feeling:

- **COMFORTED** that something will be done to help them
- **HELPED** during the transition
- **PREPARED** for the change
- **SUPPORTED** by new management

Again these aren't necessarily the only things you will want them to feel, but knowing at least these will help us craft the best possible presentation.

So on the list on page 34 simply circle those words.

HOW WOULD YOU LIKE YOUR AUDIENCE TO **FEEL**?

EXAMPLE: In your hypothetical talk, you might have wanted your audience to **FEEL** at least the following three or four things.

Activated
Aligned
Assisted
Authorized
Bolstered
Boosted
Cared for
Challenged
Comforted
Consoled
Connected
Convinced
Defended

Driven
Enabled
Encouraged
Empowered
Enlightened
Enlivened
Energized
Equipped
Excited
Fortified
Guided
Helped
Inspired

Involved
Justified
Lightened
Mobilized
Nurtured
Prepared
Persuaded
Reassured
Resolved
Revitalized
Rejuvenated
Strengthened
Sustained

Surprised
Shocked
Scared
Stimulated
Strengthened
Supported
Transformed
Unified
Validated
Warned
Wooed

Or anything else

YOU WANT THEM TO FEEL:

COMFORTED that something will be done to help them.

HELPED during the transition.

PREPARED for the change.

SUPPORTED by new management.

HOW WOULD YOU LIKE YOUR AUDIENCE TO FEEL?

YOUR TURN: Choose three or four things you would like your audience to **FEEL** in the next presentation you give.

Activated	Driven	Involved	Surprised
Aligned	Enabled	Justified	Shocked
Assisted	Encouraged	Lightened	Scared
Authorized	Empowered	Mobilized	Stimulated
Bolstered	Enlightened	Nurtured	Strengthened
Boosted	Enlivened	Prepared	Supported
Cared for	Energized	Persuaded	Transformed
Challenged	Equipped	Reassured	Unified
Comforted	Excited	Resolved	Validated
Consoled	Fortified	Revitalized	Warned
Connected	Guided	Rejuvenated	Wooed
Convinced	Helped	Strengthened	
Defended	Inspired	Sustained	Or anything else

YOU WANT THEM TO FEEL:

35

Know Your Purpose: DO

Another simple filter is knowing what **ACTIONS** your audience needs to take at the end of your presentation. That is: what is it that you want them to **DO** as a result of what you are telling them?

> **The worst presentations are ones that have no call to action.** Why should I give you my time and energy if my input, actions, or decisions are not needed?

On the next page is a list of actions that your presentation might be asking of your audience. Use this list as a way to begin thinking about actions you want your audience to take.

Remember, your presentation is not about what **YOU** will do, but rather about what action you want **YOUR AUDIENCE** to take as a result of your presentation.

Pick three or four things you want your audience to DO at the end of your presentation.

(Choose words from the list or feel free to make up your own words).

EXAMPLE

Using the scenario we talked about earlier, by the end of your presentation to current employees, you might want to make sure that everyone:

- **PLANS** for the transition
- **SUPPORTS** each other
- **VALUES** their retraining options (or severance packages)
- **VIEWS** any detailed information you need to leave behind

These aren't necessarily the only things you will want them to do, but knowing at least these is a great place to start.

You don't have to use any of the words from the list on the next page. Feel free to make up your own.

Remember that at this point you don't need to be sure about any of this. Right now you are simply brainstorming ideas to help you organize what you are eventually going to say. This will help you filter what information needs to go into your presentation versus what information might cloud your message.

For instance, as you began to think about what you want your audience to do, you might have chosen some of the words on the next page.

WHAT WOULD YOU LIKE YOUR AUDIENCE **TO DO**?

EXAMPLE: In your hypothetical talk, you might have wanted your audience to **DO** at least the following three or four things:.

Apply	Enlarge	Invest	Nurse	Qualify	Select	Troubleshoot
Assign	Establish	Improve	Observe	Quantify	Search	Uncover
Allocate	Estimate	Join	Obtain	Raise	Share	Update
Assemble	Finalize	Judge	Organize	Recommend	Simplify	Upgrade
Award	Fine-Tune	Justify	Outline	Reconcile	Strengthen	Use
Begin	Form	Label	Overhaul	Record	Sustain	**Value**
Budget	Fund	Launch	Oversee	Recruit	**Support**	**View**
Buy	Gather	List	Participate	Release	Standardize	Visit
Change	Generate	Locate	Perfect	Remodel	Target	Volunteer
Collect	Guide	Maintain	Pilot	Refine	Test	Weigh
Consult	Help	Manage	**Plan**	Repair	Time	Withdraw
Create	Hire	Measure	Preserve	Reinstate	Trade	Write
Decide	Host	Modernize	Probe	Review	Transfer	Or anything else
Discuss	Identify	Modify	Produce	Schedule	Travel	
Donate	Inspect	Navigate	Propose			
Develop	Install	Negotiate	Project			
Enforce	Inventory	Notify	Purchase			

YOU WANT THEM TO DO:

Begin to PLAN for the transition.

SUPPORT each other.

VALUE their retraining options (or for some, the severance packages).

and VIEW any information I might leave behind.

WHAT WOULD YOU LIKE YOUR AUDIENCE **TO DO**?

YOUR TURN: Choose three or four **ACTIONS** you would like your audience to **DO** after the next presentation you have to give.

Apply	Enlarge	Invest	Nurse	Qualify	Select	Troubleshoot
Assign	Establish	Improve	Observe	Quantify	Search	Uncover
Allocate	Estimate	Join	Obtain	Raise	Share	Update
Assemble	Finalize	Judge	Organize	Recommend	Simplify	Upgrade
Award	Fine-Tune	Justify	Outline	Reconcile	Strengthen	Use
Begin	Form	Label	Overhaul	Record	Sustain	Value
Budget	Fund	Launch	Oversee	Recruit	Support	View
Buy	Gather	List	Participate	Release	Standardize	Visit
Change	Generate	Locate	Perfect	Remodel	Target	Volunteer
Collect	Guide	Maintain	Pilot	Refine	Test	Weigh
Consult	Help	Manage	Plan	Repair	Time	Withdraw
Create	Hire	Measure	Preserve	Reinstate	Trade	Write
Decide	Host	Modernize	Probe	Review	Transfer	Or anything else
Discuss	Identify	Modify	Produce	Schedule	Travel	
Donate	Inspect	Navigate	Propose			
Develop	Install	Negotiate	Project			
Enforce	Inventory	Notify	Purchase			

YOU WANT THEM TO DO:

Know Your Purpose: THINK

The final chunk of planning the purpose of your presentation involves figuring out what information needs to be prioritized.

Again, **in any presentation there is always more information than time.**

> **The key to prioritizing is figuring out the difference between information your audience NEEDS to know and information that is merely GOOD to know.**

Recognizing this will allow you to prioritize what you need to say and will give you maximum flexibility if you end up short on time!

The easiest way to do this is to simply sketch out a list of what information **MIGHT** need to go into your presentation and then play around with the best way to organize it.

We find sticky notes very useful for this because they let us lay out all the information we **MIGHT** use in a way that also lets us see it all at a glance.

This doesn't need to take a lot of time. In fact, since you are still just brainstorming what information might go in you presentation, the faster you go at this point, the more likely you are to avoid getting mired in too much detail.

Write down on sticky notes as many key ideas as you think might need to go into the final presentation. Use the following page to keep track of them.

EXAMPLE

For example, in the hypothetical presentation about a company sold to new management, a quick list of information you think might be important could be laid out with the sticky note outline on the page 40.

BRAINSTORM

EXAMPLE: What information might need to go into your presentation? Here are some ideas for our hypothetical employees.

The sale of the company will be finalized on June 27.

Most people's jobs are secure.

Linda Smith will continue as VP of sales.

For those few who will lose their job, the severance package is generous.

Detailed information will be provided via one-on-one meetings that are being scheduled now.

Most of the rumors you've heard are false.

There will be job training provisions for almost everyone.

The following departments will experience almost no change at all:
- Department A
- Department B
- Department C

The following departments will be most affected:
- Department D
- Department E

The company will be more financially stable - there will be more job security in the long run.

BRAINSTORM

YOUR TURN: What information might need to go into your presentation? Write as much as possible quickly; don't edit yourself.

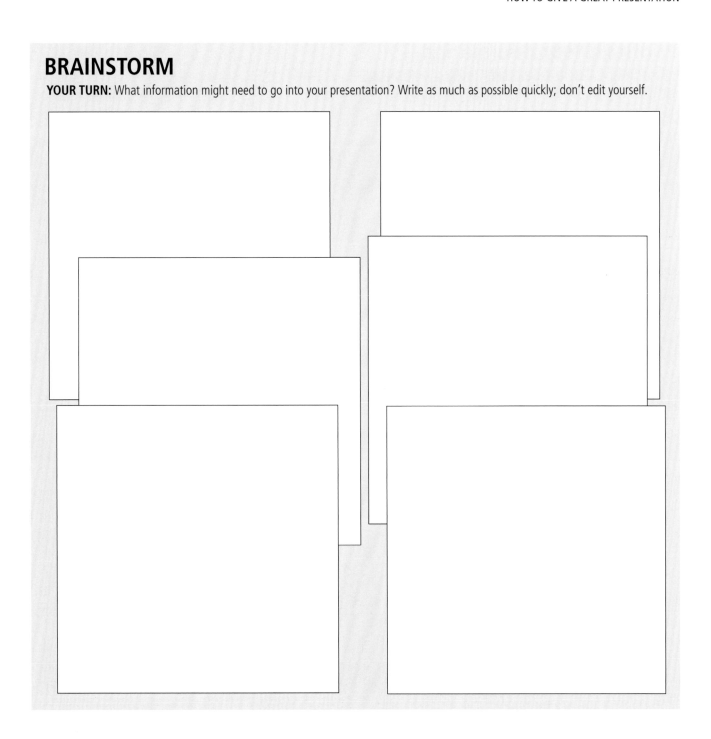

Prioritize Your Information

Take the same sticky notes you put together for the last page and place them in an order that takes into account the emotional purpose of your presentation.

Don't worry about finding the "correct" order.

We are still only brainstorming to try to begin to see how the presentation might come together.

The most important thing at this point is simply being able to step back and see a rough outline of all the information at a glance.

EXAMPLE

For instance, for our hypothetical presentation about a company sold to new management, we recognized that we needed to address the fear in the room from the very beginning. In **Chapter19: "How to Give a Persuasive Presentation,"** we will talk more about this as a way to **INOCULATE** your audience against fear. But for now it's enough to simply recognize that whenever emotions are strong, you should address any of your audience's fears as early as possible.

In our example, a quick prioritization of the information we think might be important may look like the worksheet on the next page.

PRIORITIZE YOUR INFORMATION

EXAMPLE: What information will be most useful to your audience?

NEED TO KNOW ↑

GOOD TO KNOW ↓

Most people's jobs are secure.

The following departments will experience almost no change:
- Department A
- Department B
- Department C

There will be job training provisions provided for almost everyone.

Most of the rumors you've heard are false.

The sale of the company will be finalized on June 27.

Detailed information will be provided via one to one meetings that are being scheduled now.

The following departments will be most affected:
- Department D
- Department E

For those few who will lose their job, the severance package is generous.

The company will be more financially stable – there will be more job security in the long run.

Linda Smith will continue as VP of sales.

PRIORITIZE YOUR INFORMATION

YOUR TURN: What information will be most useful to your audience?

Take the same sticky notes you put together for the last page and place them here in this space in an order that takes into account the emotional purpose of your presentation.

Don't worry about finding the correct order. You are still only brainstorming to try to begin to see how the presentation might come together.

The most important thing at this point is simply being able to step back and see a rough outline of all the information at a glance.

Remember: Keep It Short and Simple

If you have too much information to fit on one or two such pages, you have not distilled your ideas down simply enough.

Remember, the idea of using sticky notes is to force yourself to think in simple terms. If you find yourself bogged down in details by this step, zoom out and try to phrase your ideas in even more basic terms.

We are university professors. Our offices are filled with books and piles of papers from floor to ceiling: big books, little books, papers, journals, pictures, details, figures, facts. We've read all of it (okay, most of it), and we know that there is a lot of useful information in those piles. But when students ask us questions, we don't just point to the piles and say, "Read all that stuff. The answer is in there."

The students aren't asking for ALL the information we could pile on them. They are asking us to help them with their problem by filtering what we know and directing them to the information that is MOST relevant to their problem.

Giving a presentation is the same as answering a question. It's not your job to give your audience all the possible details, or even to know all the details; it's your job to point out things that **MATTER** to your audience.

Even though you would never deliberately say to an audience: "Here's a bunch of information; figure out what's important for yourself," that's exactly the way a lot of presentations are put together - as just a list of facts.

The key to NOT doing that is to be as clear as possible about your message.

Here is a good exercise to do at this point (even if you are not feeling bogged down) because it will force you to think as clearly and directly as possible:

YOUR TURN

Is your presentation as clear as it can be?

On new sticky notes, answer the questions on the next page in as simple terms as possible.

If you are having trouble paring down your information, just take the answers you have come up with to this point and pick only ONE that you think is the MOST important:

Again, don't worry about getting it right; we are still just working to make our message clear and relevant to the audience.

ZOOMING OUT
Simplifying Your Story

EXAMPLE: For our hypothetical presentation about a company being sold to new management, our answers might look like this:

MY AUDIENCE IS:

(WHO are you talking to?)

Current employees of Manufacturing Company A

THEIR DESIRE/PROBLEM IS:

(WHAT do they want?)

The company has just been sold to new management.

They want to know what that means for THEM.

THEY CARE BECAUSE:

(WHY are they listening to you?)

They are worried they will lose their jobs.

ZOOMING OUT
Simplifying Your Story

YOUR TURN: Answer these questions about the audience for your next presentation. You don't need to go into too much detail. The amount that will fit on a sticky note is enough.

MY AUDIENCE IS:
(WHO are you talking to?)

THEIR DESIRE/PROBLEM IS:
(WHAT do they want?)

THEY CARE BECAUSE:
(WHY are they listening to you?)

ZOOMING OUT

Simplifying Your Story

EXAMPLE: For our hypothetical presentation about a company being sold to new management, our answers might look like this:

If you can, list the **ONE MAIN** thing, but if you can't narrow it down to just one, try to list no more than **THREE** things for each note.

YOU WANT THEM TO FEEL:

Supported by new management.

THEY NEED TO DO:

Begin planning for the transition.

THE MAIN THINGS YOU WANT THEM TO KNOW/THINK ARE:

Most people's jobs are secure.

Only Departments D & E will experience any major changes.

One-on-one meetings to provide more details for everyone are being set up now.

ZOOMING OUT

Simplifying Your Story

YOUR TURN: Answer these questions about the audience for your next presentation. You don't need to go into too much detail. The amount that will fit on a sticky note is enough.

YOU WANT THEM TO FEEL:

THEY NEED TO DO:

THE MAIN THINGS YOU WANT THEM TO KNOW/THINK ARE:

Short, Simple, and Fast

Working up to this point should not have taken very long, and yet - just by answering some very basic questions - you now know a great deal about your audience and how they might respond to what you have to say.

In doing so, you have already sidestepped a number of possible problems that may otherwise have derailed your presentation (for instance, in our example, can you imagine the incredible pushback a low level manager would have encountered if they tried to give a presentation about how good a financial deal the sale of the company was?!).

Every day, people deliver the wrong presentations to the wrong audiences!

Don't be the person whose presentation failure is a horrible warning to others!

Know your audience, know your purpose, and have a clear, simple, message!

Doing this automatically sidesteps many of the reasons other presentations fail.

One Final Step to Simplifying

Imagine that everything that could go wrong during your next presentation does go wrong: the projector breaks down so you can't use any slides, the copier breaks down with your handouts in it, the people ahead of you talk for much longer than they should, or the boss you need to present to doesn't show up until the last minute, or you only have a moment to talk to her in the hallway, or in an elevator or as she walked to her car.

These things happen every single day in business and in life. In order to present well, you need to be prepared to present under any time pressures or without visual aids of any sort. In short, in order to present well, you need to be ready to say your main idea in only **ONE SENTENCE** if necessary.

Don't skip this step! This is one of the most important - yet too often overlooked - steps to putting together any presentation, even if you never have to use it as a fallback. If you can say the **MAIN POINT** of your presentation in one sentence, it means you have distilled your thinking down as clearly as possible. The good news is that you've already done most of the work!

Go back and look at the list of information you put together for the **"Prioritize Your Information"** worksheet on page 44. Which of those parts absolutely **NEED** to go in your presentation? Those parts - the things that absolutely need to go in - are your **MAIN POINTS**.

Now pick the ONE most important main point and pair it with some of the words from your PURPOSE.

We know this is hard. After all, there is SO much information! But remember, there is always more information than time! Consider this your last-ditch-everything-else-has-failed fallback plan. What would you say if everything that can go wrong does go wrong and you had only a moment to present?

If you could choose only ONE MAIN POINT and ONE PURPOSE for your presentation, what would it be?

SAY IT IN ONE SENTENCE

EXAMPLE: For instance, if each of the presenters we've talked about had only a single sentence to give their most important information, those sentences might look like these.

SAY IT IN ONE SENTENCE:

Our company is going to be fine with or without new government regulation.

SAY IT IN ONE SENTENCE:

I want to reassure everyone that we are doing everything in our power to make the transition to new management as painless as possible.

SAY IT IN ONE SENTENCE
Make it a compound sentence if you have to

The simpler and more direct you can be at this point, the better. However, if you are having trouble narrowing your ideas down to just one it's okay if your single sentence includes conjunctions like "and" or "but." It's even okay if you end up with two sentences (but you should try very hard to avoid having three or more). The goal of this step is not to make you perform linguistic gymnastics.

The goal is simply to make sure your message is as clear as possible.

EXAMPLE: If we were a little less confident in our abilities to be succinct in our examples we might have added a few qualifying words.

SAY IT IN ONE SENTENCE:

Our company is going to be fine with or without new government regulation ...

... because we have a good plan in place.

SAY IT IN ONE SENTENCE:

I know that there are a lot of rumors flying about the recent sale of this company and ...

... I want to reassure everyone that we are doing everything in our power to make the transition to new management as painless as possible.

SAY IT IN ONE SENTENCE
(Or as short and simple as possible)

This sentence is not necessarily something you will actually say during your presentation! Think of it as a guiding principle for you to keep in mind while organizing your talk or as an emergency fallback plan to say if everything that could go wrong does. Unless lots of things go wrong, this one sentence is mainly for you.

YOUR TURN: If you had to distill the main point of your presentation down to a single sentence, **what would it be?**

Again, don't worry about getting it "right;" instead simply focus on addressing the emotional needs of your audience (the things you want them to **FEEL**, **DO**, and **THINK**). Which of these is the MOST IMPORTANT for your presentation?

> **SAY IT IN ONE SENTENCE:**

Congratulations! You are now ready to start putting your presentation together.

PART 1   SECTION 2

ORGANIZE IT
THE IMPORTANCE OF ARRANGEMENT

**A STRESSFUL DAY IN THE BIGGEST OFFICE BUILDING IN THE WORLD
A TRUE STORY**

Ever had a rough day at the office? We know someone who's probably got you beat.

Mark (not his real name) leads a team of defense analysts in a large government agency involved in counter-terrorism. His group was (and is) charged with monitoring suspect activity in Europe and conveying information to various other agencies.

As the leader of the team, Mark is tasked with conducting briefings for high-ranking officials and as a result he is quite good at public speaking and dealing with stressful situations. In fact, one day not too long ago, he became a legend for it.

He had been instructed to give a briefing at the Pentagon to the Supreme Allied Commander for Europe. This was an intimidating task even for someone as capable as Mark. The first problem was the short turnaround time. He would have to write the brief on top of all the other tasks he was assigned AND vet the product through his chain of command before the final written version could be set – and all of this needed to be completed BEFORE he could practice delivering the information. But he was up to the task. He wrote it in time and was even able to rehearse it out loud several times before the day of the meeting.

Then he hit a little snag.

On the morning of the briefing he woke early, ate breakfast and started driving. On the way, he began to feel a little queasy. The feeling grew until he felt he had to pull off the road to throw up. He got out of the car but -- nothing -- so he got back in the car and kept going. All went well until he reached the final exit and began to merge into traffic in front of the Pentagon. Then he began throwing up in earnest ... four times in the half-mile between the exit and a nearby mall parking garage! It turned out that he had a light case of food poisoning.

If this had been any other meeting he certainly would have had one of his colleagues conduct the briefing. But this wasn't any other meeting – and by the time he realized he was sick, there wasn't time – or security clearance - to find a backup.

So Mark did what any other person would do in this situation: he changed clothes in the parking lot (into the suit he had worn the day before) and cleaned himself off with Armor All wipes from his glove box before giving his briefing anyway.

He tried hard to ignore the tray of food in front of him and the smell of fresh coffee on the table at the meeting. He also tried to ignore the fact that each of the five people who presented before him took much longer than their allotted 10 minutes to present.

Mark was scheduled to go last in a meeting strictly limited to one hour. By the time it was his turn, his own 10 minutes had dwindled to only 30 seconds! But because of the way he had organized his information – and how good he was at presenting – he managed to do it. As soon as he realized that presenters before him were running long, he modified his message – cutting some supporting details here and highlighting a key phrase or two there until the briefing was whittled down to its bare essentials.

Mark became a legend when his colleagues learned how much he had gone through just to deliver 30 seconds of content. He was able to succeed because he knew how to craft his message in a way that allowed him to adapt quickly when things went – sickeningly – wrong.

Do you know how to do the same?

THE IMPORTANCE OF ARRANGEMENT

"If I had more time, I would have written a shorter letter."
– Blaise Pascal, mathematician and philosopher

Once you know how your audience might react to the information you want to present, you can begin organizing how best to lay it out for them. As you do this, of course you need to keep your audience's responses in mind, but you also need to keep yourself in mind. After all, YOU are the one who is going to have to remember everything!

Organizing your talk is really about keeping these two things in balance: **your audience's ability to process the information and your ability to remember what to say.** Fortunately the solution is the same for both:

You need to be as clear as you can about your message and figure out how to say it as succinctly as possible.

Just having a list of information you want to convey is not enough. You also need some kind of spine to hang that information on. Principles from theatre and storytelling offer useful ways to structure all the things you might say.

In particular, it is very useful to think about the **DRAMATIC** structure of what you want to say. How does your story start? What twists and turns does it take? How does it end? Even just knowing these three signposts will help both you and your audience stay on track:

- How do you begin?
- What goes in the middle (and how do you prioritize it)?
- How do you end?

This section will walk you through the process of honing your message down to its essential ideas and structuring those ideas in a way that will yield the most impact for your audience AND will be easy for you to remember.

CHAPTER 3
MAKE AN OUTLINE

"If you don't grab your audience's attention in the first thirty seconds, your audience will tune out of your presentation."
-Akash Karia, author, <u>Public Speaking Mastery</u>

Entertainers have known for centuries that the opening moments of a story are the most important. They set the tone for everything that follows. Think about the opening scenes of any movie:

■ If the movie's theme involves action, there will almost always be action from the very beginning (think of any James Bond or *Star Wars* movie you've ever seen).

■ Mysteries almost always open with a mystery (a body discovered in the woods or an image of something out of place).

■ Romances often start with scenes that establish loneliness or a yearning for love.

■ Westerns are famous for opening scenes that establish an expansive wide-open land stretched out as far as the camera can see.

These aren't accidental. Regardless of the genre, the opening scene of every movie is meticulously crafted to have the maximum impact and set the tone for everything that follows. You should do the same for your presentation.

The opening moments of your presentation are the most important of your entire talk!

Never begin by telling your audience what you are going to tell them. Just jump right in and start telling them. You don't even need to introduce yourself first. Research suggests that it can take only seconds before a modern audience's mind begins to wander. People who grew up in a different age often lament this fact, but this tendency is not limited only to people who grew up in the Internet age. Everyone's mind works in similar ways.

How People Listen

The people in your audience are not simply empty vessels into which you dump information. Your audience will be thinking even as they listen. Sometimes they will be thinking about things completely unrelated to what you are talking about. You need something to help grab their attention up front. And even if you have their attention, they will still be thinking:

"So what? Who cares? What's in it for me?"

In order to keep their attention, you need to stay ahead of these thoughts. Keep their problem front and center from the very beginning!

Imagine two different ways to begin the same talk.

The first example is a standard, boring presentation that starts out by explaining the outline of what will be said:

What the presenter says	What you think
"Hi my name's Bob"	Who cares what your name is?
"And I'm here to talk to you today about how to navigate the university's new compliance website."	So what? Do I really need to know this?
"We need everyone to log in, create a new password and update their information so we can complete the upgrade to the new system."	Who cares what you need? How does this help me?
"Today I'm going to cover the following information …"	**Boring!** Not listening … Snore … Zzzzz …

There is a better way.

Here is the same information structured to grab the audience's attention from the very beginning and make it clear why the information is important to them:

What the presenter says	What you think
"If you don't update your information in the university's new computer system you might not graduate on time - or even have access to your student loans or scholarships."	Who cares? … Wait, **WHAT?**
"My name is Bob and I'm here to tell you how to avoid all those problems."	Okay. I'm listening Bob. Tell me what I need to know.
"The first thing you need to know is this …"	**Wait, let me get something to write this down!**

Always Have a Hook

People in the entertainment industry call something that grabs the audience's attention a **HOOK**. But a hook does more than just grab attention. It also functions as a way to organize the rest of the information you need to present. It creates a through-line on which to hang all the rest of the stuff you want your audience to know.

A HOOK is something that grabs the audience's attention in a way that draws their focus to the PROBLEM you are going to solve or the DESIRE you are going to fulfill.

■ In the CEO's story, the hook was the accidental shut down of the projector and the reassurance that everything would be fine;

- In the example of a company sold to new management, it was the knowledge that jobs are on the line;

What's Your Hook?

Without one, how will you even you know where to begin?

How can you grab your audience's attention in a way that draws focus to their problems or desires - that either addresses their fears or raises their hopes about the future?

The worst presentations start with "Well, um, I've been asked to tell you …" Don't do that. No one cares what you've been asked to do. But they might care about how that information affects them. From the very beginning, you need to find a way to make it clear to your audience why they should care about what you have to say.

One of the simplest hooks is the word "you."

In fact this technique is so effective that most infomercials use it shamelessly. Even if no one in the world actually NEEDS the particular product, many advertisements start by addressing the audience directly and describing the product as satisfying a need or desire.

For instance, if you turn on your television late at night, you are likely to see something like this:

The Bonko Egg Scrambler!

(Camera zooms in on a person in a kitchen)

Narrator: "Do YOU have trouble scrambling eggs?"

(camera shows sad face of person dropping eggs on the floor)

"Try the Bonko Egg Scrambler!"

(camera shows happy face of person using the egg scrambler)

"It slices, dices, and scrambles eggs in seconds!"

(camera shows eggs being sliced and diced and scrambled)

"Scramblers like this can sell for hundreds of dollars in stores."

(camera shows large stack of money)

"But through this special television offer YOU can own one for the incredibly low price of only $19.99!"

(camera shows flashing red "$19.99!")

"But wait - there's more! The first 100 people to order will get a second egg scrambler for FREE!"

(camera shows two egg scramblers and the word "FREE!")

"Act now - supplies are limited!"

(camera shows toll-free number)

This is a silly example, but it's not too far from the truth. In fact, some version of this commercial is running on television right now – and even as you read this, someone somewhere is calling a toll-free number to buy something they don't really need.

Why are so many infomercials structured this way?

Because it works!

We will explore more about the narrative part of this structure in a little while, but for now it's important to recognize that one of the key elements is the use of the word "you" and the immediate focus on the audience and their needs and desires. This is a classic example of using a hook to craft a sales pitch.

But hooks are used for much more than just sales.

As the examples from movie genres demonstrate, opening hooks come in many shapes and sizes. Knowing how to craft a good opening hook for any presentation is a skill that will serve you well for the rest of your life.

If there is a single theme that runs throughout this book it is this:

Your presentation isn't about your information. It's about what that information means to your audience.

This means that there is no one best hook for your information. **The best hook for your presentation is rooted in your audience, not your information.** Your job is to find a hook that will grab your audience's attention in a way that highlights the problem of theirs you are going to solve or the desire they have that you are going to fulfill.

So how do you go about figuring out the best one to use?

Here's a list of the most commonly used ideas presenters use to hook their audiences at the beginning:

- a short engaging story
- a shocking fact or statistic
- a compelling quote
- a movie or television clip
- an evocative picture
- an interesting news clipping
- an unusual prop
- a compelling question
- a humorous cartoon
- a guest visitor
- a sound bite
- a challenge

Coming up with a good hook for your presentation is simpler than you think.

The next few pages have worksheets that will help you brainstorm the best way to begin your presentation. You don't need to write much. The amount that will fit on a sticky note is enough. Right now, you are just looking for ideas that you might use to grab and hold your audience's attention.

BRAINSTORM THE BEGINNING

EXAMPLES from the Bonko Egg Scrambler pitch:

YOUR MOST IMPACTFUL PERSONAL STORY AROUND THIS ISSUE:

Someone giving a testimonial about how easy the egg scrambler is to use

THE MOST IMPACTFUL PHYSICAL OBJECT YOU COULD USE:

The egg scrambler itself

THE MOST IMPACTFUL VISUAL IMAGE YOU COULD USE:

A picture of someone's sad face as they drop eggs on the floor

THE MOST IMPACTFUL FACT OR STATISTIC:

Amount of money they can save!

BRAINSTORM THE BEGINNING

YOUR TURN: Answer the following questions. You don't need to write much. The amount that will fit on a sticky note is enough.

YOUR MOST IMPACTFUL PERSONAL STORY AROUND THIS ISSUE:	**THE MOST IMPACTFUL PHYSICAL OBJECT YOU COULD USE:**
THE MOST IMPACTFUL VISUAL IMAGE YOU COULD USE:	**THE MOST IMPACTFUL FACT OR STATISTIC:**

THE POWER OF STARTING STRONG
SUDDENLY INSIDE THE STORM

You are sitting in a theatre waiting for a play to start. It's a play by William Shakespeare: *The Tempest*. Your friend dragged you to it because they heard it was good, but you are skeptical. In your experience, plays that are supposed to be educational or cultural are always boring: all those words like "thee and "thou." Seriously, who talks like that?

People have finished filling in and sitting down and now everyone is just waiting for the play to begin. You get out your phone to play a quick game of Candy Crush. From experience you know you'll have plenty of time to put it away after the lights start to dim and people begin to "tut-tut" you for looking at your phone instead of quietly listening to all those old-fashioned words.

But then without warning, there is a giant BOOM of thunder that shakes the auditorium and the lights suddenly go out! Then the room is illuminated only by flickering light as if through lightning. Before you can figure out what's going on, you hear the sounds of two actors scrambling across ropes directly above your head! "Boatswain!" one calls. "Here, Master!" the other yells from behind you.

You pivot in your seat to try to see what's happening - and as you do so, you can feel wind on your face as if you were in the storm (are there fans somewhere?). The actors are fighting through tangled rigging directly over your head. One of them falls and is caught by another actor. The audience gasps. You find yourself holding your breath. The sounds of a storm seemingly come from everywhere – thunderous booms, howling wind, and creaking timbers. The actors are precariously holding on to the beams overhead and yelling back and forth to one another:

"We run ourselves aground: bestir, bestir!"

"Yare, yare! Take in the topsail. Tend to the master's whistle. Blow, till thou burst thy wind, if room enough!"

You still have no idea what they are talking about, but it doesn't matter. Suddenly it's as if the entire theatre were suddenly transported inside a raging storm where men are fighting for their lives! You put your phone away and hold on to your seat. If this moment is any indication, this play is going to be a wild ride!

Wouldn't it be great if the beginning of your presentation could grab your audience's attention even a fraction this much?

Good news: if you build it right, it can.

Find Your Ending

There is a saying in the entertainment industry: "**Start Strong, End Stronger.**"

The two most important parts of any presentation are the beginning and the end.

These always have the most potential to impact your audience.

So now that you've given some thought to how to begin, the next thing to do is to give some thought about the last moments of your presentation. At the beginning of your presentation your audience is deciding whether or not they care what you have to say - at the end they are mentally organizing everything you've said.

The last moment of a presentation is your last chance to leave them with something they will remember. What thoughts, images, memorable sayings, or calls to action do you want to linger with them after they leave?

Many of the very best presentations link back to the ideas or images introduced at the beginning.

"Circular conclusions" like this are satisfying because the audience can feel the **"completeness"** of the story. Improvisational performers are trained extensively in finding ways to bring stories around full circle.

They call the technique **"reincorporation"** and it is central to their craft. Likewise writers for theatre, film and television spend a great deal of time making sure to **"wrap up any loose ends"** in their story lines.

But **circular conclusions** are not the only way to end your presentation strong. Many things can have an impact and help make your talk memorable. Answer the questions on the following page to brainstorm a few that might work for you. As always, you don't need to write much. The amount that will fit on a sticky note is enough for now.

EXAMPLE

Answers about our hypothetical presentations for the Bonko Egg Scrambler might look like the examples on page 66.

CONCLUSION
End with a bang
EXAMPLE from the Bonko Egg Scrambler pitch:

OPENING HOOK TO REINCORPORATE AT THE END?

The same person who was sad at the beginning happily using the product

CALL TO ACTION?

Call the toll free number,

Buy now!

LAST THING TO LEAVE WITH THEM:

Visual image of the toll-free number and the sound of the announcer's voice reading the number three times.

ANYTHING ELSE:

CONCLUSION
End with a bang
YOUR TURN: Answer these questions for your presentation.

OPENING HOOK TO REINCORPORATE AT THE END?

CALL TO ACTION?

LAST THING TO LEAVE WITH THEM:

ANYTHING ELSE:

THE POWER OF ENDING STRONG
CALLING TO ACTION

We once had a client who ran a nonprofit group dedicated to linking local doctors with the business community in order to help create better health outcomes for underprivileged people. The group had started strong but then stagnated. The founder had been giving a talk about the group's mission in various venues for a year, but his organization had seen no appreciable growth as a result.
Our first question for him was very simple:

"How are you phrasing your call to action at the end?"

"I'm not sure what you mean," he said. "I don't have a specific call to action. I'm just informing them about our group and our mission."

"That might be the problem right there," we told him.

The rest of his presentation was very strong. He was passionate about his group's mission and his presentation made it clear that linking local doctors and businesses would benefit not only the community, but also the health care providers and the businesses themselves. The only thing he hadn't done was give his audience specific steps they could do to get involved.

It took only 15 minutes to help him craft a more useful ending. The next time he gave his talk – and every time thereafter – he ended by saying this:

"By a show of hands, how many people in this room know someone who could benefit from this information? Someone specific? By a show of hands, who knows someone who might know someone who wants these same things? I give this challenge to every one of you who raised your hand: tell that person what you heard here today and give them our website address. If even half of the people in this room do this, we will be able to implement every item in our mission statement within a year. Who's with me on this? If you think this mission is important, say 'I do.' I'm sorry - I couldn't hear you. Say it again! That's great. I could hear you that time. Now please make sure that someone else outside this room hears it as well! Thank you."

He was almost right. One year and 27 days after he first started including this call to action in his talks, his nonprofit implemented every one of the statements in its mission.

One of the most important things you can do for most presentations is be clear with your audience about what you want them to DO with the information you provide.

They say knowing is half the battle; but if you want to win the war, you also need a plan for the second half of the battle. Your ending is a great place to make sure everyone is marching in the same direction.

Find Your Middle

Believe it or not, you are almost done crafting an outline for what you might say!

If you have done all of the exercises in this book, congratulations! You've done almost everything you need to outline an outstanding presentation! You have a good idea about what you might do to grab your audience's attention at the beginning and some ideas about what you want to leave them with at the end. That means you're in a great position to recognize which of your main ideas will be most useful to your audience.

Make Some Choices

Now that you've narrowed your information down to its bare essentials and given some thought to how to begin strong and end stronger, all you really need to do is choose some the main ideas you have already identified.

Until now all we have been doing is brainstorming, trying to come up with as many ideas as possible so that we could see all of those ideas laid out in context next to each other. This is the step to give it a try.

Take a moment and look back at all the answers you have put together up to this point.

Then make some choices:

■ Look over your list of possible **HOOKS** and choose the one that you feel will make your audience pay the most attention.

■ Look over your list of possible **ENDINGS** and choose the one that you feel will best help your audience remember.

■ Then chose **THREE MAIN POINTS** you want to make that follow logically from that beginning and ending. You don't necessarily have to limit yourself to only one idea for each part, but if you include more than one point, make sure that you are clear about HOW you might include multiple ideas for each section.

NOTE: Unless you have hours to present - and will be giving your audience some kind of handout to follow along - **don't choose more than five main points!** Remember that your audience will be processing your talk mainly by listening to you.

Humans have a very hard time keeping track of multiple strands of an aural story (i.e. one they listen to). **Three to five main points are close to the maximum that people can comfortably process while listening to someone talk.**

Coincidentally, three to five chunks of information is also close to the maximum that most people can reliably remember while under stress. **Organizing your information in smaller chunks is not only the easiest way for your audience to process what you are saying, it is also the easiest way for you to make sure YOU are clear about what you are saying.**

The following pages have worksheets to help you to brainstorm a few ideas to organize the main points of your presentation. As always, you don't need to write much. The amount that will fit on a sticky note is enough for now. Sample answers appear on the left hand page. Use the right hand page for your own answers. Either move the sticky notes you wrote for **"Prioritize Your Information"** on page 44 or write new ones.

Use these pages to organize your thoughts and "see" what your presentation might look like. Try it several ways. Taking a little time to now may save you a lot of time rewriting later.

EXAMPLE

If we were trying to put together a presentation on the Bonko Egg Scrambler, our page might look something like the example on the next page.

VISUAL WHITEBOARD

EXAMPLE from the Bonko Egg Scrambler pitch:

My favorite hook:

A MESS IN THE KITCHEN!

A picture of someone's sad face as they drop eggs on the floor.

Question to audience: "Do you have trouble scrambling eggs?"

My favorite way to end with a bang:

CALL NOW!

An image of the same person who was sad at the beginning happily using the product.

The toll free number.

The words "Call now to buy the Bonko Egg Scrambler!"

Main points I need to include:

WHAT IT DOES:

The Bonko Egg Scrambler is the solution!

It slices, dices, and scrambles in seconds!

COMPETING PRODUCTS/ VALUE:

Other products cost hundreds of dollars.

Save hundreds of dollars!

URGENCY!

Limited TV offer!

Supplies are limited!

Call now and the second one is free!

VISUAL WHITEBOARD

YOUR TURN: Move some of the sticky notes you wrote earlier or write new ones. Use this page to organize your thoughts and see what your presentation might look like.

Try it several different ways to try to find the best one for your audience.

MAIN POINTS I NEED TO INCLUDE:

MY FAVORITE HOOK:

MY FAVORITE WAY TO END WITH A BANG:

THE POWER OF FLEXIBILITY, PART 1
WORKPLACE POLITICS

Jasmin came to the workshop thinking she would use the time to polish the slides for her presentation that afternoon. She was the leader of a small team that was applying for an internal "grant" within the corporation. If her pitch was successful, she and three of her coworkers would be going to a weeklong training retreat in Hawaii. If it wasn't, one of the nine other teams would be going instead.

Her company had hired us to provide presentation training to employees and Jasmin figured the class would be an opportunity to get some pointers on how to polish her slides before her own presentation.

She was initially disappointed to learn that the class wasn't about PowerPoint as much as it was about organizing a presentation and delivering it with presence. But shortly after the class began, her disappointment changed to something even worse: fear.

After everyone described their upcoming presentations, we asked them what their audience would NOT like about their information. As soon as she listed the people who would be at the meeting, she realized everything her team had put together was wrong! Much of what they had put together would trigger a landslide of corporate politics.

A large chunk of her presentation would, in effect, insult the other teams' departments by pointing out things that were not getting done in a timely manner. Jasmin realized that if she presented the information in her slides, not only would she NOT win the trip to Hawaii, but there was also a good chance that she would damage her working relationship with those other departments for months to come.

To make matters even worse, Jasmin wasn't entirely certain whether or not a particular person, named Ed, would be attending the afternoon presentations or not. If Ed did show up, there was a good chance that other parts of her presentation would trigger entirely different reactions within the group (A word of warning for business majors: this is a true story; corporate politics can be complex!).

"I don't know what to do," she said. "The presentation is at 1 p.m. There's no time to make any new slides, much less come up with a whole new presentation!"

"Maybe there's a way to reorganize what you already have," we said.

With the class's permission, we immediately re-organized what we had planned to work on that day. Instead of conducting the workshop in the way we had originally planned, we would use the morning to talk about chunking the information that goes into the middle of a presentation. The class would work together to fix Jasmin's presentation. We began by projecting her slides on the screen so that we could collectively help her redo what she was going to say . . .

(continued in PART 2: ALOHA HAWAII)

One Last Step Before Outlining

There is now really only one thing missing from this outline:

You.

In addition to the three questions all audiences always ask (So what? Who cares? What's in it for me?), there is one other question your audience might be asking themselves:

"Why should I listen to YOU?"

A good presenter is a kind of expert. Your expertise might be limited (perhaps you only need to explain that there is a new electronic signature form that needs to be used from now on), but no matter what the subject, if you present, you are asking people to give you their time and attention. Why should they give you their time? What gives you the **EXPERIENCE** or **AUTHORITY** to talk about this subject?

EXPERIENCE and AUTHORITY are not necessarily the same thing as RANK.

Of the three, rank (or job title) is the least important.

A few pages ago we mentioned that students often come to us asking for help, and that when they did we never just point to the pile of journals and books in our office and say "the answer is in there somewhere." The students don't come to us for help because we have important sounding titles, they come to us because they believe we have the **EXPERIENCE** to filter all that information and point them in the right direction.

If you are going to ask someone to give you their time to listen to your opinion, you should also **let them know why they should TRUST you.** Do you have any information that they couldn't find themselves by just looking up the topic on Wikipedia?

EVERY presentation you give needs to be more than just a list of facts that your audience could find on its own.

Use the following questions to help you identify your **EXPERIENCE** and **AUTHORITY** on to this particular topic.

EXAMPLE

If we were trying to put together a presentation on the Bonko Egg Scrambler, our page might look something like thexample on page74.

WHY SHOULD THEY LISTEN TO YOU?

EXAMPLE from the Bonko Egg Scrambler pitch:

YOUR EXPERIENCE WITH THIS TOPIC:

I personally own three Bonko Egg Scramblers and use them every day.

I love them

They make my life better.

HOW LONG YOU'VE SPENT WORKING ON THIS PROBLEM:

I've been using it ever since it first came out.

RESEARCH YOU'VE DONE ON THIS TOPIC:
(experiments done, articles and books read, etc.)

I owned other similar products and they weren't as good.

YOUR RANK THAT COMPELS THEM TO LISTEN:

I'm a colonel in the newly formed Bonko Army (it's a new online thing).

Note: Title and rank are the LEAST convincing reasons anyone should listen to you.

WHY SHOULD THEY LISTEN TO YOU?

YOUR TURN: Answer the following questions. You don't need to write much. The amount that will fit on a sticky note is enough for now.

YOUR EXPERIENCE WITH THIS TOPIC:

HOW LONG YOU'VE SPENT WORKING ON THIS PROBLEM:

RESEARCH YOU'VE DONE ON THIS TOPIC:
(experiments done, articles and books read, etc.)

YOUR RANK THAT COMPELS THEM TO LISTEN:

Note: Title and rank are the LEAST convincing reasons anyone should listen to you.

THE POWER OF FLEXIBILITY, PART 2
ALOHA HAWAII

We helped Jasmin create a hook to grab her audience's attention in a way that didn't require any slides. There wasn't time to make new ones and her original presentation didn't start strong enough otherwise.

The next thing we did was even more critical: we helped her reorganize her existing slides into "groups" or "chunks" of information and identify how different audience members would respond to each chunk.

The class then helped her come up with two different ways of presenting that information: she'd present it one way if certain committee members were there, and a different way if others showed up.

There was a lot to work with. Jasmin and her team had done their homework well. Her slides contained good information and her overall argument was strong. The main difficulty was that her slides weren't designed to be organized in a way that made the new arguments she wanted to make.

After we reorganized the information in chunks, we emphasized the grouping by changing the headers in each group of slides to highlight the new underlying message (and to help Jasmin remember the new order). We also helped her delete any data that might be interpreted as disparaging of anyone. All of this fundamentally changed the way her slides looked.

"The slides don't look as good now," she said. "We spent A LOT of time putting those together."

"It doesn't matter how much time YOU spent," we said. "Your audience doesn't care bout how much effort you put in, they care about what your message means to THEM – or in this case to the company. You presentation isn't about how pretty your slides look. It's about how clear your message is."

"This IS a much better message," she agreed.

Over lunch, Jasmin rehearsed giving the presentation both ways in front of the class. Everyone agreed that both ways made very strong arguments.

The main difference between the two presentations was the order of the central points. One way emphasized one aspect of the company's strategic vision, while the other emphasized a different aspect of that same vision that would have particular appeal to a particular group of leaders. She saved both versions on her laptop under different names to help her remember which one to choose depending on who she saw when she got to the room.

Just after lunch, Jasmin left to give her presentation. The rest of the class went back and covered the material we had skipped earlier. It was hard to concentrate because we all knew that Jasmin was giving a presentation two floors above us.

Two hours after she went upstairs, Jasmin came back into the room triumphant. Not only had her presentation gone well, they had already announced her team as the winner. Ed HAD been in the room and his presence had made all the difference.

Luckily for her, we had organized our training session in a way that allowed us to reorder the information we presented. Because of this, Jasmin was able to reorder the information in her own presentation in a way that also allowed her to plan for contingencies.

Could you reorder your presentation at the last minute as well?

Outline It!

That's it! **Congratulations,** you now have nearly everything you need to put together an outline of your presentation!

> In fact, you have TWO versions of your presentation to choose from:
>
> 1. You have a very **quick version** in which you could simply **state your main point in ONE SENTENCE.**
>
> 2. And now, you are ready **to outline a longer version** that you can expand or contract as much as you want anytime you need to.

The following two pages show an overview of all the pieces you've already put together. To make things simple, it's shown on a single page in outline form.

The only parts you'll see that we haven't mentioned yet are the **TITLE** of your presentation, **HOOKS** for each of your main points, and a holding place for a **QUESTION** and **ANSWER** session.

The **TITLE** is simply what you might call the purpose of your presentation if you had to give it a name. Titles are not something you necessarily have to show your audience, but they are nice to have.

You already know how to put together **HOOKS**. So all you really need to know is that if you want your presentation to have maximum impact, you will want to have some kind of hook for each of your main points (i.e. a story, a fact, or a memorable example of some kind). At this point, these will be easy to design. If you have any trouble, simply glance back at pages 62 and 63 to remind yourself how to brainstorm possible hooks.

Also for some presentations, you may want to include a **QUESTION** and **ANSWER** session. For clarity, we've shown at what point in your talk you might want to include it. We discuss Q&A in more detail in the second part of this book. For now, if you have any trouble imagining what might go in that part, just leave that section blank until you read the chapter on **"How to Conduct a Q&A."**

If you've completed all the worksheets up to this point, you have all the tools you need to put together a powerful presentation.

If you were to zoom out and think of your presentation in outline form, it would look like this:

EXAMPLE

<u>**BACKGROUND NOTES:**</u> Stuff you will keep in mind but not necessarily say out loud:

TITLE: *The Bonko Egg Scrambler*

PURPOSE

    Audience should FEEL: *Excited about the product!*

    Audience should DO: *Buy!*

    Audience should THINK: *I need one!*

IN ONE SENTENCE: *The Bonko Egg Scrambler saves time and effort in the kitchen!*

<u>**PRESENTATION:**</u> Stuff you will say out loud and/or otherwise include in your presentation:

BEGINNING / INTRODUCTION

    Hook: *Images of someone having trouble scrambling eggs*

    Desire/Problem: *"Do you have trouble scrambling eggs?"*

    Solution: *"Try the Bonko Egg Scrambler."*

    Name / Credibility: *[Not needed for infomercials unless it is an individual endorsement]*

MIDDLE / BODY

    Point 1: *"It slices, dices, and scrambles eggs in seconds!"*

        Hook or evidence: *Images of the product doing its thing*

    Point 2: *"Scramblers like this can sell for hundreds of dollars in stores."*

        Hook or evidence: *[There is absolutely no evidence this is true, but infomercials leave that part out]*

    Point 3: *The first 100 people to order will get a second egg scrambler for free!"*

        Hook or evidence: *"Special TV offer"*

END / CONCLUSION

    Question and answer session: *[Not used on television ads]*

    Call to action: *"Act now; supplies are limited!"*

    Last thing they leave with: *The toll-free number and image of person using the product*

YOUR TURN

BACKGROUND NOTES: Stuff you will keep in mind but not necessarily say out loud:

    TITLE: _____

    PURPOSE

        Audience should FEEL: _____

        Audience should DO: _____

        Audience should THINK: _____

    IN ONE SENTENCE: _____

PRESENTATION: Stuff you will say out loud and/or otherwise include in your presentation:

    BEGINNING / INTRODUCTION

        Hook: _____

        Problem: _____

        Solution: _____

        Name / Credibility: _____

    MIDDLE / BODY

        Point 1: _____

            Hook or evidence: _____

        Point 2: _____

            Hook or evidence: _____

        Point 3: _____

            Hook or evidence: _____

    END / CONCLUSION

        Question and answer session: _____

        Call to action: _____

        Last thing they leave with: _____

BACKGROUND NOTES

What's your purpose?

YOUR TURN: To make this even easier, we've included space on the following pages to organize your outline using the same sticky notes you've been working with.

Either move them from the other sections of the book, or write new ones to answer the questions on the following pages and make your outline as simple and clear as possible.

These are thing to keep in mind but not necessarily to say.

WORKING TITLE OF YOUR PRESENTATION:

YOU WANT THEM TO FEEL:

YOU WANT THEM TO KNOW OR THINK:

YOU WANT THEM TO DO THIS:

ONE SENTENCE TO ENCOMPASS EVERYTHING:

THE INTRODUCTION

YOUR TURN: What will you say, do, and show them first?

YOUR HOOK:
(How will you get their attention?)

YOUR DESIRE OR PROBLEM:
(What do they need to know about?)

YOUR SOLUTION:
(This is your BIG IDEA)

CREDIBILITY ON THIS TOPIC:
(Why should they listen to you?)

THE BODY OF YOUR PRESENTATION

YOUR TURN: What are your main points?

FIRST MAIN POINT IS:

HOOKS YOU CAN USE:
(stories, evidence or examples)

SECOND MAIN POINT IS:

HOOKS YOU CAN USE:
(stories, evidence or examples)

THE BODY OF YOUR PRESENTATION

What are your MAIN POINTS?

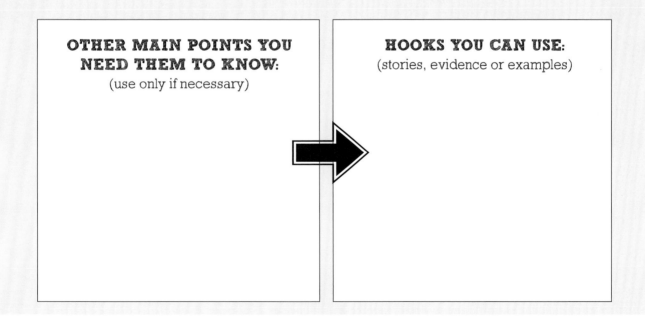

THE CONCLUSION

YOUR TURN: What final thoughts or images will you leave them with?

END WITH A BANG BY DOING THIS:	QUESTIONS: from the audience you should anticipate are:

YOUR CALL TO ACTION IS: (what do you want them to DO?)	THE LAST THING YOU WILL LEAVE THEM WITH:

What's Next?

Congratulations! You've come a very long way in a very short time. You're way ahead of most people. Most people start developing their presentations by opening up their computers and starting to type. If you do that before organizing your thoughts, what could you type? No wonder most presentations are just long boring lists of information!

Even if you do nothing else from here on, you have already sketched the outline of a presentation that can be made as short or long as necessary on a moment's notice, is rooted in your audience's needs, is in touch with their hopes and fears, and is directly relevant to them!

The next chapter will help you craft some of the stories you will use to demonstrate your ideas. After that, **Section 3: "Write It"** will help you learn how to write the words you might want to say, and **Section 4: "Design It"** will help you design any visual aids you might want to accompany you as you give your presentation.

CHAPTER CHECKLIST - MAKE AN OUTLINE

☐ Have you brainstormed your opening **hook**?

☐ Have you brainstormed how to **end** with a **bang**?

☐ Have you brainstormed several ways you could put it all together?

☐ Have you identified what gives you **credibility** to speak about your topic?

☐ Have you **outlined** a version of your presentation?

If so, you are ready to move on to the next steps.

CHAPTER 4
TELL A STORY

"Presentations are a powerfully persuasive tool, and when packaged in a story framework, your ideas become downright unstoppable."
- Nancy Duarte, author, Resonate: Present Visual Stories that Transform Audiences

Several years ago we gave a workshop at one of the nation's largest banking systems. It was a very fancy event. The room was filled with VIPs from the world of finance. The spread of food was impressive, as was the list of speakers. Part of the day's events included presentations by banking leaders about their plans for the upcoming year. Two speakers in particular stood out – one because his presentation was very bad; the other because his presentation was really good. Interestingly, both used the exact same slides and both discussed the very same data. **What made the difference?**

Both speakers were presidents and CEOs of units within the banking system. After lunch they were brought up one after the other to describe lessons learned from the then-recent financial crash and to lay out policy plans to solve problems that were still happening.

The first speaker put up a slide of a recently published analysis of the causes of the crash and then proceeded to list responses for each of its 27 points. The gist of each of his points was basically the same: "We need to find a way to pay more attention to details even when things are changing quickly," but he didn't say it as simply as that. It may have been the most boring presentation ever given.

The second speaker used the exact same slide about the exact same report but his presentation was memorizing. He didn't talk about the list of things in the report. **Instead he told a story** about his love of car racing.

Unbeknownst to almost everyone, he'd been racing cars for nearly 20 years. As he told his story, he placed his audience behind the wheel and talked about what it feels like to go 200 MPH. Everyone sat on the edge of their seats as he spoke. There wasn't a sound in the room. He talked about the importance of knowing everything about the car, everything about yourself, and everything about the other drivers. Then he tied it all back to the findings in the report:

> "When I read this report, I think of car racing," he said. "You've got to be able to keep up your speed and pay attention to every detail along the way. You have to be able to go fast on the outside but slow on the inside. You need absolute focus at all times. One small oversight and you're done."

Both speakers had the same message, but the first person's talk was boring. It was like listening to a school principal giving morning announcements. The second person's presentation glued us to our seats. His message was engaging, inspiring and clear. After his car analogy, he proposed many of the same remedies the first speaker had, but in a far more engaging context. The difference is that the first speaker gave us information while the second speaker told us a story.

The Power of Stories

Humans are hardwired to listen to stories. Since the dawn of mankind, people have huddled around campfires, gathered in groups, or snuggled in their beds to hear them. Stories take us on a journey. They make us feel and help us see. They motivate us, teach us, warn us, and help us define who we are. Stories can excite us, scare us, or inspire us. And, best of all, they're easy to remember.

If you want to make your message memorable, tell a story.

The best presentations are told through stories. There are two ways to do this: the simplest way is to use stories to highlight, prove, or illustrate points within a longer presentation. The second way is to design your entire presentation as a single story. Both approaches are easy if you know the basic ways that stories are structured. Let's start by taking a look at how you might use short stories within a longer presentation.

Audience First

No story exists without an audience. Any presentation you give - even if it's only about data - still needs to focus on WHY that information is important to the people who will be listening and why the actions you're suggesting are worth taking.

Before you can start putting together stories for your presentation, you need to know the MESSAGE you want the stories to convey.

The message is not the same as your single sentence. The sentence is the overall message but **each main point may have its own message.**

Think back to the example of the Bonko Egg Scrambler from the last chapter. The overall message of the commercial "Buy!" But this message was in turn divided into smaller points. The message of the first point was: "It slices, dices, and scrambles eggs in seconds," and the message of the second point was "scramblers like this can sell for hundreds of dollars in stores."

Each of these messages could be illustrated with stories of their own.

In the story about the bank CEOs above, the message was the same in both presentations: "We need to pay attention to details even when things are changing quickly." The first presenter chose to present this message in the form of a list, while the second one chose to convey this message by telling a story about what it feels like to drive a racecar. **His presentation was memorable because of that story.**

Make a Story File

When you present, you can tell stories about anyone or anything. However the closer the stories are to your own experiences, the more impact they will have. So how do you know what stories to use for a particular audience? The best way for you to have the right story at the right time is to have several stories at your fingertips at all times.

The way to do that is to make a list of personal stories and keep them in a file or notebook. You don't have to write out each one in full but you should make a few notes to help you remember.

Right now you might be telling yourself that you don't have many good - or appropriate - stories. That's not true. You create stories every day. That means you have thousands at your disposal just based on your life alone.

There's a story in everything you do.

Your Whole Life Is a Story

In this section, we're going to help you dig deep into your life to uncover some of your stories. When you make a story file, the important thing for you to remember is this: don't edit yourself.

Make a few notes and move on. Try to make it fun for yourself instead of a hardship. You'll also find that one story often leads to another and soon you'll have way more than you can possibly imagine.

After you finish your first pass through, set it aside and then go back to it another day. Ask your close friends and family members to help you out. Your parents and siblings will tell you stories about yourself that you didn't even know!

There's a story in everything you do. For instance, maybe:

- Your car died and you had to be at work in 30 minutes. Things went downhill from there.

- You found a lost dog, called its owner and changed her day.

- Your parents called to let you know they were getting a divorce.

- You got accepted into an honor society only to be told that they mistakenly sent the letter to you when it was meant for someone else.

- You won an award for something you did in high school.

- There's even a story about how you ended up taking this class.

YOUR TURN

In order to help you recall some stories about your life, let's do an exercise called "**Mine Your Life**."

Look at the categories in the sticky notes boxes on the next page. We've included some notes in boxes as examples of the kinds of things you might write. Note how little you need to write to jog your memory.

The more boxes you fill in, the more you'll remember.

The important thing is just to jot down as many story ideas as possible in each box. Use multiple sticky notes for each category if you run out of room. As you write, you'll naturally create even more categories of stories.

Some people like to divide their stories up into stages of their life; for example: through grade school, middle and high school, college, post college, family, work, etc. It doesn't matter how you do it.

Categorize them in any way that makes sense to you.

The important thing at this point is just to keep adding stories to your list. The more stories you compile, the easier it will be to find a good one to use when need to. Place your own sticky notes on top of these and fill in your own stories.

OVERCOMING ADVERSITY:

Growing up no money
Sledding accident
Car crash

JOYOUS/HAPPY EVENTS:

Swim team state meet
Trip to see shuttle launch
First car

PEOPLE/MENTORS WHO SHAPED YOU:

Coach Datilio
Carol self-designed major
Jewel, Tom, Charles H

MENTEE STORIES:

Story hour at library
Sarah J, woodworking
Steve, Chip and Wayne

PROBLEM SOLVING:

Figuring out application process
Parks & Rec summer job
Getting to NYC for interview

MISTAKES/FAILURE & WHAT YOU LEARNED:

Getting fired from Sheraton
UM interview
Overcommitting 3 jobs

GREATEST ACCOMPLISHMENTS:

National Spelling Bee
Story accepted for publication
Raising my sister

BIGGEST RISKS:

Joining military
Quitting NK
That time on the boat

HARD TO BELIEVE:

Sheraton job
Finding the diamond
Missed me by an inch!

VOLUNTEERING, SERVICE:

Retirement community
Meals for homeless
HS coaching

LEADERSHIP:

Captain of football team
Eagle Scout
Mary and TC

BIG IDEAS:

Starting a business
Parks & Rec
Guinness Book record attempt

Pick the Story that Illustrates Your Message

Once you have a list of stories, it's time to dig into them and figure out which ones you can use to illustrate the message you want to convey. Look through your list and pick out a few that might contain elements of the message you are working on at the moment. Most stories can be modified to illustrate several different messages. The next section ("**Write It**") will give you some tips on how to polish these stories and bring them to life through the use of dialogue and other strategies. But for now, let's look at the basic elements that all stories have in common.

Note: There will be times when you won't have a story from your own life that illustrates the point you're trying to make. When that happens, it's perfectly acceptable to ask friends and family, use the Internet or do whatever possible to find an anecdote or story that reinforces your message. However you gather your stories, we're suggesting that you make it as personal as you can. Here's an example of how you might transition to a story that you found on the Internet:

> "Last week, I came across a compelling story on business.com about a company that turned its loss into a gain just by changing one word in its mission statement. I think it's appropriate that I share it with you now."

The Elements of Story

Every story in your list can be told in many different ways depending on the order you present it and what you want to emphasize.

The simplest stories have at least two parts: **Character** and **Action.** For instance, a very short story might be:

Character: "She"
Action: "fell."

Of course there are many ways to make this story more dynamic, but for now it's enough to recognize that all stories need to include some combination of character (a subject) and action (something that happens).

There are lots of different words to describe the main character in a story. Hollywood scripts sometimes use the words "lead" or "principal." "Protagonist" is a common term, but some people prefer the word "hero" or "heroine" (or "anti-hero" if the story has a darker tone), or any one of a dozen other ways of describing the idea.

To keep things simple we'll keep using the term **MAIN CHARACTER.** But it's important to realize that the main character of a story doesn't have to be a person. It can be an animal ("The dog fell") or a group ("We fell") or an object ("The car crashed") or really anything that can be tied to action ("The light faded").

The first thing you need to do when crafting a story is to decide WHO or WHAT the story is about.

The main character of your story needs to be someone your audience can relate to. **The very best stories for presentations place the audience as close to the center of the story as possible.** This is why direct address to the audience is used so much in advertising ("Do YOU have trouble scrambling eggs?").

The next thing you need to do is to identify the action or actions that move the story forward. This may sound simple, but the implications for presentations are enormous. Have you ever listened to a presentation that was only a list of facts? Even the most basic presentation will benefit from knowing what **ACTION** is at play.

If you are asked to present some facts about your company's financial situation, you can make that presentation much better simply by defining the **ACTION** those facts suggest.

For instance:

"We're improving." Or, "we're falling behind."

Facts may be facts, **but your job as a presenter is to make those facts tell a story.** The easiest way to do this is to identify the **ACTION** behind the facts.

Just as there are many ways to describe the main character, there are also lots of ways to describe the action in a story. The word "plot" is used a lot, as is the word "thread" or "line" (as in "storyline"). But by far the most common way to describe the action in a story is to divide it up into different parts or "plot points." For example, from school you are probably familiar with the idea of an "inciting incident" that creates "rising action" that culminates in a "climax" that then gives way to "falling action" (or "dénouement") and ends in a "resolution." You have probably seen this visually as a "dramatic arc" that looks like this:

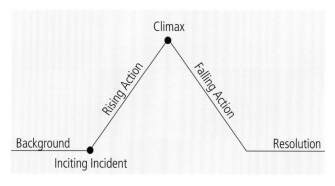

The problem with this model is that not all stories are structured like this. For instance many plays or movies have dozens of twisting plot points, many television series tell multiple interlocking stories at the same time, and most fairy tales include multiple reversals of fortune (for example: Red Riding Hood initially escapes the Big Bad Wolf in the woods – but foolishly tells the Wolf where she was going – so the Wolf runs ahead and disguises himself in Grandma's clothes – and then talks to Red Riding Hood before eating her – and in some versions Red Riding Hood is then saved by a Woodcutter with an axe – etc.). **Clearly not all stories follow the standard "dramatic arc" shape.**

But the "dramatic arc" diagram is useful nevertheless because it visually shows how **many stories change direction.** These changes of direction are essential for good storytelling. The best stories change in unexpected ways.

A Journey

Not all stories are structured the same way but all stories have action. Think about this in terms of movement. The main characters are trying to move toward something they desire (profit, love, etc.) or trying to escape something they fear (pain, loneliness, etc.). But then something gets in the way.

Usually – but not always – things that get in the way involve **OBSTACLES** or **ANTAGONISTS** that need to be overcome. For instance, while it's possible to make a movie about a man who does nothing but sit on a couch and eat potato chips all day, very few people will want to watch that movie.

Most stories describe a **JOURNEY** of some sort. For instance, "We're improving" is a story about successful forward motion, while "we're falling behind" implies that something is getting in the way. Likewise, "she fell" is a very simple story about a sudden change in elevation.

When you structure a story, think of it in terms of change.

Something about your main character's understanding or situation needs to change. In fact, many business presentations are simply ways to discuss strategies for change. For instance, right now someone somewhere is presenting a variation of this basic story:

"Our company is making less profit than we'd like. How can we change this and make more money?"

One of the main things you need to do to craft your story is to identify the **CHANGE** that takes place (or that your main character wants or needs to take place).

Conflict and Crisis

When you structure your story, pay attention to any **CONFLICT** that will drive the action forward. Or better yet, see if there is a way to describe that conflict in terms of a **CRISIS** – why is this important **NOW**? Or why did things **NEED** to change when they did?

Look back at the drawing of the dramatic arc. The period of "rising action" is also the period of "conflict." This is the part of the story in which things aren't going as well as they could for the main character. There are problems, but nothing really changes until those problems come to a "climax" (a moment of ultimate tension). Your story, too, needs a moment like this – a moment when things **HAVE TO CHANGE.**

Identifying why change **NEEDS** to take place is a very useful storytelling skill. When playwrights, script writers, actors or directors have trouble crafting a story or bringing it to life, one of the first strategies they turn to is "raising the stakes" – **or finding a way to make the action more important.**

This principle is particularly useful for business presentations. Few decisions are made because of low-grade conflict. In business, things that "probably should get done someday" rarely get done. If you ever have to give a presentation about making changes in your organization, **you need to know why the change is important NOW.** Otherwise it is unlikely that anything will change.

This principle is one of the fundamental strategies for sales of all sorts. "Identify a need" "solve a problem" and "create a sense of urgency" are among the most common pieces of advice given to new salespeople in every industry.

This is also good advice for storytellers. **It is easier to tell a good story about things that matter.** This is another reason why you rarely see movies about someone sitting on a couch eating potato chips all day – not only is there no action and no conflict, there is also no **NEED** for action.

Basic Pieces

The basic parts of most stories are the same things that you've already thought about for your presentation:

- **Who** is your story about?
- **Where** does it take place?
- **Why** is it important?
- **What** does your main character want?
- **When** do they want it?
- **How** does the action unfold?

It's possible to build a story using these questions, but it's even easier to think of the answers in terms of the **DRAMATIC** elements they represent.

Who is the MAIN CHARACTER?
Who is your story about?

What is the SETTING?
Where does the story take place?

What is their DESIRE or PROBLEM?
What does your main character want and when do they want it?

What CONFLICT/ CRISIS is happening?
Why is this important to them now?

What is the TURNING POINT (CLIMAX)?
At what point in the story do things change?

What SOLUTIONS do they attempt?
How does the story unfold?

In the end, WHAT CHANGES?
(Or if you are leading a discussion about possible solutions, what will change as the result of each proposal?)

Illustrated Example

Think back to the Bonko Egg Scrambler story from the previous chapter:

Narrator:

"Do YOU have trouble scrambling eggs? Try the Bonko Egg Scrambler! It slices, dices, and scrambles eggs in seconds! Scramblers like this can sell for hundreds of dollars in stores. But through this special television offer YOU can own one for the incredibly low price of only $19.99! But wait – there's more! The first 100 people to order will get a second egg scrambler for free! Act now; supplies are limited!"

This infomercial follows a very basic narrative structure:

What is the SETTING?

An average kitchen

Who is the MAIN CHARACTER?

An average person just like me.
(The announcer says "You.")

What is their DESIRE or PROBLEM?

Wants to scramble eggs, but is having trouble.

Other egg scramblers cost hundreds of dollars!

Why is this a CRISIS? / Why is this information important now?

Supplies are limited!

Special TV offer!

First 50 people get second one free!

What SOLUTIONS will help?

Buy the Bonko Egg Scrambler!

What is the TURNING POINT?

Call now!

What will CHANGE if the audience attempts those remedies?

No more trouble scrambling eggs!

Slices, dices, scrambles in seconds!

Save hundreds of dollars!

The second one free!

This is an example of using a single story to craft an entire presentation.

Business Presentations as a Single Story

This is also the way a lot of business presentations are organized. For instance, right now someone somewhere is giving a presentation that goes something like this:

Main Character:

A team in a manufacturing plant. The presenter says "We" or "Us."

Setting / Background:

"We've been using the same manufacturing machines for years. Our current ones are 25 years old."

Problem / Conflict or Crisis:

"Unfortunately, because they're old, these machines are starting to break down."

Turning Point (Climax):

"We've been nursing them along as best we can, but last week one of them failed completely."

Possible Solutions:

"We have three options at this point:

1. We can do nothing and continue nursing the remaining machines along as best we can.

2. Or, we can replace the machine that broke down.

3. Or, we can replace ALL the machines to fix the problem for good and upgrade our system."

Change:

Here's how each of those options play out:

1. "Doing nothing seems like it would cost nothing, but it means we'll have diminished manufacturing capability and so will make less money."

2. "Replacing only the machine that failed is the minimum we can realistically do. This will return us to our current manufacturing capacity."

3. "We should also consider using this as an opportunity to upgrade the entire system. It will cost more up front, but it will stop similar problems from occurring in the future as our machines continue to age."

What's the Best Order?

As we discussed, not all stories are told in the same order. For instance, mysteries usually begin by first describing the change (a body is found in the woods) and then work backwards to try to figure out how this change occurred (How did it get there? Who was the killer?). Many business presentations are set up like mysteries. The presentation in the previous example could also begin like this:

What has CHANGED?
"Last week we discovered that one of our machines had broken down."

What SOLUTIONS were tried?
"So we did some digging and found out that all of the machines have advanced wear."

What is the CONFLICT / Why is this a CRISIS?
"This is a big problem because it means at any moment any of the other machines could break down too."

The difference between the two stories isn't the information; it's the **MOOD** or the **TONE** of the telling. There is no "correct" order. The best way is simply the one that fulfills your **PURPOSE** (Do you want to calm them or do you want to warn them? – each approach has a different emotional flavor).

There is no one best order to lay out all the pieces of your story. Also not all stories need to include every piece (for instance "she fell" includes only the main character and the change).

The best advice is the same as it is for any presentation:

Know your purpose, start with a hook, end strong, make sure your story has a clear beginning, middle and end, and keep it short and simple.

However if you want to keep your audience on the edge of their seats, also give some thought to including some twists, turns, or changes of direction along the way. For instance the business presentation above can be made more interesting by including an unexpected change of direction:

"Last week we discovered that one of our machines had broken down. So we did some digging and uncovered something we were hoping we wouldn't find . . ."

This simple technique can help you craft stories that have impact. The next section – **"Write It"** – will give you more tips and techniques for crafting stories and bringing them to life.

But for now, look back over the presentation you outlined in the previous chapter and give some thought to the dramatic – storytelling – elements in it.

Your Presentation: One Story or Several?

Look over the presentation outline you drafted in the last chapter. Does it tell a story? Does it describe a change? Are there twists and turns or other unexpected elements in it?

Consider laying your entire presentation out like a **simple story** or use **several stories** to illustrate and reinforce your message.

Use the outline on the next page to brainstorm some story ideas. If you're having trouble coming up with story ideas to support your message, flip forward to the section in **Chapter 23: "How to Give Other Types of Presentations."**

In that chapter is an example of how you can use the questions about the elements of your story to brainstorm ways to create an entire presentation.

In fact, throughout the second part of the book you'll also see lots of examples of how to use stories in presentations of all types.

Consider your story's:
- setting
- main character
- solution
- desire/problem
- conflict.crisis
- changes

DRAMATIC PARTS

YOUR TURN: Answer these questions about the next presentation you have to give:

SETTING:
What is it?
Important background information?

MAIN CHARACTER:
Who is the main character?
(It should be someone the audience can relate to.)

DESIRE or PROBLEM:
What does your main character want and when do they want it?

CONFLICT/CRISIS:
What's in the way?
Why is this important now?

TURNING POINT/SOLUTION:
At what point do things begin to change?
What do they do to overcome the conflict?
What actions do you want your audience to take?

CHANGES:
How can the solution solve the problem, overcome the obstacle, or make things different?

Once you have all the elements of your story in place, play around with different orders in which to tell it:

Is it a story about chronological change (i.e. rags to riches, or once upon a time)?

> If so, try laying out the **SETTING** or **BACK-GROUND** first.

Is your story about an unusual person (or a "fish out of water")?

> If so, try describing the **MAIN CHARACTER** first.

Is your main character unsatisfied, or setting off on a quest?

> If so, try explaining their **PROBLEM** or **DESIRE** first.

Is it an action story?

> If so, try jumping right into the **CONFLICT** and **CRISIS** and/or **TURNING POINT** first.

Is your story about the journey rather than the outcome?

> If so, try starting with the **SOLUTION** first and then showing how it came about.

Is the story a mystery?

> If so, try telling the **CHANGE** first and then working backwards.

There are nearly as many ways to organize a story as there are stories to tell. Find the way that suits the purpose of that part of your presentation. You can re-order the same stories in different ways to serve different purposes. Your only limits are imagination and creativity.

Ten Additional Tips

Use these guidelines to help you pick out the best stories to use when you need them:

1. Make sure it's relevant.

When you choose to tell a story, make sure it's relevant to the situation at hand. It's best if the story is authentic and close to you, but other people's stories can sometimes be just as effective if you frame them well.

2. Pick stories that demonstrate values or lessons without having to name them directly.

One of the best things about stories is that they illustrate rather than state. After your story is finished, you can point out the lessons you think are in it, but these lessons will have more impact if they are revealed through the actions within the story.

3. Make sure your story has conflict, suspense, emotion, surprise, fun, or something unexpected.

You might tell yourself that none of your stories have these elements but almost every event in your life is filled with them. Any one or combination of these elements will keep your audience interested and engaged. Don't let your audience get ahead of you.

4. Write out the entire story or at least write down key words and phrases.

It's easier to shape and edit your stories once you see them on paper. It may seem time consuming at first, but in the long run writing them down will actually save you time and make your stories FAR more compelling. You can also use one story for many different situations. The next section – "Write It" – will help you do this.

> Note: there's no need to write out every story in your story file. For now just write out the ones that you think you'll use in your next presentation.

5. Use descriptive words and short pieces of dialogue.

Using descriptive words brings your story to life. Dialogue makes your story more immediate. Dialogue also brings your story to the present time instead of something that happened years ago. The next section – "Write It" will give you tips for how to do this quickly.

6. Tell it with passion.

Your body language and paralanguage (vocal tone, breath sounds, and other non-word verbal sounds) are often more important for successful storytelling than the words you use. The chapters on "How to Use Your Voice" and "How to Use Your Body" will give you tips on how to do this effectively.

7. Keep it short.

The length of a story depends upon your audience, where you are, what the situation is and so on. Stories look longer when written out. When you tell them with passion, they engage the listener. When your listeners are engaged, they stop looking at their watches. It's a good idea to speak your story out loud once or twice and time it so you have an idea of how long the story actually is.

Note: Don't go overboard doing any of this; remember, you're not competing in a storytelling contest. You're just taking a moment to organize your thoughts.

8. Make it conversational.

Your delivery should always be conversational rather than sound like you're reciting something that you've memorized. Again, remember: you're not competing in a storytelling contest. This is an actual story. Tell it like you're talking to your friends. It's not a question of getting it "right." Just be you.

9. Practice it out loud.

When you say it out loud, you'll know whether or not it sounds like you. And by saying it out loud, you'll hear it the way your listeners will hear it.

10. Tell it to a friend or group of friends.

Conversely, it is often difficult to feel authentic while practicing out loud by yourself. A better way is to tell the story as many times as possible in front of friends to help you feel confident. You won't have to worry about forgetting what you're going to say because it's your story.

Final Thoughts About the Elements of a Story

Your presentation should have stories in it. In fact, in many ways your presentation IS a story - a story about your audience's problems or desires and your proposed solutions. When you tell this story to them – when you give your presentation – it's important that you also lay out for them the **CHANGE** that will result from the **ACTIONS** you are asking them to take.

Your stories and the outline of your presentation go hand in hand. Remember, you can craft your entire presentation as a single story or – even easier – craft stories to illustrate points.

Give some thought to **HOW** you tell each story. This includes changing things up to keep it interesting for your audience as well as paying attention to your body language and tone of voice.

There is an art to storytelling that can only be learned through practice. The easiest way to practice is do it outside of class. You tell stories every day. From now on, just do it a little more deliberately. In no time at all, you'll be a great storyteller and your presentations will carry your audience on the journey that you create.

CHAPTER CHECKLIST - TELL A STORY

☐ Have you started a story file? Are you adding to it?

☐ Have you identified the **main character** of the story you want to tell?

☐ Have you identified the **action** within that story?

☐ Do you know what **changes** over the course of the story?

☐ Have you identified your main character's **desire**?

☐ Have you described a **possible solution** for them or described the things they attempted to do?

☐ Have you identified the **conflict/crisis** in your story? Will your audience recognize why the change needs to happen?

☐ Do you know the **setting** or **background** of your story?

☐ Have you tried laying out your story or presentation in different ways so that there are elements of the unexpected in it?

☐ Is it relevant? Does it reinforce your message?

☐ Did you practice it out loud?

PART 1   SECTION 3
WRITE IT
WRITE LIKE YOU TALK

PUBLIC SPEAKING'S DOUBLE STANDARD

Do you know that most people have a double standard when it comes to public speaking?

When they go see a presentation, listen to a speaker or attend a meeting, they expect to hear something meaningful and important. If they don't, they'll often complain about having their time wasted.

However, when it's their turn to present, unless they're reading a speech word for word, they often don't figure out exactly what to say until they get up to talk. Sometimes – if they're prepared – they'll have given some thought to what to say (a rough outline or bullet points) but often they haven't decided how to say it (the actual words).

In her book *The Message of You*, Judy Carter says:

> "Whether you're writing a one-hour keynote, a half-hour presentation, or even a ten-minute sales pitch, the first sixty seconds of your speech are absolutely the most important."

If this is true (and it is), it means you only have 60 seconds to "hook" your audience. Those first words are very important. You should give some thought to exactly how to say them.

Getting it right means writing it down and editing what you want to say – in advance. If you don't, you run the risk of delivering a long-winded, meaningless, and unimportant presentation. And this time, those complaints will be directed toward you! Justifiably.

You've gotta write it if you want it right.

How much of it do you need to write?

It depends on how important the message is.

If you have tell your employees that the company is being sold to new management, or that their equity stake dropped 57.5% over the past quarter, you can bet that every word you say is important. And the only way you can do that is to make sure you write them all down.

On the other hand, if your message isn't as "weighty," you usually only need to write down a few key words and phrases about your hook, intro, main ideas, and conclusion.

But either way, at least some part of your presentation needs to be written down and finely crafted.

This section will help you do that with a minimum of time and effort.

WRITE LIKE YOU TALK

"What is well conceived is expressed clearly."
– Nicolas Bolieau-Despreaux, French poet and critic

When you deliver a speech or give a presentation, you talk and people listen. If you're not clear, they won't understand you. And since you're speaking live, your audience can't rewind or reread your words to understand what you just said. That's why it's so important for you to make sure that your presentation is clear.

Your audience will give you their attention when you talk TO them, not AT them. When you write it down, write it in a conversational manner and make sure you practice it that way. There is a difference between written grammar and conversational grammar.

You don't need to know exactly what the differences are, but you do need to know that the ways you were taught to write "properly" in school are not necessarily the best ways to write for speaking. Luckily, you've had a lot of practice with conversational grammar. You use it every day when you talk and also when you send texts and emails.

Most of this book is also written using a conversational style. You might've recognized that we use more contractions and smaller words than some of your other textbooks. We've done this deliberately – and not just to make the book user friendly – but also because we wanted to get you used to reading the same way we want you to write.

Write conversationally.

Remember - Make It About Them

Focus on your audience. You know that. We're just saying it again because it's easy to forget them when you start to write.

For maximum impact, use the word "you" in your first sentence. Look at the difference in these two openings. The first one excludes the audience.

> "This morning, I'm here to share with you how I can breathe new life into this community."

The next one's better because it includes them.

> "Would you be happy if there were 900 new jobs created in your community over the next two years? With your support, we can make that happen."

Even if you can't include the word "you" in your opening, at a minimum, it's essential that your audience knows that what they're about to hear is all about them.

Your audience will stay interested when they know it's about them.

CHAPTER 5
MAKE IT CLEAR

"When I write short, it is to honor and enshrine, … to summarize and define, to sell and persuade, to report in real time and narrate, to link and think, and, probably most of all, to get attention."
– Roy Peter Clark, author, <u>How to Write Short</u>

When you talk with others, you process what you hear, figure out what you want to say and then reply accordingly. They do the same. This back and forth exchange is called dialogue.

A dialogue with friends is a spontaneous exchange. You don't edit while talking. And because the conversation is casual, you rarely think about how long you're talking or what words to say. You just talk. If you want to argue about something, you do that. If you can't figure out how to say something, you search for the words or ask for help. Either way, it's okay if it gets long-winded. You and your friends start on one topic, jump to another, begin a third one, and move sideways here, there and everywhere and no one gets lost.

But when you give a presentation or speech, you don't have the luxury of free time. **If you wait until you get on your feet before deciding on the words you want to use, you'll waste valuable time.** In business, time is money, but to individuals, time is their life. No one wants to sit and listen to your message if it's not short, simple, and clear. **One of the worst things you can do is to try to cram everything you want to say into your presentation or speech.** Audiences expect to hear something important and they want it presented in a manner that is short, simple, meaningful, and clear. Use the following tools to help you write:

How to K.I.S.S.

When you talk more, your audience understands less. The average spoken sentence is only between eight and 16 words - in other words **"Keep It Short & Simple!"**

Use these 10 tools to keep your writing short and simple:

1. Write in the active voice.

Bad: The beach is where she went.

Good: She went to the beach.

Bad: The speech was completed by me in five minutes, 15 seconds.

Good: I presented the speech in five minutes, 15 seconds.

2. Active verbs are good.

Bad: All of the people in the room had decided to get up and leave the building.

Good: Everyone left the building.

Bad: The speaker had chosen to end his speech five minutes earlier than expected.

Good: The speaker ended five minutes early.

3. Reduce clauses to phrases and phrases to a single word.

Bad: A person who is honest…

Good: An honest person…

Bad: Personally, I think that…

Good: I think …

4. Eliminate wordiness.

Bad: When you read you stop, gaze, identify, re-read, process, and finally give meaning to the words before moving on to the next sentence.

Good: You read text and give meaning to the words.

Bad: You might not like the idea of writing down all or parts of your presentation because you think it'll take more time than you want to spend.

Good: You're worried it'll take too long to write your presentation.

5. Avoid redundancy.

Bad: The millionaires who could afford nearly anything they wanted decided to close the restaurant to the public and feast on a 12-course meal.

Good: The millionaires decided to close the restaurant to the public and feast on a 12-course meal.

Bad: I plan to write my presentation out and write my outline out before I start to practice.

Good: I plan to write my presentation before I practice.

6. Avoid the obvious.

Bad: It goes without saying that unbeknownst to almost everyone in the room, he'd been racing cars for nearly 20 years.

Good: Unbeknownst to almost everyone, he'd been racing cars for nearly 20 years.

Bad: We sat in the driver's seat when we got in the car and learned how to drive.

Good: We sat in the driver's seat and learned how to drive.

7. Avoid ambiguity.

Bad: The essential first step in beginning to ensure that your audience comprehends your message is to generate your idea and articulate it in a way that is precise and stated in a straightforward manner.

Good: Make it short and simple if you want your audience to understand your message.

Bad: Even the most self-assured autoists might become somewhat distracted when they're unaccustomed to navigating their way through early evening automobile congestion.

Good: Even confident drivers can get distracted when rush hour traffic is bad.

8. Avoid jargonitis and 50-cent words.

Bad: If you don't update your programs and operating system regularly, you will acquire a legacy code that is living in your system yet not performing any function and possibly affecting other key functionalities in the back-end operating system.

Good: You'd better update your software.

Bad: You have an inflammatory response to an invasive microbe affecting your upper respiratory epithelium and eliciting febrile tussive fits with disturbing nasal congestion.

Good: You're sick because you have an infection in your nose and throat.

9. Stay away from intensifiers.

Bad: Public speaking is extremely scary especially when you know you're not really prepared.

Good: Public speaking is scary when you're not prepared.

Bad: Writing is ridiculously easy for me because I majored in English.

Good: Writing is easy for me because I majored in English.

10. Break the rhythm.

Bad: Break up the structure of your sentences by making some of them short and some of them long because if they're the same length your audience gets lulled to sleep especially if you deliver them at the same pace.

Good: Break the rhythm of your speech. Some sentences can be long and others short. When you do that, you keep your audience interested.

Bad: Practice your presentation alone and get to know it well before rehearsing with others so you don't waste their time.

Good: First, practice your presentation alone. Then, rehearse with others after you know your part well.

How to Make It Clear

When you deliver a purposeful speech, don't be lazy with your words.

You have a limited amount of time to make your point clear and in order to do that, you need to use every available tool. **Use these tools to make your message clear:**

■ Use figurative language: metaphors, similes and analogies

Figurative language in the form of metaphors, similes and analogies are like paintbrushes on a canvas. **You can use them to create a vivid picture for the listener.** They're powerful tools that can move your audience when inserted at the right time and place. You don't need to know the names of all the figurative language types, but knowing how they work is useful:

Metaphors

A metaphor is a figure of speech in which a person, place, or thing is directly compared to an object that is unrelated and seemingly contradictory but has at least one common characteristic. For instance:

> "Everyone stormed out of the principal's office and said 'that man is a monster.'"

We know that he's not really a monster but the metaphor creates a visceral impression of what people think of him. Here's another example:

> "Susan thought John was a snake for cheating on her. When he begged for forgiveness, her heart turned to stone."

Obviously these things are not literally true, but the imagery paints a vivid picture.

Similes

A simile is a figure of speech that explicitly compares two unlike things. The words "like" or "as" are always used in a simile. For example:

> "The speaker was like a frightened baby bird when she stood up to address the crowd."

We know the speaker is not actually a frightened baby bird but the comparison gives a strong, visual impression of what it was like to watch her stand up and face the crowd. Another example:

"The crowd packed the room like sardines in a can when she started to speak."

The simile "packed the room like sardines" created a visual image of people squashed together so tightly that they can hardly move.

Analogies

An analogy is a comparison of one idea or thing to another thing that is quite different from it. One thing is like another.

The main difference between an analogy and a simile or metaphor is that **an analogy isn't a figure of speech as much as it's a rational argument** that tries to explain one thing through another: a thing that is comparable to something else in significant respects.

There's a famous story about the pitching of the movie *Aliens*. In Hollywood, movie ideas are "pitched" to producers and executives with the hope of attracting money to develop the project.

Steven Spielberg's *Jaws* had been a major box office success (it made $471 million worldwide). At this same time, outer space movies like *2001 Space Odyssey* and *Star Wars* were also huge money-makers. But at the time the plotline of *Aliens* was like nothing anyone had seen before and (because movies are so expensive to make), Hollywood executives were (and still are) reluctant to bankroll unknown or unproven ideas. But wisely, *Aliens* was pitched using an analogy that everyone could understand:

"It's like *Jaws* in space."

The pitch worked. The producers invested $9 million and the movie made $204 million. That's a good return on an investment – based on a simple analogy.

Why did the *Jaws/Aliens* analogy work so well? Because *Jaws* evoked strong feelings and stunning images: fear, terror, horror, and monsters – and "space" was a great shorthand for a whole other type of known movie types. The analogy argued that *Aliens* had all the ingredients of a summer blockbuster hit. And it did. Here's another analogy:

"When the tornado hit, it sounded like a freight train was splitting our house in two."

The audience can almost see and hear the tornado ripping the house apart because the language makes the image so vivid. The analogy tries to explain something the listener hasn't experienced by comparing it to more familiar things. Note the use of the words "hit" and "splitting." Those particular choices add color and the make the image more potent.

Again, you don't need to know the exact differences between these language types.

Simply find ways to use figurative language or arguments in your writing. They will bring new colors to your writing and so can deepen your audience's understanding.

Metaphors, similes, and analogies can increase audience understanding.

YOUR TURN
Respond to these prompts.

THREE METAPHORS THAT MIGHT BE USEFUL:

THREE SIMILES THAT MIGHT BE USEFUL:

THREE ANALOGIES THAT MIGHT BE USEFUL:

■ Repetition

Repetition is different from redundancy. A redundant sentence unnecessarily repeats a word or phrase. **Repetition is the deliberate use of the same words to reinforce an idea.**

For instance the Rev. Dr. Martin Luther King Jr. repeated the phrase "I have a dream" eight times in his most famous speech. In real life, you use repetition all the time when you want to make a point. For instance, you might say:

> "I can't believe I got stopped for speeding. I was only going two miles over the speed limit! Do you believe that, two miles! Two stupid miles!"

Another useful way to make your message is clear is to ask your audience to repeat a word or phrase that you just mentioned. For instance you might say:

> "Whether you're giving a presentation or speech, the first 60 seconds of your speech – that's right, I said the first 60 seconds – are absolutely the most important." Then you might ask your audience: "What part of your speech is the most important?"

■ Ask Questions

What's the most direct way to engage with your audience? Ask them a question. (See what we did there?) **Questions move your audience from passive spectators to active listeners.** They can also challenge assumptions and serve as a bridge from one chunk to another.

Here are three types of questions you might use:

Rhetorical

They're frequently asked to make a point or to produce an effect without eliciting a reply. They are particularly useful in transitions from one chunk of information to the next. For instance you might say:

> "Let's do a quick review. Can you remember the difference between a metaphor and a simile? Can you remember the last time you used a metaphor or simile?"

Polling

Many speakers use this as a technique to check in with their audience. These types of questions are useful because they keep the listeners actively engaged even if some people are too shy or timid to respond out loud. For instance:

> "Of those who raised their hands, how many used a metaphor?"

Direct

These are intended to draw a verbal response. For instance:

> "Would anyone like to give an example of a metaphor you used?"

You can also ask different types of direct questions. For instance:

Yes/No questions:
"Do you like to speak in public?"

Choice questions:
"Do you prefer giving a speech or listening to a speech?"

Direct questions functioning as audience-wide polling questions:
"Does this make sense?"

Rhetorical, polling, and direct questions deepen understanding.

YOUR TURN: Make a list of questions to help make your ideas clear.

RHETORICAL QUESTIONS:
Three examples you might use

POLLING QUESTIONS:
Three examples you might use

DIRECT QUESTIONS:
Three examples you might use

■ Paint a Picture

A sure way to guarantee that your audience will be bored is to make bland choices for descriptive adjectives and adverbs. Without adjective and adverbs, your speech will have no color. It's like trying to paint a picture with a few shades of gray. Note the analogy?

When you deliver your presentation, don't be lazy with your words.

You have a limited amount of time to make your point clear. Descriptive language can help you get there faster.

Adjectives
An adjective is a word that modifies a noun (or pronoun) in order to make it more specific. For instance:

- a raging fire
- a conniving thief
- a smoldering look
- the crystal-clear water
- a sickly child
- an elegant necklace

Use adjectives to make your nouns and pronouns vivid and bring your images to life.

Adverbs
An adverb is a word that describes or gives more information about another word or phrase (especially a verb, adjective, or other adverb). For instance:

- financially independent
- eternally grateful
- wearily trudged home
- sorrowfully bowed her head
- cheerfully jumped up
- delightfully quirky young man

Paint the air with adjectives, adverbs, and active verbs.

YOUR TURN: Go through your outline and see what ideas can be made clearer or more colorful by using some adjectives or adverbs.

Write two sentences to give the listener a vivid picture of what you describe.

Note: Don't overwrite. If you do, when you speak the text aloud, your descriptions will call too much attention to themselves.

ONE SENTENCE:

ANOTHER SENTENCE:

Before You Start

Writing down at least some of what you are going to say will help you and your audience.

Never use more words when fewer will do.

For instance, don't say things like this: "The single best tactic you can employ in the service of verbal communication is to avoid any extraneous, particularly florid or filigreed elaborations of style, diction, form, and presentation."

A simpler way to say the same thing is: "Don't use jargon or long-winded sentences."

**Shorter is better. Simpler is better.
Make it short and simple.**

Keep it short and simple.

■ Avoid ambiguity and redundancy and don't overstate the obvious.

■ Metaphors, similes, and analogies can deepen and enrich the connection between your ideas and your audience.

■ To make your message clear, try repeating a word or phrase.

■ Ask your audience questions at strategic points and paint a vivid picture.

■ Use any and all tools at your disposal to clarify your overall message.

CHAPTER CHECKLIST - MAKE IT CLEAR

☐ Write in the active voice.

☐ Use active verbs when possible.

☐ Reduce clauses to phrases and phrases to single words.

☐ Avoid wordiness.

☐ Avoid redundancy.

☐ Avoid the obvious.

☐ Avoid jargonitus and 50-cent words.

☐ Stay away from intensifiers.

☐ Break the rhythm.

☐ Use figurative language: metaphors, similes, and analogies.

☐ Repeat words or phrases to reinforce your message.

☐ Ask rhetorical, polling, and direct (yes/no or choices) questions.

☐ Paint a picture using adjectives and adverbs.

CHAPTER 6
WRITE A STORY

"Experience of the best teacher. A compelling story is a close second."
Paul Smith, *author,* <u>Lead with a Story</u>

Writing well is hard. The best writers dedicate their lives to honing their skills. Luckily, you don't need to be a fantastic writer to give a fantastic presentation. You just need to know a few basic skills.

When you use storytelling in the world of public speaking, you need to put thought behind your words. You need to know how to write and tell a story that communicates your message in a short, simple, clear, and meaningful way.

Chapter 4: "Tell a Story" describes the basic structure of a story. This chapter – **"Write a Story"** describes how you transform your story ideas into words.

Analyze Stories

One of the best ways for you to learn how to transform your ideas into words is to analyze and evaluate great stories. When you can break them down and identify what made them successful, you can apply those same techniques when drafting stories for your own presentations and speeches.

The story you're about to read is real -- it's part of a presentation called **"The Five Fundamentals of Success."** It's been delivered many times to college seniors who want to know what it takes to be successful.

■ The first fundamental of success is **DISCOVER YOUR PASSION.** Find something you love and do it. Even better, find something you "have to do" and do it.

■ The second is **DEVELOP SELF-CONFIDENCE.** It's essential that you believe in yourself and your abilities, otherwise "real-world stuff" will get in your way.

■ The third fundamental is **HAVE GREAT PEOPLE SKILLS.** If you have great people skills, your ability to network will pay huge dividends in your career.

■ The fourth is **KNOW YOUR STUFF.** Make sure that you are properly trained and have the requisite skills to do the job.

In the presentation, we tell stories to illustrate each of these main points.

■ The message behind the fifth fundamental is told through the story you're about to read. Read it and then we'll analyze how all the parts fit together.

As a side note, stories always look longer when written out. However, when you deliver a well-crafted story with passion, your audience won't be worried about how long it takes you to tell it (assuming you tell it well).

A TRUE STORY WITH A MORAL

Have you ever had a goal you wanted to achieve? Have you ever stopped short of reaching it because something or someone got in the way?

Back in 1994, Wayne Duvall was a struggling actor in Los Angeles. He wasn't alone in looking for work. At the time, 97,000 other actors were also looking. The competition was fierce but there was something different about Wayne.

Earlier that same year, Jeffrey Kluger, a college classmate of Wayne's, co-authored the nonfiction novel *Lost Moon* that Ron Howard decided to make into the movie *Apollo 13*.

Wayne naturally hoped his old college friend could help him get an audition. But when he called Jeffrey to ask if he could help him out, Jeffrey said that he wasn't comfortable asking for favors like this. It was his first feature film.

Not content with a no, Wayne set out to find a way in the door anyway. He called everyone he knew to see if anyone knew someone connected to the film. But no matter where he turned, the answer was still no. He called the casting office but was told that they weren't seeing any more actors. He tried again a day later hoping someone else would pick up and give him a different answer. Still no. He tried a third time but the answer was still no. Again and again the answer was always "No."

The film was being cast by Jane Jenkins, one of the biggest names in Hollywood. Clint Eastwood, Whoopi Goldberg, Kurt Russell, Robert DeNiro and hundreds of other stars have appeared in movies cast by her. Wayne knew he was perfect for the part. If he could just get Jenkins to see him, it could be his big break.

Wayne wanted this audition more than he had wanted anything before in his life. "All I want is a chance to audition," he told himself. "Just let me step up to bat and take a swing. If I strike out, fine, it's over, but I can't let it go before then." Those thoughts just kept going through his head. Over and over and over.

Wayne refused to give up. A few days later, he bought a box of chocolate chip cookies from a Mrs. Fields cookie store. The box had a cellophane window on the front that let you see the gourmet cookies inside. Then he wrote a short letter to the casting director saying that he wanted a chance to audition and placed it in an envelope and taped it to the top of the box.

As an added touch, he folded his resume and tucked it inside. He also placed a photo of his face (called a headshot) right behind the cellophane window so you could see him looking out of the box.

continued on the next page

Wayne rushed to the casting director's office with renewed confidence and high expectations. He parked his car, practiced what to say and then opened the door and entered.

But . . . the room was empty. There wasn't a soul around. No one was anywhere to be found.

Wayne's expectations died on the spot. In spite of his all-out effort, his strategy had failed. He placed the box of cookies (his "special delivery") on the receptionist's desk and drove back home.

But on the way home, he thought "Maybe I'm not done just yet." He was defeated, yes, but he still wasn't going to quit. So he called his answering machine to check his messages. To his surprise, there was a message from a woman who sounded like she was talking with a mouth full of cookies! It was the receptionist from the casting office calling to let him know that he was scheduled to audition first thing Monday morning.

Wayne knocked his first audition out of the ballpark! The next day he auditioned for director Ron Howard who agreed with him that he was perfect for the movie.

After he left, Ron turned to the casting agent and asked "Where'd you find this guy?!" So they told him the story about the cookies.

Wayne got the job - his first big-time movie with an all-star cast. He acted opposite Gary Sinise and Ed Harris. But that was only the beginning. His work on *Apollo 13* led to more and more casting. Today, Wayne has done nearly 100 TV shows and films with stars such as George Clooney, Tommy Lee Jones, Charlize Theron and many more.

As a side note, news of Wayne's success quickly spread throughout the entire industry. In fact, Jane Jenkins' casting office still receives many "special delivery" packages even today.

Wayne has talent. There's no doubt about it. But he also has another ingredient that might matter even more: perseverance - the drive to succeed even when times are tough.

The world is full of talented people. The world is full of smart people. But talent and smarts alone aren't always enough. Even Albert Einstein, one of the most brilliant physicists of all time, once said: "It's not that I'm smart; it's just that I stay with problems longer."

You too can achieve your goals as Wayne did. Are you willing to keep driving until to get where you want to go?

Now that you've read Wayne's story, let's break it down and show you what techniques we used to try to keep you interested and engaged. We wrote it in the form we did specifically so you could see how many of the techniques you've read about can work in an actual story.

First, there were a few questions about story structure we needed to answer before we began to write:

Story Structure

What is the SETTING?
Los Angeles, CA. 1994.

Who is the MAIN CHARACTER?
Wayne Duvall, struggling actor.

What's his DESIRE?
To improve his life by getting an audition and landing a part in the feature film *Apollo 13*, directed by Ron Howard.

What's the CONFLICT/PROBLEM?
■ Wayne is a struggling actor.
■ There are 97,000 other actors competing for work.
■ His college buddy isn't willing to help him get an audition, and
■ The casting office is not auditioning anyone else for the film.

What SOLUTIONS does he try?
■ Perseverance (calling, driving, preparing, visiting the office in person),
■ Ingenuity (the box of cookies).

What's the TURNING POINT (the climax)?
The receptionist calls to let him know he can audition.

What will CHANGE if the audience attempts those same remedies?
Their opportunity for success will improve.

Begin With a Hook and Build the Story

Once we had all the parts in place, organizing the story was easy. Let's go through it from the beginning to see how it was laid out and why.

The entire story is written and presented in a **conversational** manner.

We opened Wayne's story with a **you-focused question** to hook the audience in. The question requires **audience participation**. For your next story, consider doing this to pull your audience in.

> "Have you ever had a goal you wanted to achieve? Have you ever stopped short of reaching it because something or someone got in the way?"

The next paragraph **sets the scene** in Los Angeles and introduces the main character, Wayne. The sentence ending "… but there was something different about Wayne" creates **intrigue** because it makes you want to know what that "something" is.

Some people call this a **tease**. Craig Valentine, the 1999 World Champion of Public Speaking, says "Tease them before you tell them." TV and radio broadcasters do that all the time when they say things like "I have a secret tip about how you can get a new iPhone for free by doing one simple thing. Stay tuned and I'll tell you what that is right after the break."

Colorful phrases such as "struggling actor" and "the competition was fierce" are also used here to **paint a picture** for the audience.

> "Back in 1994, Wayne Duvall was a struggling actor in Los Angeles. He wasn't alone in looking for work. At the time 97,000 other actors were also looking. The competition was fierce but there was something different about Wayne."

Sometimes you need to give your audience background information about the setting and characters in order for them to understand the story. This is called "**exposition**." Be careful about putting too much of it into your story because it temporarily stops the action from moving forward. Tell them only what they need to know and no more.

> "Earlier that same year, Jeffrey Kluger, a college classmate of Wayne's, co-authored the non-fiction novel *Lost Moon* that Ron Howard decided to make into the movie *Apollo 13*."

Then we introduce the **CONFLICT**. For your own story, establish this as soon as possible after you introduce your **main character.**

> "But when Wayne called Jeffrey to ask if he could help him out, Jeffrey said that he wasn't comfortable asking for favors like this. It was his first feature film."

We add even more **CONFLICT** to heighten the **PROBLEM**. Conflict keeps your audience on the edge of their seat because they want to know what's going to happen next.

> "Not content with a no, Wayne set out to find a way in the door anyway. He called everyone he knew to see if anyone knew someone connected to the film. But no matter where he turned, the answer was still no."

We continue to **INTENSIFY THE CONFLICT**. This is the best way to captivate your audience. Notice that we also **break the rhythm** of the sentence structure by mixing up long, medium length, and short sentences. The short ones figuratively stop him in his tracks. It's as if he had a door slammed in his face. We do this three times as emphasis. Note: your conflict doesn't necessarily have to happen three times, but the problem must be "big" enough to make your audience care.

> "He called the casting office but was told that they weren't seeing any more actors. He tried again a day later hoping someone else would pick up and give him a different answer. Still no. He tried a third time but the answer was still no. Again and again the answer was always 'No.'"

We raise the stakes even more by demonstrating our main character's desire and showing how important this one audition could be.

> "The film was being cast by Jane Jenkins, one of the biggest names in Hollywood. Clint Eastwood, Whoopi Goldberg, Kurt Russell, Robert DeNiro and hundreds of other stars have appeared in movies cast by her. Wayne knew he was perfect for the part. If he could just get Jenkins to see him, it could be his big break."

DIALOGUE brings Wayne's emotional state to life and makes the story more immediate. This figuratively transports us inside his head. Even though the story took place in 1994, his thoughts spoken out loud make it seem like it's happening right now.

Wayne's inner thoughts are expressed as an **ANALOGY**. The reference to swinging a bat helps define his character. For your own story, **use figurative language, adjectives,** and **adverbs** to paint a clear picture for your audience.

> "'All I want is a chance to audition,' he told himself. 'Just let me step up to bat and take a swing. If I strike out, fine, it's over, but I can't let it go before then.'"

We also use **REPETITION** to emphasize Wayne's desperation.

> "Those thoughts just kept going through his head. Over and over and over."

The next bit of action creates **INTRIGUE**. What's he doing? It's part of the **SOLUTION** to his problem but it's presented in a way that keeps the audience guessing.

> "A few days later, he bought a box of chocolate chip cookies from a Mrs. Fields cookie store. The box had a cellophane window on the front that let you see the gourmet cookies inside."

We add even more **action** and more **intrigue**. His action is part of the solution but the audience doesn't realize that it will initially fail. This failure later allows us to **change the direction of the story** more than once.

> "He wrote a short letter to the casting director saying that he wanted a chance to audition and placed

it in an envelope and taped it to the top of the box. As an added touch, he folded his resume and tucked it inside. He also placed a photo of his face (called a headshot) right behind the cellophane window so you could see him looking out of the box."

We **RAISE THE STAKES** even more by describing Wayne's emotional state. The words "Wayne rushed" and "renewed confidence" tell us that he's excited and revved up.

"Wayne rushed to the casting director's office with re-newed confidence and high expectations."

Then we include something **unexpected**. This piles on even more **CONFLICT** and **CHANGES THE DIRECTION of the story**. The term "special delivery" is introduced now. When this is read out loud, this phrase needs to be high-lighted through tone of voice so the audience can then hear when the phrase is repeated at the end.

"But . . . the room was empty. There wasn't a soul around. No one was anywhere to be found. Wayne's expectations died on the spot. In spite of his all-out effort, his strategy had failed. He placed the box of cookies (his 'special delivery') on the receptionist's desk and drove back home."

The next part of the story is the **turning point - the climax**. This is the result of all of his hard work and determination – his perseverance. Note that the turning point only occurs after the point of **maximum conflict** (his "defeat"). The "mouth full of cookies" sentence also adds **humor** and paints a clear picture.

"To his surprise, there was a message from a woman who sounded like she was talking with a mouth full of cookies! It was the receptionist from the casting office calling to let him know that he was scheduled to audi-tion first thing Monday morning."

His perseverance leads to a great **resolution**. His efforts pay off big time.

"Wayne knocked his first audition out of the ballpark! The next day he auditioned for director Ron Howard who agreed with him that he was perfect for the movie."

The **RESOLUTION** contains an **IDIOM**: "knocked it out of the ballpark." An idiom is a phrase that has a figurative meaning whereby one thing means another. You use idioms all the time when you say things like "I'll drop you a line" or "that puts me back to square one." In this instance, the **figurative language** describes Wayne's sense of elation and **reincorporates** the baseball imagery from his earlier inner monologue.

Finally we end by describing the **change** that takes place through the **actions** in the story (changes both to Wayne and to the industry itself).

"But that was only the beginning. His work on *Apollo 13* led to more and more casting. Today, Wayne has done nearly 100 TV shows and films with stars such as George Clooney, Tommy Lee Jones, Charlize Theron and many more.

As a side note, news of Wayne's success quickly spread throughout the entire industry. In fact Jane Jenkins' casting office still receives many 'special delivery' packages even today."

At this point we can finally state the **main message** more explicitly.

"Wayne has talent. There's no doubt about it. But he also has another ingredient that might matter even more: perseverance - the drive to succeed even when times are tough.

The world is full of talented people. The world is full of smart people. But talent and smarts alone aren't al-ways enough."

Albert Einstein is thought of as one of the smartest people ever. His **quote** succinctly **ADDS WEIGHT** to make the message even more apparent.

"Even Albert Einstein, one of the most brilliant physi-cists of all time, once said: 'It's not that I'm smart; it's just that I stay with problems longer.'"

For your own story, if there is a moral or message you want to explicitly state, don't give your takeaway message until the end. If you mention the lesson too early or make the mistake of saying it a lot, it'll sound like you're preaching at them rather than taking them on a journey. In our story, we end by explicitly **REINCORPORATING THE OPENING QUESTION** to highlight the completeness of the narrative.

> "You too can achieve your goals as Wayne did. Are you willing to keep driving until to get where you want to go?"

An Afterthought

We didn't include this story an example of perfect writing. We're including it because Wayne Duvall is a great guy and his story is inspirational. His journey to success also has enough twists and turns to be a great example of how to write many parts of a story.

Wayne's story is neatly structured but not all stories are (or should be) so tidy. You can arrange your story any way you want to suit your purpose. The easiest way to begin is just to make sure you have the main ingredients you need (as a minimum you need **CHARACTER** and **ACTION**). Remember, with a few small changes you can also use the same story to convey several different messages. For example, Wayne's story could easily be restructured to emphasize ingenuity or self-confidence.

As a final note, sometimes you don't need a full story to make your point. Sometimes you can also use an anecdote to interest your audience and add humor to your presentation. **An ANECDOTE is a short account of an event told to support or prove your point.** Since they illustrate just an event and not an entire story, anecdotes don't need as much emphasis on all parts (beginning, middle, and ending).

The side-note in Wayne's story that "Jane Jenkins' casting office still receives many 'special delivery' packages even today" is really an anecdote. The larger story really doesn't need it but it's a short and amusing side-note. As such, it doesn't need to become a fully developed story of its own.

YOUR TURN

Go back to your outline. Look it over and see if you can find a way to use a story or anecdote to hook your audience, illustrate your main points, and wow them at the end. If you can't find one, then perhaps a stunning visual or unusual prop will do the job. We'll talk about that more in the next section, **"Design It."**

With the tips and tools described in this chapter and the last one, write and edit some of your stories. Use every tool available to bring your stories to life. Then practice saying them out loud by telling them to friends. In no time at all, you'll be great at it.

CHAPTER CHECKLIST - WRITE A STORY

For each story, double-check the following:

☐ The MESSAGE of my story is clear.

☐ The story is RELEVANT to the point I'm trying to make.

☐ The SETTING is defined.

☐ The MAIN character is evident.

☐ Their DESIRE is clear.

☐ The CONFLICT/PROBLEM is introduced early and often.

☐ The SOLUTIONS to the problem are logical and helpful.

☐ The TURNING POINT (the climax) is evident.

☐ The actual or desired CHANGE is evident.

☐ I made it conversational.

☐ I avoided wordiness, redundancy, and jargonitis.

☐ I used figurative language and active verbs.

☐ I asked questions at appropriate times.

☐ I used rhetorical, polling, or direct (yes/no, choices) questions.

☐ I painted a picture using adjectives and adverbs.

☐ I broke the rhythm by using long, medium length and short sentences.

CHAPTER 7
TRANSFORM YOUR OUTLINE

"Precision of communication is important, more important than ever, in our era of hair trigger balances,
when a false or misunderstood word may create as much disaster as a sudden thoughtless act."
— James Thurber, cartoonist, author, journalist

When you start to transform your outline notes into words, double check to make sure each chunk of your outline is crystal clear. If you've gone through the exercises in the first two sections of this book, then you've already created a solid outline.

Take a good look at your outline and make sure you've filled in every chunk. If you've left anything blank, take a moment, go back and fill it in. Once you have a complete outline, you can begin writing. Let's go through some tips on how to do that one chunk at a time.

How to Write Your Hook

Your hook sets the scene and prepares your audience for what they're going to hear next. If you start your presentation without a good one, you stand a chance of losing your audience before you even begin.

> Never start with "Hi, my name is _____ and today I'm going to talk to you about ..."

If you want them to sit up, lean in and listen, write it down. After that, edit your hook and make sure you practice it out loud.

Here are a couple of examples:

Use an object

The purpose of this speech is to recruit a group of science, engineering and technology college students to do a summer internship with a new start-up company, Biotech Products.

> "Raise your hands if you've ever cut or scraped yourself? How many of you have ever needed medical attention to stop the bleeding?"

> (Look around hold up a 5-inch-long metallic object shaped like a pencil.)

> "Does anyone know what this is?"

> (Dim the lights in the room and turn on the laser pen and wave it around the room while making sure that the beam avoids everyone's eyes.)

> "That's right, this is a laser pointer. And not just any old laser pointer. Our research scientists developed these lasers to seal wounds. Surgeons are using the first ones now. In a few short years, they'll also be in every household in America."

> "Imagine getting into a bike accident 50 miles away from a hospital and instead of panicking, you simply

take out your laser pen and seal the wound. Then you get back in saddle and go on your merry way."

Use a visual

The purpose of this speech is to convince your colleagues to use a voice recognition software program because it will save them valuable time when working on their computers.

(Your computer sits on a table at the front of the room. The projection screen is empty. You walk to the computer, look at your audience and begin to speak.)

"Most of you are afraid to use voice recognition programs, especially when doing important business, because up until now they didn't always work perfectly."

(Immediately, as you speak, the very words you just said appear instantly on the screen.)

"But as you can see, our program can keep up with anything I'm saying."

Both hooks create interest and grab attention. In many ways, the first words of your presentation are the most important. Writing down exactly what you want to say is important.

When you write your hook, remember the key ideas:

DO

- Make sure it's true.
- Make sure it relates to the premise of your speech.
- Write it conversationally.

DON'T

- Make it too long.
- Start with your premise.
- Start with "Hi, I'm _____ and I'm here to . . ."

Once you've chosen the best hook for your presentation, take a few moments to write out exactly how you might begin.

OPENING SENTENCE:

Use "you" or "imagine" or another focus word.

PERSONAL STORY:

First lines of a personal story you could use.

INTRODUCE A PROP, VISUAL, OR FACT:

How to Write Your Introduction

Immediately after you hook them, your introduction needs to identify your topic and preview your main points. The next two examples immediately follow the hooks you just read.

> "Today I'd like to show you a few technological wonders that Bio Tech is working on right now. Each of these products has the potential to improve your quality of life. In the next few minutes, you'll learn how to join our company as a paid intern and earn credits toward your college degree."

> "Public opinion says that there are three reasons why people don't use voice-recognition programs. One, because they're not accurate; two, because they're too hard to learn; and three, because they're too expensive.

> Well I'm here today to show you a program that addresses each of these concerns. In the next few minutes, you'll see how accurate, easy to learn, and cost effective they are."

Tease them with your topic and preview your main points.

Let's try it with your presentation:

YOUR TURN: Write your introduction.

INTRODUCE YOUR TOPIC:	YOUR PREVIEW POINTS: How will you describe them?

NOTE: It's a good idea to write your introduction and your conclusion at the same time so that they complement one another.

How to Write Your Main Points

The main points, or key points of a speech are the most important ideas that you want your audience to remember. In a persuasive presentation or speech, your main points prove your premise or demonstrate exactly why you want your audience to change their point of view.

Determining the main points of your speech is usually the easiest part of the writing process. In **Chapter 3,** we walked you through narrowing your list down to the three most compelling, engaging, interesting, or convincing ideas that back up your big idea or prove your premise. Now is the time to spend a couple minutes figuring out how you will introduce or explain each point.

Main points prove your premise.

YOUR TURN: Write out a sentence or three that will help you introduce or describe each of your main points.

INTRODUCE YOUR FIRST MAIN POINT:

INTRODUCE YOUR SECOND MAIN POINT:

INTRODUCE YOUR THIRD MAIN POINT:

INTRODUCE OTHER MAIN POINTS:

How to Write Transitions

Transitions are your way of letting your audience know that you are changing ideas. **A transition is a shift from one topic to another.**

It's more difficult for a speaker than a writer to signal a change from one point to another because your audience doesn't have printed words to let them see the transitions. For that reason, it's important to make your transitional sentences short, simple and easy to understand.

Transitional words are used in many different ways to help the listener understand how one idea relates to another.

The FLOW of your presentation is important.

As a general rule, use transitions:

- **after your introduction**
- **between each main point**
- **before your conclusion**

Some move the listener forward and imply the building of a thought or idea. Others help your audience make connections from one preceding thought to another.

EXAMPLE: There are many types of transitions. Use these to guide you in your writing.

To give an example
for example
for instance
in this case
in another case
on this occasion
in this situation
to demonstrate
to illustrate
to show how

To show sequence
first, second, third
first, next, last
A, B, C

To emphasize a point
for this reason
In fact
to point out
another
the most important
to repeat
to emphasize
in order to
and again

To clarify
for example
for instance
in other words
to put another way
stated differently
simply stated
to clarify
to make a point
said a different way

To contrast ideas
although
as opposed to
conversely
counter to
however
in spite of this
contrary to
on the other hand
still yet

To summarize
to conclude
to summarize
in brief
as I have said
therefore
as a result
in closing
as a result
lastly

To compare ideas
also
likewise
in the same manner
comparable to
in the same way
similarly

Transitions show how one idea relates to another.

Examples of transitional phrases might include:

"Now that we've established a need to learn better study habits, let's see which ones might be most effective. "

"Why learn better study habits if you're already a good student? Here are five reasons."

"Let's begin our journey by looking at your first week of classes."

"During your second week of college life, the excitement wears off and reality sets in."

"Did you know that 35% of freshman college students study less than five hours per week? Here's a story about how I went from a National Honors Society GPA high school student to a college dropout in 15 short weeks."

YOUR TURN: Write a transitional sentence to move from each point to the next.

TRANSITIONAL SENTENCE FROM HOOK TO FIRST MAIN POINT:

TRANSITIONAL SENTENCE FROM FIRST MAIN POINT TO SECOND:

TRANSITIONAL SENTENCE FROM SECOND MAIN POINT TO THIRD:

TRANSITIONAL SENTENCE FROM THIRD POINT TO CONCLUSION:

How to Write Your Conclusion

Your last words spoken will be the first words they remember. The conclusion is your final chance to make an impression, leave them inspired, or change their perspective and call them to action.

Write your conclusion with a sense of urgency. As a reminder, keep your sentences short (no more than eight to 16 words if possible). A well-constructed conclusion begins with a **brief summary of your main points**. You don't need to include each and every main point when writing your summary - just do a quick overview.

Here's an example of a conclusion related to the presentation on voice-recognition software.

> "Over the last 15 minutes, we measured the accuracy of three different voice recognition programs. I spoke 125 words into each of them. Out of 375 words, there were only 12 mistakes.
>
> You also saw that the set up time for two of them was under five minutes. For the other, it took next to no time as all. Set up time was easy breezy. Each of these programs sells for under $200. Not a bad price knowing how much time you can save."

How to Write a Closing Statement

A closing statement is the very last sentence or sentences that your audience will hear you say. A well-written one can drive your message home and help you achieve your purpose.

When possible, tie your closing back to the beginning of your presentation. As an example, let's revisit Wayne's story.

The Hook: "Raise your hand if you have a goal you want to achieve? Now, raise your hand if you've ever had a goal and stopped short of reaching it because something or someone got in the way?"

The Closing: "You too can achieve your goals as Wayne did. Are you willing to keep driving until to get where you want to go?"

How to Write a Call to Action

Persuasive speeches and presentations end their conclusions with an explicit appeal to your audience to take specific action on the content of your speech. That appeal is called a **Call to Action**.

Use active verbs when writing your call to action otherwise your audience won't know what you want them to do. No matter how influential you are, they won't respond to your appeal if you don't make it clear what you want them to do.

Possible calls to action are to:

- buy this product
- shut off technology 1 hour daily
- exercise daily
- register to vote

Inactive and passive verbs like "try to exercise," "think about shutting off your smartphone," and "plan to register to vote" are far less effective. Passive verbs don't ask your audience to take immediate action. **Active verbs are better.** Use them.

Make your call to action easy for them to follow through. For instance if you want your audience to sign a petition, bring the petition with you and pass it around. If you want them to shut off technology one hour per day, pass out stickers that say "Shut down tech and start to connect."

Here's an example of a call to action that uses active verbs and makes it easy to follow through:

> "Yesterday, I went to our local software store and told them I was going to pitch the value of using a voice-recognition program to all of you. They gave me these discount coupons to hand out and said that if you buy one of their programs by midnight tonight, they'll give you 40% off the total cost."

Focus on the benefits to your audience. Describe the results that your audience will get if they decide to follow through. For example:

> "These voice-recognition programs will save you money and get your reports done in half the time so you can do the things you really want to do."

YOUR TURN: Write the conclusion for your presentation.

SUMMARIZE YOUR MAIN POINTS:

STATE YOUR CONCLUSION:

STATE YOUR CALL TO ACTION:

STATE HOW TO HELP THEM DO THIS:

CHAPTER CHECKLIST - TRANSFORM YOUR OUTLINE

☐ Does your HOOK peak interest?

☐ Is your MESSAGE clear?

☐ Are your TRANSITIONS clear?

☐ Are your KEY POINTS clear?

☐ Is your CONCLUSION engaging and brief?

☐ Is your CALL TO ACTION clear and active?

☐ Is it easy for them to FOLLOW THROUGH?

PART 1　　SECTION 4

DESIGN IT
MORE THAN SLIDES

THE BEST DESIGN OFTEN HAS NOTHING TO DO WITH SLIDES

One of the most memorable presentations of all time was given to a small audience in a boring looking conference room as part of a regularly scheduled meeting for a large corporation.

The people in the room were heads of various departments. Each took turns reading from prepared slides and updating one another about various projects. Few people had anything of substance to report, but the meeting was scheduled for two hours regardless.

When it was Stewart's turn to report on the Information Technology Department, he stood up and said simply:

"For the past few weeks we've been trying to get information from all the departments and authorization to do some maintenance, but not everyone has gotten back to me. So instead of putting together another set of charts to explain how important this is, I thought I would just show you why we need to act now."

He projected a single slide with an illustration of the company's internal network system and dialed a number on his cell phone. "Unplug it and bring it in," he said into the phone. He turned back to the audience and pointed at the illustration on the slide:

"Every circle you see there is a digital router. Every time you talk to someone on the phone, send an email, or look something up on the Internet, your stuff runs through one of those routers. We need them to operate flawlessly."

The person he had called on the phone entered the room carrying a small black box. It was 18 inches wide with input and output wires on one side. And it was smoking slightly. The smell of overheated electronics was unmistakable.

> "That is one of the routers. They're not supposed to smoke like that," he said simply. "Don't worry, they're not all this bad. But our system is old. It needs updating. I'm going to resend the questionnaire and follow up individually with everyone. Please respond as soon as you can so we will know what we need to get to replace the old ones. This problem belongs to all of us. I'm happy to answer any questions you have at this time."

Everyone in the room immediately agreed to Stewart's request. There was no discussion about required paperwork or additional committees or any of the other things normally associated with regularly scheduled meetings at large corporations. The only questions anyone asked was how they could help.

Within one week all the old electronics were replaced with new ones and the company is stronger than ever.

Stewart used only a single slide – and yet his presentation was the most impactful one anyone at that company can remember. The moral of the story?

A presentation is NOT a slide show!

MORE THAN SLIDES

"My best advice is not to start in PowerPoint. Presentation tools force you to think through information linearly, and you really need to start by thinking of the whole instead of the individual lines."
- Nancy Duarte, author, <u>Resonate: Present Visual Stories that Transform Audiences</u>

Most people create their presentations backwards: First they turn on their computer and open up PowerPoint, and only then decide what they are going to say. This always results in terrible presentations. Almost always, **your presentation will be better served with something other than projected slides.** The smoking router in the previous story had way more impact than ANY slide ever could have.

If you turn on your presentation software before you know what you need to support your points, you aren't just wasting your time, you're also likely to end up with slides that have lots of words and lots of bullet points.

Worst of all, if you haven't taken time to clearly organize your thoughts, when you present, you'll have a hard time remembering what to say - so you'll end up just reading directly off your slides. If you want to avoid giving a truly bad presentation, don't do that!

Lots of slides + lots of words + reading directly off the sides = Worst. Presentation. Ever.

In the last section, you put together your thoughts about both what to say and how to say it. But it's important to re-member that the words you wrote down are NOT necessarily the words you'll put on your slides. In fact, you might not need any slides at all.

Think of your presentation as having three different parts:

1. Words you actually say out loud (The focus of the first three sections of this book was on figuring those out).

2. Images or props you need to ACCOMPANY those words.

3. Anything else you have to leave behind to help people follow up with what you've said. (This might include handouts or other documentation in the "Notes" sections of your slides).

Unfortunately, many audiences have grown so used to presentations using PowerPoint or similar software that it can be jarring to them if you don't use slides. How crazy is that?

In fact using slides for presentations is so common that some people will ask you to email your "presentation" in advance. Those people mistakenly think that your slides ARE your presentation. They're not. Never use slides to take your place! This section is about designing visual aids (when you need them) to **SUPPORT your IDEAS.**

CHAPTER 8
REVISIT YOUR PURPOSE

"I don't start with a design objective, I start with a communication objective.
I feel my project is successful if it communicates what it is supposed to communicate"
- Mike Davidson, former VP of design at Twitter

Slideuments are Bad

Lawyers for large corporations know that anything written by an employee at work might be subpoenaed in a lawsuit. As a result, many companies institute "brand standards" or other internal rules saying that you have to include certain things in your PowerPoint presentations to insulate the company from liability. This is one of the main reasons many corporate presentations are so awful. **Any slide show written by committee is bound to be bad.**

"Presentations" like this are sometimes called "slideuments" – an unwieldy combination of an actual presentation and a legal document. The term was coined by a designer named Garr Renolds to point out how bad slide shows like this are at accomplishing either thing: they aren't complete enough to be a good document and they aren't clear enough to be useful to your audience during an actual presentation. **Don't make them!**

The good news is that you **DON'T** actually have to put all those disclaimers and extra information in the part of the slides your audience sees. Most presentation software has a "Notes" section. Use it! The more information you try to cram onto a single slide, the less important everything else becomes. Don't clutter your main points with caveats.

Always keep your central message clear and simple.

Your presentation isn't about your slides. Your slides are there to support you – not the other way around!

Your presentation is about making your audience **FEEL** something. It's about getting your audience to **DO** something. Yes, it is also about getting your audience to **KNOW** or **UNDERSTAND** something too, but don't confuse knowledge with reading. If you put lots of words on your slides, you are forcing people to read at the same pace.

A presentation is a time-based thing. Everyone begins and ends at the same time. The average rate of speech for normal conversation is around 110-150 words per minute. Books on tape are read at an average of 150-160 words per minute. Anything faster than that is hard to follow. In contrast, the average reading rate is 200-300 words per minute. This means that if you read your slides out loud, you are forcing your audience to process the information at **HALF the speed** they could on their own.

Worse, many people read much **FASTER** than this. Some speed-readers can read over 25,000 words per minute (no kidding). You are unlikely to have anyone in your audience who can read that fast, but no matter what, you will have people in your audience who can read at different speeds.

This means that even if you don't read directly off your slides, you are still forcing your audience to read at the rate of the slowest reader there. Or, if you switch your slides over to the next one faster than that, you are leaving some of your audience members behind!

Don't think of your presentation as something to be read!

In fact it's best not to even THINK about slides until after you've designed your entire presentation from beginning to end. If you do it right, there is a good chance you won't need any slides at all – or that you can get by with very few.

Putting together slides is one of the last things you need to do.

The first thing you need to do when creating a presentation is to **CLARIFY YOUR MESSAGE.** If you went through the exercises in **Section 1** then you have already done that.

The next thing you need to do is to **ORGANIZE WHAT TO SAY.** If you went through the exercises in **Section 2,** then you have already done that too.

Many of the questions you answered in those sections will give you insight about the best way to design your presentation.

For instance, in the story about the smoking router presentation, Stewart's worksheet answers may have looked like this:

I want them to FEEL:
  A sense of urgency and ownership.

They need to DO:
  Respond to the questionnaire I sent!

I want them to THINK:
  This problem impacts all of us.

Note that these answers kept the **focus on the audience**.

When you focus on the audience, it's harder for them to ignore or be bored by you.

What's my MOST IMPACTFUL PERSONAL STORY on this issue?
  It isn't about me – It's OUR problem.

What's the MOST IMPACTFUL PHYSICAL OBJECT I could use?
  I want to figure out how to SHOW them how old these routers are.

What is the MOST IMPACTFUL VISUAL IMAGE I could use?
  That one router is smoking! Wow, that would get their attention!

What is the MOST IMPACTFUL STATISTIC or FACT?
  That nearly EVERYTHING they do runs through old routers!

What part of your opening HOOK can you REINCORPORATE at the end?

I can just point back at the visual diagrams and the smoking router.

What is your CALL TO ACTION? Answer the dang questionnaire!

I can keep them ACCOUNTABLE for this by follow up with each of them individually.

What is the LAST THING you want to leave with them

Send the link to the questionnaire again so that everyone will have it fresh at the top of their email chains. I don't want anyone having to dig to find my last email.

For some presentations (and all speeches), the next thing you will want to do is to **WRITE IT**. If you went through the exercises in **Section 3**, then you have done this. At a minimum you should have a few key phrases written out. Doing this before opening PowerPoint (or other presentation software) will ensure that you have thoroughly considered your entire presentation.

If you've done all of that, **THEN** – and only then – you can begin thinking about slides.

Think of slides as merely **ONE POSSIBILITY** for relaying information to your audience. More often than not, slides are the least useful tools in your arsenal. Stories, props, activities, and handouts are usually much more impactful than slides.

Storyboard It

Before filmmakers begin to get out all their technology (cameras and microphones, lights and recorders), they first create something called a **STORYBOARD** – a visual flow-chart of all the parts of their story. The reason they do this is that doing so saves them a **LOT** of time and money in the long run. Storyboarding your presentation offline before you open up your computer will save you a lot of time and energy too!

The easiest way to figure out whether or not to use slides - and what to put on them if you do use them - is to quickly revisit the purpose of each part of your presentation. Doing this will help you recognize when slides are appropriate and what needs to go on them when you do use them.

The fastest way to do this is simply to answer the following questions (partial examples are given for the first few to illustrate how little you need to write):

Are you absolutely sure you NEED to use slides at all?

Many of the best presentations don't.

If the answer is "yes, I do need slides," then use the worksheets on the next pages to help you figure out what to put on them. On each page, simply answer the questions on the left and then use the space on the right to sketch in some rough drafts of what the slides might look like.

VISUAL DESIGN BUILDER

Do you need a title slide?

Visuals that could accompany this:

> How to Give a Great Presentation
>
> by
>
> Aaron Anderson
>
> &
>
> David Leong

Best way to introduce and support your opening HOOK:

> Let's start by asking them a list of T/F questions about presenting.
>
> Question 1: "True or False, in national polls, fear of public speaking is ranked second only to fear of death?"
>
> Answer: FALSE!
>
> Fear of speaking is the number one fear. Here's the list:
>
> 1. Public speaking   2. Spiders
>   3. Flying   4. Death

Visuals that could accompany this:

> TRUE or FALSE!

VISUAL DESIGN BUILDER

Demonstrate their desire or problem by:

Visuals that could accompany this:

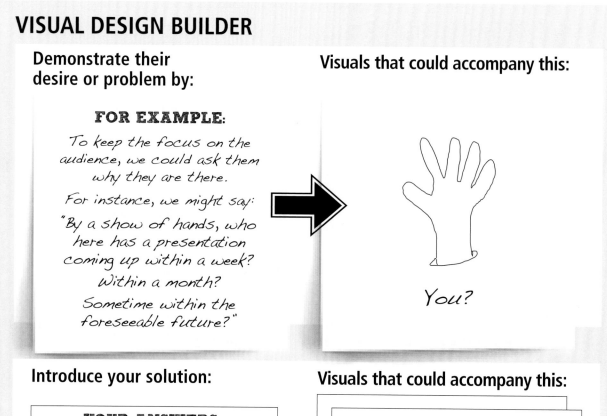

FOR EXAMPLE:

To keep the focus on the audience, we could ask them why they are there.

For instance, we might say:

"By a show of hands, who here has a presentation coming up within a week?

Within a month?

Sometime within the foreseeable future?"

You?

Introduce your solution:

Visuals that could accompany this:

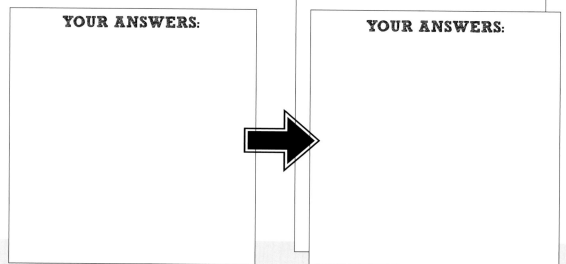

YOUR ANSWERS:

YOUR ANSWERS:

VISUAL DESIGN BUILDER

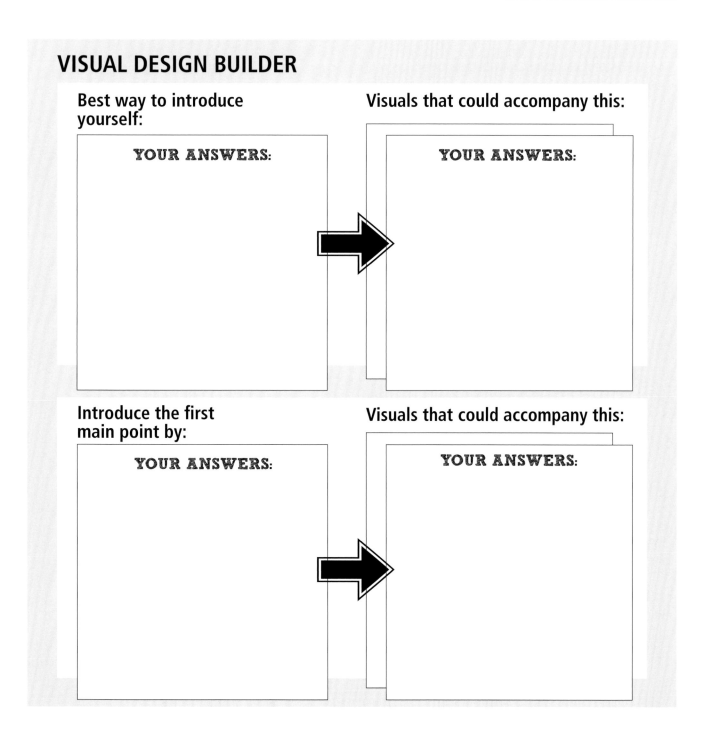

Best way to introduce yourself:

YOUR ANSWERS:

Visuals that could accompany this:

YOUR ANSWERS:

Introduce the first main point by:

YOUR ANSWERS:

Visuals that could accompany this:

YOUR ANSWERS:

VISUAL DESIGN BUILDER

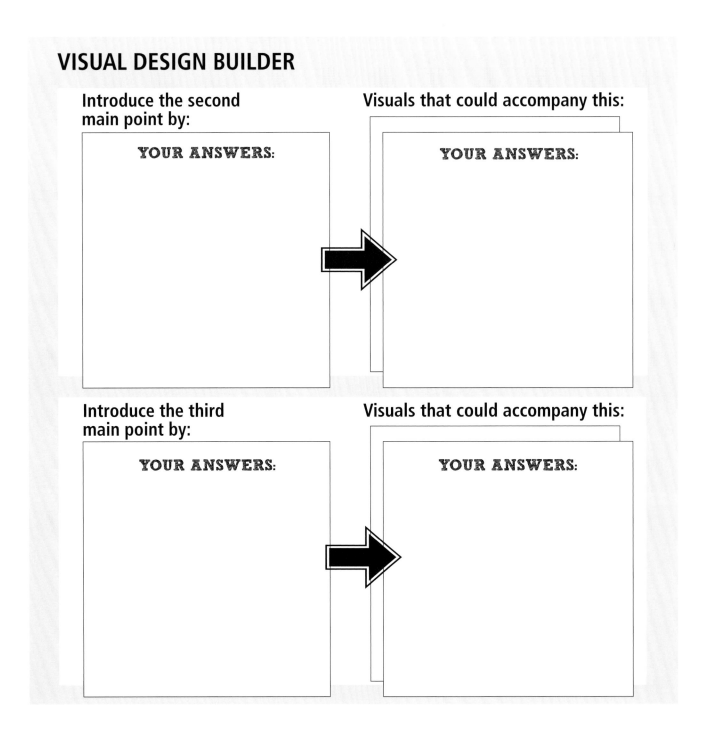

Introduce the second
main point by:

YOUR ANSWERS:

Visuals that could accompany this:

YOUR ANSWERS:

Introduce the third
main point by:

YOUR ANSWERS:

Visuals that could accompany this:

YOUR ANSWERS:

VISUAL DESIGN BUILDER

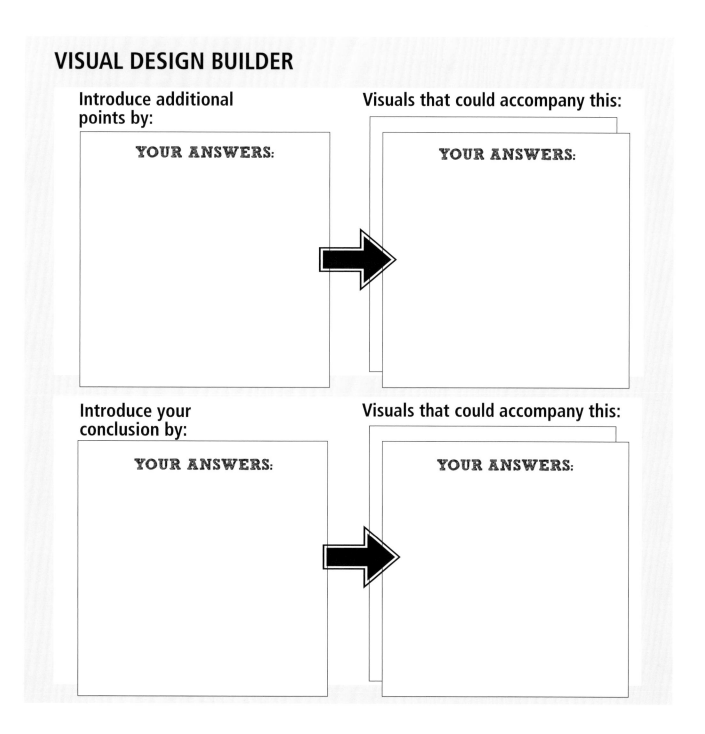

Introduce additional points by:

YOUR ANSWERS:

Visuals that could accompany this:

YOUR ANSWERS:

Introduce your conclusion by:

YOUR ANSWERS:

Visuals that could accompany this:

YOUR ANSWERS:

VISUAL DESIGN BUILDER

Introduce and support your call to action by:

YOUR ANSWERS:

Visuals that could accompany this:

YOUR ANSWERS:

Last thing you want to leave with them:

YOUR ANSWERS:

Visuals that could accompany this:

YOUR ANSWERS:

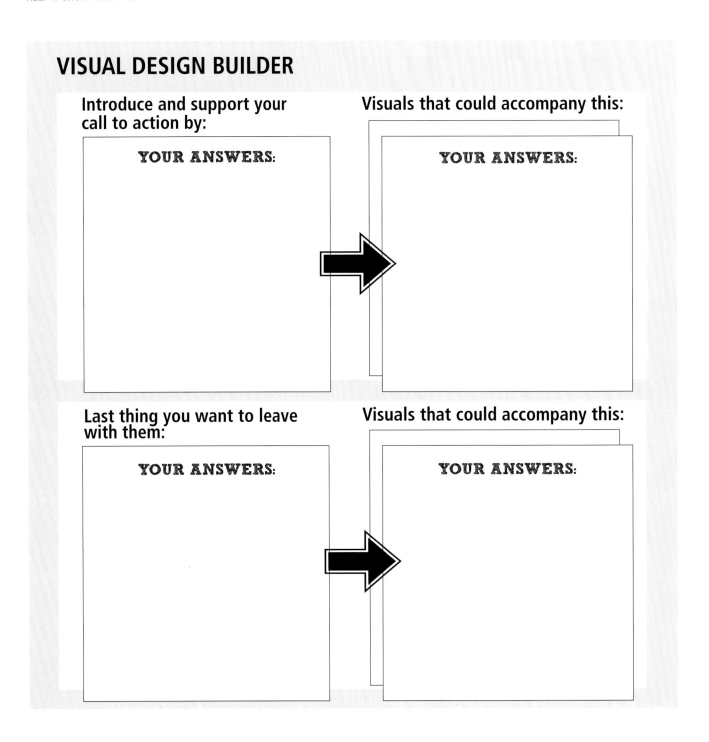

Congratulations! You've just saved yourself a ton of time. Now you have a very clear blueprint for what slides you actually need and some idea of what to put on them. You have just created a storyboard for your slide show. The next chapter will provide you with some more advice about how to design the slides you use.

CHAPTER CHECKLIST - REVISIT YOUR PURPOSE

☐ I've looked back over my answers from earlier in the book to see what design ideas I've already come up with.

☐ I've considered not using any slides at all.

☐ I know whether I need a TITLE slide.

☐ I know whether I need slides for my HOOK.

☐ I know whether I need slides about their DESIRE or PROBLEM.

☐ I know whether I need slides about the SOLUTION or my BIG IDEA.

☐ I know whether I need slides to demonstrate my CREDIBILITY.

☐ I know whether I need slides for any of my MAIN POINTS.

☐ I know whether I need slides for my ENDING or CALL TO ACTION.

☐ I know whether I need slides for TRANSITIONS.

☐ I've SKETCHED out ideas for what these slides should look like.

CHAPTER 9
DESIGN BASICS

"Well-designed visuals do more than present information; they bring order to the conversation."
- Dale Ludwig and Greg Owen-Boger, authors, The Orderly Conversation: Business Presentations Redefined

PowerPoint is not the enemy of good presentations - using it WRONG is the enemy of good presentations.

There are LOTS of great books on how to make your slides better-looking and more effective. We recommend pretty much everything Nancy Duarte and Garr Reynolds but there are dozens of other authors who are just as good.

In the meantime, if you do decide that the best way to get your message across is to use slides, you need to know a few simple concepts about visual design.

The first, and **MAIN concept** is simple:

IMAGES, GRAPHS, and CHARTS ARE ALWAYS BETTER THAN WORDS.

Your brain processes words differently than visual stimuli.

Think of it as a continuum with images and stories on one side and words and facts on the other:

EASIER FOR BRAIN TO PROCESS   **HARDER FOR BRAIN TO PROCESS**

← ─── →

Images / Stories with Imagery   **Graphs**   **Charts**   **Words**

This chapter will explain the eight simplest - and most important - ideas you need to know about visual graphic design.

The concepts in this chapter are in two groups: **four basic elements** and **four tips about composition**. Think of the basic elements as the logic underlying everything and the tip as the art of using those elements. Let's start with the basic elements first.

The Basic Elements

Each element is important, and each works in conjunction with all the others. In no particular order they are:

- Proximity
- Repetition
- Direction and Alignment
- Contrast

. . . Let's look at each in turn:

Proximity

This is the visual equivalent of the idea of chunking your information.

When items on your slides are close to each other, they become **VISUALLY RELATED**. Your audience will understand the whole group as a single unit of information. This makes it possible for you to convey the relationship without having to explain it.

Group ideas or images together to make it easier for your audience to see the structure of what you are trying to explain.

DON'T

Here is an example of some text put together without consideration to proximity.

Notice how hard it is to differentiate individual concepts within the single block of words. Since the words are visually related, your mind lumps all the elements together into a single thought

> The goal for this presentation is to help everyone recognize how emotion spurs action by engaging your hopes and fears around an issue. Some presentations make you make you feel cared for, or challenged, or confronted, or convinced, or driven, or encouraged, or energized, or excited, or inspired, or prepared, or resolved, or strengthened, or shocked, or scared, or supported, or validated, or warned. Each of these is linked to hope or fear, or sometimes a combination of the two.

DO

In contrast, notice how much easier it is to see the underlying concepts when the ideas are linked together using PROXIMITY to help visually clarify the meaning

Goal for this Presentation
Emotion Spurs Action

HOPES	FEARS	BOTH
Cared For	Resolved	Challenged
Comforted	Shocked	Convinced
Encouraged	Scared	Driven
Strengthened	Warned	Energized
Supported		Inspired
Validated		

Direction / Alignment

This is the idea that even though your audience will be able to SEE all the visual elements on your slide in a single glance, they will nevertheless read individual elements in a certain order.

Native English readers scan images from top to the bottom and from left to right (the order and direction is different in different cultures).

Don't place anything on your slide arbitrarily.

Your audience's eye will naturally flow from one visual element to the next in the order they are accustomed to reading. Use this to your advantage.

The easiest way to think of this is to imagine your audience reading the visual elements on your slide in a "Z."

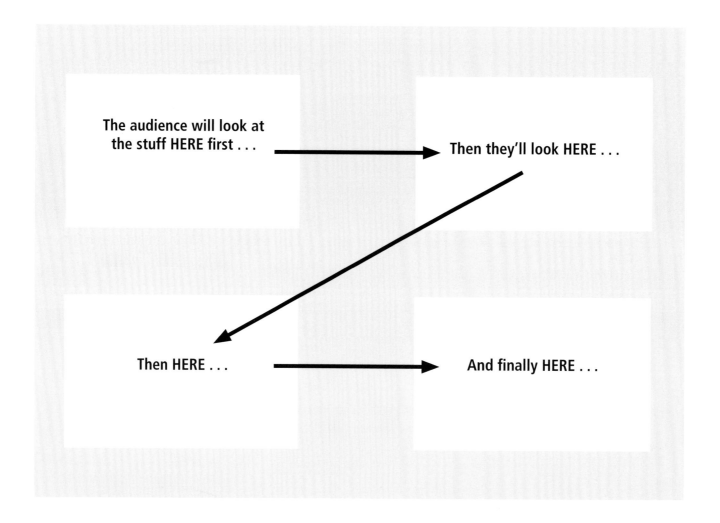

You can do the same thing with pictures or graphs.

They'll read THIS chart first ...

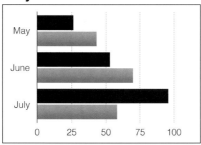

... then look at stuff HERE

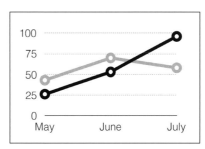

followed by things HERE ...

... and finally HERE.

But look how much clearer it is with only ONE IDEA on the slide.

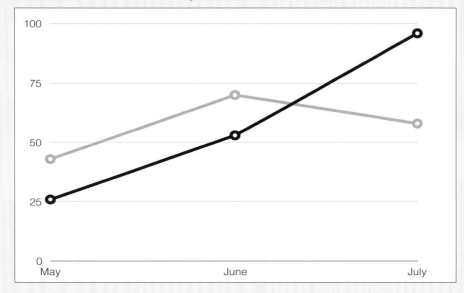

145

Repetition

Continuity in background elements will help your main message stand out. If your first slide has a blue background, but your second slide has a pink background, your audience will wonder if the change in colors mean something important (this is also part of the idea behind corporate "brand standards").

An even more important idea is that visual images that are repeated more than once **REINFORCE** the impact of the first image. Advertisers all over the world know that repeating an image, idea, or phrases makes it more likely that you will be able to recall it later. You can use this same trick.

For example, the main ideas in this chapter might be reinforced through repetition on a series of slides like this:

FOUR BASIC VISUAL DESIGN IDEAS

1 - Proximity
2 - Direction / Alignment
3 - Repetition
4 - Contrast

FOUR BASIC VISUAL DESIGN IDEAS

1 - Proximity
2 - Direction / Alignment
3 - Repetition
4 - Contrast

FOUR BASIC VISUAL DESIGN IDEAS

1 - Proximity
2 - Direction / Alignment
3 - Repetition
4 - Contrast

4 BASIC VISUAL DESIGN IDEAS

1 - Proximity
2 - Direction / Alignment
3 - Repetition
4 - Contrast

Fixed Point

Consistency / repetition in your background imagery creates a **fixed point** that can help your audience stay oriented. For instance, we could show that:

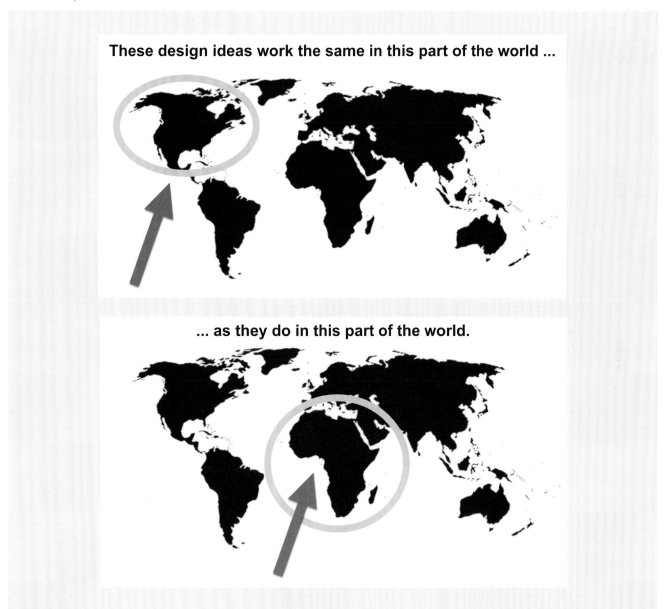

These design ideas work the same in this part of the world ...

... as they do in this part of the world.

Contrast

The most important concept here is that the human eye sees primarily through **difference / contrast**. For instance when you look up at the sky at night, the reason it appears to you that there are more stars in the sky when it is darker out is simply that when it is lighter there is less contrast between the light emitted by dim stars and ambient light in the sky. The number of stars remains the same. Darker skies just create more contrast.

Something similar happens when you design slides on a computer that will eventually be projected on a screen in a room for a viewing audience. Few projectors use lights strong enough to create the same contrast your computer screen emits easily. Thus the images you see on your computer might look different when projected on a screen or wall.

Ambient light in the room will have exactly the same impact on your slide show that ambient light in the sky has on stars - your audience will not necessarily be able to see as much detail as is "really" there.

For example:

It's easier for your eyes to read THIS

Than it is to read THIS

Simply because the contrast between the black ink and shaded space is greater.

For instance, our last few example slides wouldn't work as well without a white background.

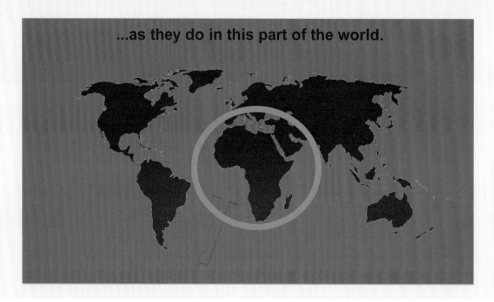

This lack of contrast will be even worse once the image is projected in a room (can you make out the arrow?).

...as they do in this part of the world.

Color

Technically color falls under the category of **CONTRAST**.

In school you probably learned that light has different wavelengths. We won't go into detail about color theory here, but you should know that the light source in many projectors is not pure white.

The colors you see on your computer can emerge VERY differently when routed though a projector. If you're not careful, this can make your slides unreadable. Never assume that what you see on your computer screen is the same thing that will be projected on the screen. Look at your slides in the room beforehand and be prepared to make changes if necessary.

But even before that, the easiest way to make sure the audience can see your slides the way you want them to is to consider **CONTRAST** as you design - contrast in terms of not only light and dark, but also in the colors you choose to use.

As a general rule, more contrast is better.

EMOTION AND THE COLOR WHEEL

Designers talk about color as existing on a wheel. They do this to help them see the way colors will interact when mixed together and to spatially visualize the the emotional aspects of the colors (ie. how they will complement or clash when used together). It's difficult to illustrate too much about color in a book that's printed in black and white - so you'll need to use your imagination a little bit here - but this rough guide will help you visualize the concepts:

Cool colors:
■ Can convey calm

■ On slides, they work best for backgrounds because the colors appear to recede away from us.

When using color on slides:

■ Don't use every color available. Keep your palette simple.

■ You can use color to punch up important points.

■ Colors on opposite sides of the wheel are jarring when used together (ie, green-red, blue-orange).

■ Colors that are close to each other on the wheel are hard to tell apart when projected (eg. highlighting something blue-violet on a blue slide will not make the idea stand out).

■ If you need to put words inside color, use white lettering in most colors (except yellow and pastels) to increase contrast and make it easier to read.

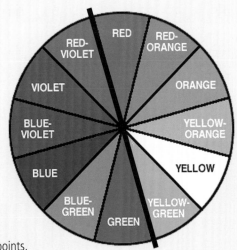

Warm colors:
■ Can convey emergency.

■ On slides, they work best for objects in the foreground because the colors appear to be coming toward us.

Images Are Better Than Words

When you project slides, you force your audience to process the information visually. Do your best to make sure your audience can easily process the ideas in your slides. This means using pictures, illustrations, graphs, and charts wherever possible instead of words and/or using images to set off the words.

For instance, in the examples below, notice how the lines and shapes in the images and the overall composition help draw the viewer's attention to the words.

Ideally, you should have only ONE idea per slide.

Composition Tips

In addition to those basic design concepts, there are also some basic tips about composition that are useful to keep in mind.

Composition is placement or arrangement of visual elements or ingredients within a frame. So when we talk about basic design concepts, we are also talking in part about composition. Remember - the concepts we've talked about up to this point are the underlying logic of design and the rest of this is the art of putting it all together.

Visual artists know that there are a lot of things that you can keep in mind about composition. However, to keep things simple, we'll stick to just the **four most important ideas** about composition for putting together slides. Also, to avoid getting too far into the weeds, we'll include only one example for each.

These tips are pretty straightforward. In fact, you're probably already familiar with each of them (or at least, you will recognize the ideas when you see them).

The most useful ideas about composition for slides are:
- **focus**
- **white space**
- **scale and hierarchy**
- **balance**

SIDE NOTE
Since we're on the subject of composition, here's a good place a quick note about how to size digital images.

One of the key concepts for all two-dimensional art is the idea of **PROPORTION**. Since this is a book about presentations rather than art, you don't really need to know that much about proportion except for this:

If you stretch a digital image wrong, you'll change its proportions and make it look weird.

On your computer, when you click on a digital image that your software is able to manipulate, eight little boxes will show up on the image. To resize the image with the same proportions, "grab" the image from the corners. If you grab from the non-corner boxes, you will change the proportions within the image.

To change size

Use these

Not these

Focus

Focus is where you want your audience to look.

We've used focus in every example so far:

For instance, we used **PROXIMITY** to draw focus, then we used **DIRECTION** and **ALIGNMENT** to direct focus across a page, then we used **REPETITION** to draw focus to a concept with words and we used a circle and an arrow on a map to draw focus to specific parts of the map, then we used **CONTRAST** to demonstrate how hard it is to hold focus when colors or shades blend together.

The best advice for putting together slides is to include only ONE main focus per slide.

Think of it visually like this:

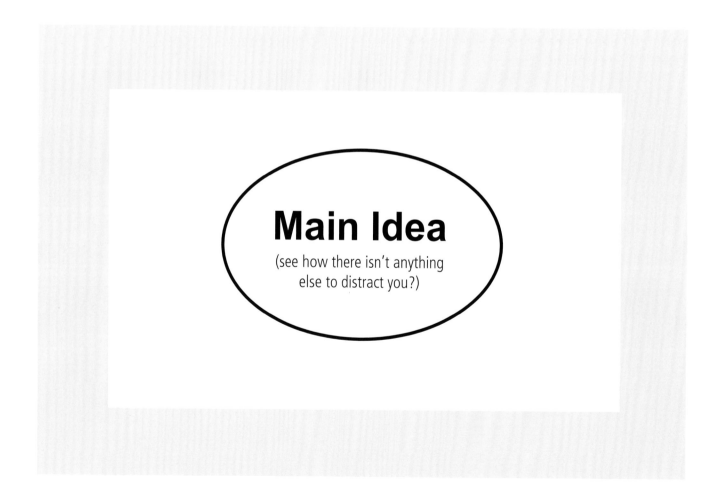

White Space

White space doesn't have to be white. Designers also sometimes call it "negative space." It is the part of the page that is left unmarked.

The most important thing to know about it is that the more stuff you have on your slides, the less important everything is. In this way, white space is also about focus. The more stuff on the page, the less focus you have.

The best advice for putting together slides is to never try to cram too much information onto a single slide.

For instance, look how hard it is to focus on the **MAIN IDEA** in our example when we fill the negative space with lots of other things:

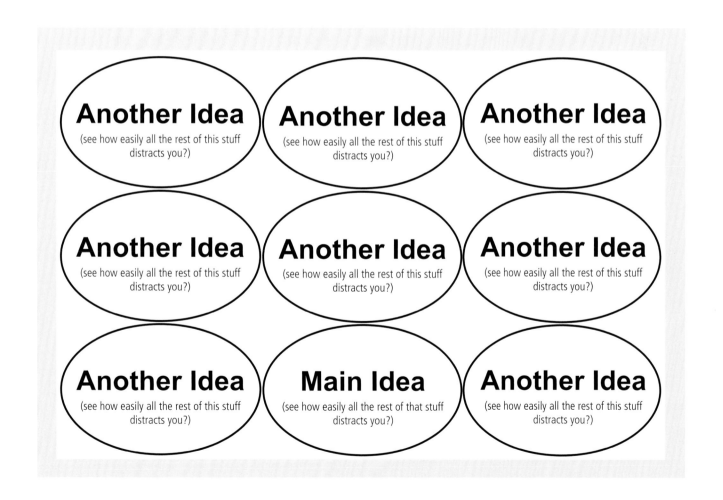

Scale and Hierarchy

Scale is a way of creating focus through **CONTRAST IN SIZE.** In this way, it also creates white space.

Hierarchy is **WHY** you use scale - it allows you to visually illustrate that the bigger thing is more important than the smaller thing.

You can also use hierarchy based on where your eye flows on the page. For instance, in the **DIRECTION** and **ALIGNMENT** example, we used the "Z" pattern to take advantage of the way you read information on a page. We created a hierarchy by putting the more important ideas earlier in the Z.

The best advice for putting together slides is to use contrast in scale when you want to direct focus in groups of words.

For instance, we could gain back some focus on our **MAIN IDEA** just by scaling down the clutter around it and putting it in the middle:

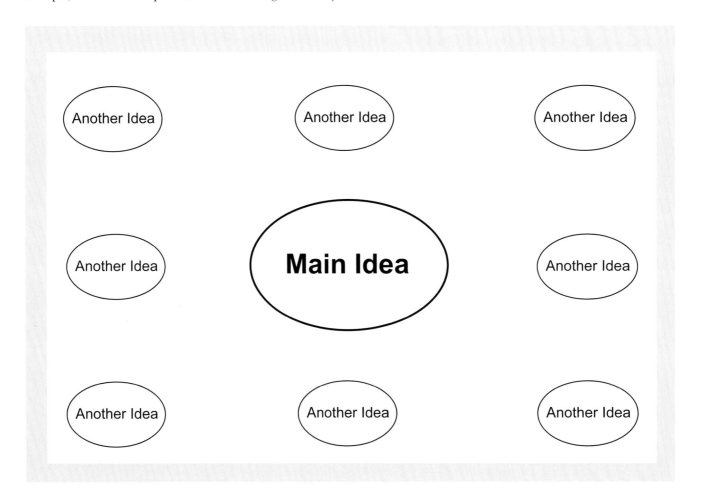

Balance

Balance is the geometric relationship between your visual elements. It's easiest to think about this in terms of **symmetry** and **asymmetry**.

Symmetrical designs place things equally distributed around the center. Symmetrical slides can seem boring because they don't have much "movement" in them. All of our examples about composition have been symmetrical so far

But for slides, some degree of **asymmetry** is usually desirable. However, to keep things focused, pay attention to balance (i.e. the geometric relationship of elements to each other).

The easiest way to do that is to pay attention to what visual designers call the "RULE OF THIRDS."

Imagine that your page is equally divided into three parts up and down (top, bottom, and middle) and into three parts left to right (left, right, and middle). Each of those areas gives you a useful place to put visual elements.

The best advice for putting together slides this way is to use the rule of thirds to make your slides more dynamic.

For instance, if we place elements in relationship to each other using those lines, we create a more dynamic slide that is still balanced:

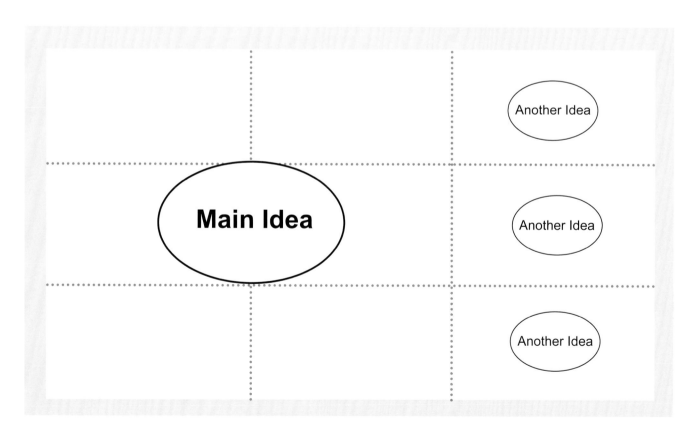

Additional Thoughts About Design

These basic design concepts and tips about composition are enough to help you design most of the slides you'll ever use in your career.

In the meantime, here are a few other tips that will help keep your visual design on track:

■ Only use slides when you absoluteley NEED to.

■ When possible, use pictures or other images instead of words.

■ If you do use words, never - ever - read directly off of your slides. Seriously - don't. We can read it ourselves.

■ Graphs and charts will help you display information visually.

■ Include no more than **ONE IDEA** per slide.

■ Think of your slides as **BILLBOARDS** that need to be seen from the back of the room - use large fonts and full bleed images whenever possible (i.e. images that go all the way to the edge of your slides).

■ Don't let your slides take your place! Your interaction with the audience is more important than anything you put up on a screen.

■ Verbally transition from one slide to another. Don't just click on a new slide and assume it will speak for itself.

■ Practice and rehearse the timing of when to change slides. Sometimes you will want to verbally set up the slide before you show it and other times you might want to show the slide before you explain it. The next section, **"Practice and Present"** will give you more tips on how to do this.

Presentation Software

PowerPoint is the most commonly used presentation software in the world. But it is not your only option. If you decide that you do need / want to use slides, then you should use the software that will best suit your needs at that moment.

Each presentation you give might be best served with DIFFERENT software tools.

The four most widely used presentation programs at the moment are:

■ PowerPoint   ■ Prezi

■ Keynote   ■ Emaze

But even these are not your only options - there are new tools being developed all the time.

Choose the one that best suits the needs of each presentation.

There are benefits and drawbacks to any program. Choose the one that best fulfills your presentation's purpose.

Below are some benefits and drawbacks for the four most widely used programs:

PowerPoint

What it is: The grandaddy of all presentation software.

Benefits: Very powerful, very versatile.

Drawbacks: Not as intuitive to use with images as others.

Tip: Unless you use Apple products exclusively, PowerPoint should probably be your default option.

Keynote

What it is: Apple's answer to PowerPoint.

Benefits: Easy and intuitive to use.

Drawbacks: Only available with Apple. Most places will not be able to "plug and play" your file.

Tip: Good option if you use Apple products, but unless you intend to travel with your computer and presentation cables, you might have to convert your files to PowerPoint before presenting anyway (and some transitions will be lost in the conversion).

Prezi

What it is: First and most powerful of a new breed of online presentation software platforms.

Benefits: Free. Entirely image based, with a smooth flow.

Drawbacks: Unless you purchase the full version, you will need Internet access to open and store your file. Not all companies will allow you to store presentations on outside servers.

Tip: A good option for many presentations, but will not in and of itself make your presentation better.

Emaze

What it is: A follow-up to Prezi, growing in popularity.

Benefits: Free. Image-based, with a smooth flow.

Drawbacks: Limited control of flow and visual templates. Not all companies will allow you to store presentations on outside servers.

Tip: Sort of a lazy person's version of Prezi - simply plug your images in and the program takes over creating interesting transitions between slides. **Again, this will not make your presentation better.**

More options are being developed all the time and each platform takes time to learn.

Chose the presentation software platform that is right for YOU and for EACH PRESENTATION.

Where to Find Images

If you've storyboarded some of the images you'd like to use, and have decided on the best presentation software to accomplish your goal, then you're almost ready to start putting together your slides.

So **WHERE** can you find the visuals you've sketched out? The answer is that there are several possible places, depending on your specific needs.

If you work for a large company, the odds are the company has specific rules that they need you to follow. These are called **"brand standards"** and they represent a lawyer's eye view of any document you create as an employee of that company. If you want to stay employed, you should follow those standards.

Luckily, most brand standards include the ability to use pictures or other images as long as they are acquired legally, or copyright-free, and that you can demonstrate that you have the rights to use them.

There are three basic ways to go about finding visuals:

- Look on free online sites
- Look on paid online sites
- Take your own

Each way has its advantages and drawbacks.

Free online sites

URLs: everystockphoto.com, freedigitalphotos.net, depositphotos.com

Benefits: Free.

Drawbacks: Legal use hard to verify.

Tip: Choose large images to avoid pixilation when enlarged.

Paid online sites

URLs: istockphoto.com, shutterstock.com, bigstockphoto.com

Benefits: Legal use explicit.

Drawbacks: Not free.

Tip: Save purchased images in a file for future use. Over time you will develop a "photo morgue" that you can go to again and again.

Take your own with phone or camera

Benefits: Free, imminently customizable

Drawbacks: Can look amateurish if done carelessly.

Tip: For best results, pay attention to focus, lighting and composition.

Final Thoughts On Digital Imagery

■ If you download images from free Internet sites, you'll need to double check that the image doesn't have copyright restrictions that could prevent you from using it legally.

■ Always assume that images found on free sites are protected by copyright. For some class projects, "fair use" laws for education **MIGHT** permit you to use them in class, but this is not always true. Double-check who owns the rights to the image. Some sites give explicit permission to reproduce their images. Other sites specifically restrict it. When in doubt, ask your professor for advice.

■ Pay attention to the **SIZE** of the image file. Making **SMALLER** images **BIGGER** often results in a loss of resolution. If you're not careful, that perfect image will look terrible projected on a big screen.

■ Most of all, keep your audience in mind! Will they think your images are too sexy, not diverse enough, too humorous, not humorous enough, etc.

■ Again, your presentation isn't about your slide show! It's about your audience and the purpose behind your message. Make sure your slides do what you and your audience need them to do.

Okay, You Can Open Up PowerPoint Now

If you've gone through all the exercises in the book up to this point, then you are finally ready to start building your visual aids online.

Go ahead and open up PowerPoint (or similar software) and begin putting together a slide show if doing so will make your presentation better.

Just remember:

PowerPoint and other presentation software are merely TOOLS for you to use.

Your presentation is NOT a PowerPoint deck.

YOU and your INTERACTION with your AUDIENCE are the presentation!

CHAPTER SUMMARY - DESIGN BASICS

■ Using presentation software wrong is the enemy of great presentations.

■ Images or stories are better than words.

■ Use PROXIMITY to group ideas or images together.

■ Use DIRECTION and ALIGNMENT to help your audience follow your presentation.

■ Use REPETITION to reinforce key concepts.

■ CONTRAST is important for your audience to be able to read your slides.

■ Use only ONE IDEA or one FOCUS for each slide.

■ WHITE SPACE helps your audience focus on what is important. Don't clutter your slides.

■ SCALE and HIERARCHY help your audience see which parts are most important.

■ BALANCE is the geometric relationship of elements on your slides. ASYMMETRY is more dynamic than SYMMETRY.

■ Use the RULE OF THIRDS to help you align asymmetrical elements.

■ Chose the best presentation software for each presentation.

■ You can find images online or take your own.

■ Your presentation is not a PowerPoint deck. You and your relationship to the audience are the real presentation.

PART 1   SECTION 5

PRACTICE AND PRESENT
THE VALUE OF PRACTICE

READ LESS, DELIVER MORE
A CASE STUDY

The room was abuzz as Mr. Z stepped up to the podium. He looked the part. He had a nice looking three-piece suit with a handsome Ralph Lauren tie. On the way to the podium, he shook a few hands. He stepped to the podium and gave a warm welcome. He looked out and smiled. The audience leaned in. This could be good...

He took a sip of water. Then he put his head down and read. His speech was well crafted and he read the words exactly as they were written - but no one cared. He read without passion – looking up only a few times. He continued to read, and read, and read. His hands gripped the podium throughout. His attention was only on the words - which he spoke down into the podium. By the time he neared the end, no one was listening, but he didn't notice.

During his speech, he showed a slide full of stunning information. It might have been a highlight of the speech - except he left the slide for the remainder of his speech. He was a bad presenter competing with a good slide. While the slide was up, the only thing anyone could think about was how those results might affect their future with company.

His message was solid. He had some useful things to say - when you could hear him. Reading his speech wasn't the problem; it was how he read his speech, and how he didn't use his body to communicate his ideas.

He did everything he thought he was supposed to do. He did his research and organized his thoughts. **But he didn't practice HOW to deliver.**

This section will help you make sure you don't make the same mistakes Mr. Z. made.

THE VALUE OF PRACTICE

"A great message delivered poorly becomes a poor message."
-Craig Valentine, 1999 Toastmasters World Champion of Public Speaking

Do you think a football team can win a game without practicing?

Or even be competitive on the field?

Would you like to hear an orchestra play Beethoven's Fifth Symphony if they never rehearsed?

Of course not.

But that's what happens a lot when people get ready to present. They don't practice. They don't practice for several reasons.

First of all, they spend all their time making slides, (most of them badly) and falsely believe that that their presentations will be good.

Second, they don't practice because they're (unconsciously) afraid of speaking in public so they avoid it hoping that their fear will go away when they start to present.

Third, they don't know how. They don't know how to practice, rehearse, or deliver.

Practice is what you do on your own. Every presentation you give requires you to repeat it over and over for the purpose of getting better at it.

Rehearsal is what you do with other people. Even if you present by yourself, it's always good to rehearse in front of others to get yourself more comfortable speaking in public. When you present with other people, you'll rehearse with them after you've practiced your part.

Delivery happens from the moment you arrive on premises until the time you exit. It includes everything from greeting your host through saying farewell and exiting the building.

How much time should you practice and rehearse? The amount of time depends upon your experience speaking in public and the importance of the event. The more important the event, the more you need to practice. Eventually, when you gain more experience, you'll be able to shorten your preparation time.

For now, the following tools will help you know exactly what to do and how to do it to make your next presentation great!

BY THE END OF THIS SECTION, YOU WILL KNOW:
- How to use your voice and body.
- How to use the stage to support your message.
- How to learn your presentation.
- How to practice on your own and rehearse with others.
- How to use props and handouts.
- How to work with slides.
- How to build good presentation routines.
- How to deliver with confidence and clarity.
- How to deal with stage fright.
- How to recover if things go wrong.
- How to end your presentation as strongly as you began.

CHAPTER 10
HOW TO USE YOUR VOICE

*"Actors learn and practice all these techniques and many more until they become automatic.
And that's the point—to make the voice an instrument of marvelous variety that can
effortlessly and unconsciously play whatever music your passionate purpose dictates."*
- Kathy Lubar and Belle Halpern, authors, Leadership Presence

Your first obligation as a speaker is to make sure you can be heard. In order to do that, you need to know how to use your voice. Your vocal tools include volume, pitch, articulation, tempo, and variety. When you get good at using them in real life, you'll be good when speaking in public as well.

How Your Voice Works

Your voice works very much like a musical instrument. And just like a musical instrument, the more you practice with your voice, the better the quality of the sound you can use. Here is what that instrument looks like and some of the ways you can play it:

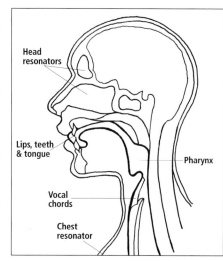

Head resonators

Lips, teeth & tongue

Pharynx

Vocal chords

Chest resonator

■ When you pass air across your **vocal cords**, they vibrate like a reed on a musical instrument. The more air you pass over your vocal cords the louder the sound you can make.

■ You can move your "voice box" (or **pharynx**) up and down in your throat to raise and lower the pitch of the vibrations (like moving your fingers across a guitar strut). Variation in pitch is one of the most important things for conveying meaning.

■ Those vibrations **"resonate"** in different places throughout your body (like sound does inside an acoustic guitar). Some people routinely resonate from their head or nose, causing an irritatingly high pitched or "nasally" voice. This is easily fixed by practicing resonating from your chest.

■ Your **lips, teeth, and tongue** further shape the sound (like pushing the keys on a wind instrument). Paying attention to articulation is often the key to using your voice well.

■ The sound emerges as waves that exit your mouth (the larger you open your mouth the more sound can emerge). A common mistake bad speakers make is not opening their mouths enough for the sound to come out clearly.

■ This sound is directional (when you speak TOWARDS someone, they can hear you better than when you speak AWAY from them). This is especially important to keep in mind when speaking in large rooms without a microphone.

How to Breathe

Thought you already knew how to breathe, didn't you? You probably do; but maybe just not in the way that makes your voice work well. Most people have a tendency to breathe shallowly (or only in their chest) especially when nervous.

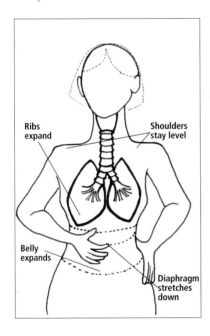

Breathing for vocal power requires that you breathe not only with your chest, but also with your stomach, back and sides. This is called "deep breathing" and it's the best way not only to project your voice, but also to relax at the same time.

So how exactly do you do this?

Deep breathing is also called **"breathing into your diaphragm."** Your diaphragm is a huge dome shaped muscle at the bottom of your rib cage. The bottom of it is attached lower on the inside of your spine and when you activate it, it descends. As it does, it creates negative pressure in your lungs – which allows them to take in air (your lungs don't have any muscles to expand or contract on their own).

When you breathe in, it's your diaphragm working, not your chest. In order to do this well, your stomach and lower ribs need to be able to move aside a little bit to create room. The deeper you breathe, the more the rest of your body needs to make space.

The simplest way to do this is to first think about breathing from your stomach (or to think about filling up the bottom of your lungs first). To do this, you need to allow your stomach to soften and stretch outward.

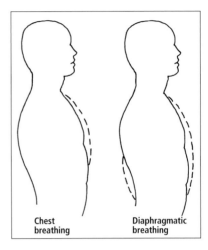

Chest breathing   Diaphragmatic breathing

Secondly, **allow your lower ribs to "swing out and up"** on your sides and lower back (you can feel this in yourself or in others).

Finally, to keep tension out of your neck and throat, simply **keep your shoulders down as you do all of this.** Then when you breathe out, think of squeezing from your stomach area first (there are lots of specific muscles involved in all of this, but you don't need to know all their names to use them).

Proper breath support is the foundation of a strong voice.

Your diaphragm supports your breath. Your breath supports your voice.

One last word about the breath: **The first step toward proper breathing is proper posture.** Good posture (or what is nowadays called proper "alignment") is the best way to keep tension out of your body, which in turn will keep tension out of your voice and keep it strong and healthy.

For those who are interested in learning more about vocal anatomy (and who isn't, right?), there is more to learn. But for the rest of us, this simple explanation is enough.

Here are some of the key elements of using your voice well:

Volume

One of the things you can always control is the amount of sound you make. You can raise or lower your volume for dramatic effect. The appropriate volume is determined not only by the drama of the moment, but also by the size of the room, the number of people in the audience, and whether or not you have a microphone.

Projecting your voice isn't a matter of shouting or yelling. Those can possibly damage your voice. If you want to speak louder, simply support with more air from your abdomen and open your mouth in the direction you wish to be heard.

Soft and loud can tame a crowd.

YOUR TURN

Say "Ha" (elongate the vowel). **Practice making the sound get louder or softer by only using more or less air.** Try the same thing with different parts of your presentation. Don't think about speaking louder, think about using more air. Air is free. Breathe or die.

Change the directionality of your voice: imagine that you are standing talking to a large crowd. First look down and speak only to the people on the front row. Imagine that the sound emerging from your mouth is shaped like a cone with the small end at your mouth and the larger end away from you. Notice how when you speak to the front row this cone is directed mostly at the ground. The sound will have a hard time reaching the back of the room. Also notice how the downward tilt of your neck constricts your airway slightly, making louder sounds more difficult to achieve.

Now raise your head slightly and speak to the people on the last row (don't raise your head so much that you are pointing your chin at the back of the room – only lift your head enough to straighten the back of your neck and point your mouth at the back row). Notice how the cone of sound now touches not only the people in the back, but also the people in the middle and the people in the front. Notice how allowing your neck to straighten also releases some of the tension in your throat. Not only is it easier to get more air across your vocal cords and make more sound, it's also easier for those in the back of the room to hear you anyway.

If you can't be heard, speak UP and OUT.

Pitch

Pitch is the highness or the lowness of your voice (as in notes on a musical scale). The higher you raise your pitch, the higher the note; the lower you drop your pitch, the lower the note.

People often raise their pitch when they get excited and lower it when they calm down. Conversely, sometimes a word delivered with a lower pitch can have a dramatic impact.

Changing the pitch in a word or phrase is known as **"inflection."**

Inflection is used to punctuate ideas. It can help your audience understand the story or how the speaker feels about something.

YOUR TURN

Say the following sentence: "I am so excited that I can jump out of my skin!"

Say it again and vary the pitch of your delivery:
- with no pitch change
- raise pitch on "excited"
- raise pitch on "jump"

Try it again and see what happens if you lower the inflection on some of the words. How does that change the meaning? How does changing the inflection change the meaning of the sentence?

Beware of using only upward inflection or of routinely using it at the ends of sentences.

Try the same sentence again, this time raising the inflection upward at the end (on "skin"). Notice how this inflection turns the statement into a question ("I'm so excited that I can jump out of my skin?"). Some people routinely use upward inflection at the ends of their sentences. These people are easy to make fun of and hard to take seriously.

Try this. Raise the inflection at the end of each statement:

"I'm, like, so excited? That I could, like, jump out of my skin?"

Annoying isn't it? We bet you know someone who talks like that all the time. Don't be that person. Likewise some people routinely end sentences with a downward inflection. In theatre we call this "dropping the ends of the lines" and it is considered the easiest way to become boring. If your message is going to continue beyond any one sentence, it is sometimes useful to think of the punctuation at the end as an ellipsis that connects one thought to another.

Open up your Internet browser and look up Taylor Mali, world-renowned author, slam poet, humorist and advocate for teachers. His YouTube video "Totally like whatever, you know" expounds on the importance of speaking in declarative sentences. It's a great and funny explanation of the importance of inflection and well worth three minutes of your time.

Say the end of the first sentence with a downward inflection, allowing the energy in the thought to drop and stop. Then start the next sentence and drop the end of that line as well:

"I am so excited that I can jump out of my skin."

"But yesterday, I was so tired, I just wanted to sleep all day."

Now try it as a single longer thought connected with an ellipsis:

"I am so excited that I can jump out of my skin . . . . But yesterday, I was so tired, I just wanted to sleep all day."

Notice how this small change in inflection changes both the rhythm and the import of the story. One starts and stops. The other builds and sustains.

As a general rule, statements should end strong – with neither an upward nor downward inflection at the very end. Beware habitually lifting or dropping the ends of your lines. Related to this, if you want your message to be clear, pay particular attention to the final consonants of the words you say.

High and low pitch makes your voice sound rich.

Articulation, Diction, and Pronunciation:

In order for your audience to understand you clearly, you need to develop good speech habits. You don't have to be perfect but it's important that you become aware of how your speech habits impact your audience and can support or impede your message. Good speech habits include articulation, diction and pronunciation.

Articulation is the practice of using your articulators (lips, tongue, teeth, jaw, and throat) to form the sounds of the speech. Using your articulators well means the difference between saying "I picked up a fluffy rabbit" versus "I picked up a flubby wabbit."

Diction is how you pronounce your words. It means the difference between saying "the title of the book is "The Catcher in the Rye" versus "Catch Her in the Rye." Notice the difference in meaning when the word "catcher" is mistakenly pronounced with a hard sounding "h" instead of a silent "h" in the word. Even subtle changes can make a big difference!

Pronunciation is the way in which a word is said in a given language in order for its meaning to be understood.

It means the difference between pronouncing the word "library" correctly as two syllables instead of pronouncing it as "li-berry." It means saying the word /PIK-TURE/, and not /pitch-er/. A "picture" is a visual image. A "pitcher" is a serving vessel with a handle - or someone throwing a ball.

In the theatre, we think of emotion as carried by vowels and meaning by consonants. If you want your meaning to be clear then you need to make sure your audience can understand what you are saying. **The final consonants of words are often key. Pay particular attention to them!**

Articulation, diction, and pronunciation are so important that Shakespeare's most famous character, Hamlet, devotes an entire speech to making sure a group of actors speak clearly and lightly:

> *"Speak the speech, I pray you, as I pronounced it to you, trippingly on the tongue: but if you mouth it, as many of our players do, I had as lief the town-crier spoke my lines."*

If you want your message to have impact, you would do well to follow Hamlet's advice to the players!

Even the best words are useless if the audience can't understand you.

Vocal Warm-Ups

Just like an athlete warms up their body, speakers need to warm up when they prepare to practice. Say these tongue twisters out loud, paying close attention to your diction, articulation and pronunciation.

YOUR TURN

Say the following as clearly as you can:

Did Doug dig David's garden or did David dig Doug's garden?
Do drop in at the Dewdrop Inn

Four furious friends fought for the phone
Five flippant Frenchmen fly from France for fashions

You know New York,
You need New York,
You know you need unique New York.

Peter Piper picked a peck of pickled peppers.
If Peter Piper picked a peck of pickled peppers,
Where's the peck of pickled peppers that Peter Piper picked?

Now say any two parts of your presentation out loud paying particular attention to the beginning and ending consonants in the important words.

Don't "bang" the ends or over-articulate. Simply make sure that the words are clearly separated one from another.

This next passage comes from Gilbert and Sullivan's operetta *The Pirates of Penzance.*

It's a great tongue twister that requires you to practice everything you have just learned.

I am the very model of a modern Major-General;

I've information vegetable, animal, and mineral;

I know the Kings of England, and I quote the fights historical,

From Marathon to Waterloo, in order categorical;

I'm very well acquainted too with matters mathematical,

I understand equations, both simple and quadratical,

About binomial theorem I'm teeming with a lot o' news,

With many cheerful facts about the square of the hypotenuse.

I'm very good at integral and differential calculus,

I know the scientific names of beings animalculous,

In short, in matters vegetable, animal, and mineral,

I am the very model of a modern Major-General.'

Trippingly on the tongue saves speeches.

Speed

Speed is how fast or slow you speak. The average native English speaker in America speaks at a rate between 120-150 words per minute. Speaking too fast can make listeners lose track of what you are saying and speaking too slowly can be boring. Find the pace that works for you; however, be aware that in order for your message to sound important, it needs to be delivered with urgency.

Urgency means that you might need to deliver your presentation at a speed slightly faster than your normal rate of speech. In order for you to determine a proper rate of speed for you, you will most likely need to get other people to listen and give you feedback.

Please note that speaking with urgency is not the same as speaking as fast as you can. Some people talk fast because they want their talk to be over with quickly. Remember, it's not about you - it's about your audience and whether or not they understand your message.

Don't be afraid to add variety. Slow down when you have an important point to make and speed up when you are trying to excite the audience.

Speak with urgency.

YOUR TURN

Read this sentence at a fast speed.

"I am so excited. I feel like I can jump out of my skin!"

Read this sentence at a slow speed.

"I am so tired and just want to go to sleep."

Next, identify any parts of your presentation that might benefit from an increased tempo and other parts that might benefit from a slight slowing of the pace. Experiment with different paces throughout.

Pauses

Sometimes silence communicates better than sound. It's always best to pause just before you begin your presentation. When you do that, you pique the interest of your audience and encourage them lean in to hear what you're going to say.

You can also insert pauses at other times to help you communicate more persuasively. Pauses create anticipation and suspense and give your audience time to process what they heard.

You help your cause when you know when to pause.

YOUR TURN

The pause in the following sentence builds suspense and creates emphasis. Say this out loud:

"The total sum of money we raised from tonight's banquet was (pause) $294,322."

The pause in this sentence gives your audience time to process. Say this out loud:

"Management says that 32% of our sales are return customers. (Pause) That's less than our competitors (pause). Starting next week, here's what we're going to do about it..."

Vocal Variety

Vocal sounds have many other nuances (tone, color, warmth, etc.). For presentations, it's simplest to think of all of them as **VOCAL VARIETY**. A skilled singer can use a range of over 20 notes, but some boring speakers use fewer than five! If you are one of them then your voice has all the dynamics of a dripping faucet. Your drip-drip-drip monotone isn't helping you OR your audience. **A face that doesn't smile or frown or otherwise show emotion is deadpan and dull.**

A voice without variety is dead and dull as well. Let it come to life!

If there is an emotional aspect to what you need to say, allow your body and voice to reflect how you feel. For instance, one of the easiest ways to add "brightness" to your voice is to smile a little as you speak. Sometimes it really is that simple:

When you're sad, let your voice sound sad. When you're happy, let it sound happy. If you're excited, let your voice sound excited. It can be just as easy as that.

In fact, you do this all the time. It's only when you're asked to speak in public that you talk in a monotone voice or talk so softly that we can't hear you. This is the opposite of what you really need to do.

When you present, use all of the tools at your disposal to aid expressiveness within the bounds of your own authenticity.

Believe it or not, you can be expressive and authentic and sincere all at the same time.

Variety is the key to vocal life!

YOUR TURN

Read these sentences out loud without emotion or vocal variety.

"I am so excited. I feel like I can jump out of my skin."

"But yesterday, I was so tired, I just wanted to sleep all day."

• Now say the first sentence at a fast speed and a higher pitch so you sound excited and happy.

• Say the second sentence at a slow speed with a lower pitch so you sound tired.

• Say the first sentence with a vocal tone that makes you sound angry.

• Say the second sentence with a vocal tone that makes you sound sad.

A good way to practice vocal variety is to tell a children's story out loud either to yourself or in front of friends. Better yet, read it aloud to children. Concentrate on conveying the character's emotions and give each one a different vocal quality.

Don't be afraid to use vocal variety throughout your presentation.

Putting It All Together

Some people like to warm up by saying the *Jabberwocky* speech from Lewis Carroll's famous story *Through the Looking-Glass, and What Alice Found There*. It's a nonsense poem about killing an mythical animal called the Jabber-wock. **This is a challenging way to use all of the skills you've just learned, including volume, articulation, pitch, pronunciation, speed, pauses and vocal variety. Give it a try:**

YOUR TURN

Say the following as dynamically as you can:

> `Twas brillig, and the slithy toves
>> Did gyre and gimble in the wabe:
> All mimsy were the borogoves,
>> And the mome raths outgrabe.

> "Beware the Jabberwock, my son!
>> The jaws that bite, the claws that catch!
> Beware the Jubjub bird, and shun
>> The frumious Bandersnatch!"

> He took his vorpal sword in hand:
>> Long time the manxome foe he sought --
> So rested he by the Tumtum tree,
>> And stood awhile in thought.

> And, as in uffish thought he stood,
>> The Jabberwock, with eyes of flame,
> Came whiffling through the tulgey wood,
>> And burbled as it came!

> One, two! One, two! And through and through
>> The vorpal blade went snicker-snack!
> He left it dead, and with its head
>> He went galumphing back.

> "And, has thou slain the Jabberwock?
>> Come to my arms, my beamish boy!
> O frabjous day! Callooh! Callay!'
>> He chortled in his joy.

> `Twas brillig, and the slithy toves
>> Did gyre and gimble in the wabe;
> All mimsy were the borogoves,
>> And the mome raths outgrabe.

How to Stop Saying "Uh" or "Um"

"Uh, um, er, like, you know, kinda, sorta" and other similar words are called **FILLER WORDS** (because they are used to "fill" empty space or silence between other spoken elements). Filler words exist in every culture and in every language, and you have doubtless been told that they are bad things to use when speaking in public.

But here's the thing: they don't really make that much difference. **No one cares if you use a filler word every now or then.** In fact there is some research to suggest that people prefer speakers who use them occasionally over speakers who don't!

Filler words happen most frequently when you are trying to speak and think at the same time. This is not always a bad thing. For instance:

■ **They can be used as a placeholder to let your audience know that you're going to continue speaking.** We do this most commonly when we are under pressure to have an answer or when there is a possibility that someone else will step in and interrupt us ("so the answer to your question is . . . um . . . wait, I got this!")

■ **They can be a way to signal that you need help** (for instance if you've forgotten someone's name: "Your name is um, uh . . . um . . ." – "Bob." – "Right! I knew that!")

■ **Or they can indicate that you are searching for the right word** ("It's an . . . um . . . uh . . . filler word! Yeah, that's it!")

None of these things are bad. In fact, all of them are useful in communicating subtle ideas that would be hard to say otherwise. Unfortunately, because filler words happen most often when you think and speak at the same time, they can also broadcast to your audience that you are unprepared. For instance:

■ **They are more common when you are speaking about an abstract concept** that you have not worked out in advance how to describe (because you are having to think about how to explain it while explaining it).

■ **They are more common when you are not as confident in what you are saying** (because part of your brain is gauging how much conviction you really have in what you are saying).

■ **They are more common when you are transitioning to a new subject** and have not planned the transition in advance (because your brain is trying to plan what to say next even while beginning to say it).

■ **They are more common when your vocal energy is low.** Filler words are less common when the presenter believes what they are saying is urgent! We know you think you say them more when you are nervous, but you really say them more when you don't care as much about what you are saying!

■ **They are more common when your hands are in your pockets.** Informal body language reflects (to your audience and to your own subconscious) that you don't care that much about the subject.

So, how do you get rid of them? **The best way is to BE PREPARED and REHEARSE what you are going to say to be PASSIONATE about your message!** That way you won't have to be thinking and speaking at the same time. This is the secret formula for getting rid of filler words!

However, there are also some people who use these words habitually. If you are one of those people, this means that you do not even know that you are saying them (habits are largely subconscious). If this is the case, then the best way to begin to get rid of them is to first draw your own attention to the fact that you are saying them. **The easiest way to begin hearing yourself say them is to deliberately say them a LOT:**

YOUR TURN

Identify a filler word or words you habitually use. Now rehearse your presentation using those words as often as possible, inserting them at the beginning and throughout each chunk.

Notice we didn't say practice your presentation – it'll be easier for you to recognize that you use filler words when others are present. They can also give you feedback.

Now go back and say each chunk without using your filler words. See if you can hear yourself if you do use them. If you catch yourself saying it, this is a good thing. **It means now you can at least hear it!** Eventually you will get through your entire presentation with minimal filler words.

Want to know what the secret to that exercise really is?

Practice, rehearsal and focus on your audience! After you've given your presentation out loud a few times in front of an audience you will be more confident in your underlying message. You will be less likely to have to think and speak at the same time! That's really all there is to it.

When you have to give your presentation for "real," don't worry if the occasional "uh" or "um" slips out. Focus on your audience and making sure that they understand the import of what you are telling them. If you do that, no one will care if what you say isn't perfectly clear of all fillers. In fact, research suggests they will see the occasional word filler as a sign of authenticity. So don't worry about it! Just focus on them!

Here are the four main ways to get rid of using filler words:

■ **Prepare rigorously.** Practice saying your presentation out loud while standing. Rehearse making sure your audience understands why this is important to them.

■ **Tell a story.** Filler words happen less often when you are telling stories rather than relating facts.

■ **Make eye contact with someone.** Filler words happen less in face-to-face conversations. Talking directly to someone in your audience will help you lessen the urge to focus on yourself.

■ **Keep it short and simple.** The longer the sentences or thoughts you try to relate, the more likely you are to struggle in the middle. Also the fewer hedge words you use in other parts of your presentation (like, sort of, kind of), the less likely filler words are likely to show up when you don't want them. Short declarative sentences are often the key to making presentations clear.

Prior preparation prevents poor use of otherwise perfectly proper filler words.

How to Use a Microphone

Sometimes your unaided voice is not enough to reach your audience. No matter what kind of business you are in, at one time or another, you'll undoubtedly need to use a microphone. Unfortunately they can be tricky for novices to use well.

If you are just learning how to speak in public or haven't used a microphone often, it is essential that you practice with one from as early in your rehearsal as possible. Even if you don't have the actual microphone you will be using on the podium or in your hand, find a substitute prop to stand in for it.

Just like any skill, you need to practice a lot in order for your technique to become invisible to your audience. A good presentation will immediately become a bad one if your microphone technique is distracting.

Ask in advance if you will be using a microphone, and if so, what type. Some facilities offer you a choice between **wired or wireless** microphones. If that's the case, you'll need to decide what type best serves your presentation.

As the name suggests, **wired microphones** are connected by a wire to an amplifier. They are most often used on lecterns, podiums, or stands. Their benefit is that they reduce most chances of interference, dropouts, static or signal blockage and produce a good

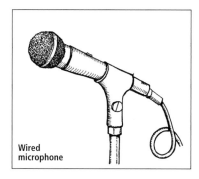

Wired microphone

audio result. If you present from one location for the entire length of your presentation, a wired microphone would be a good choice. They're also usually more dependable than wireless ones.

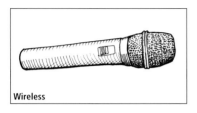

Wireless

Wireless microphones, on the other hand, have some kind of break between the microphone and the amplifier. Their benefit is that they allow you to go almost anywhere on stage (or nearby) within reason without worrying about trailing a long cable behind you. A handheld wireless microphone can look like a standard microphone or it can be shaped like a tiny microphone that is clipped to your clothing on your upper chest area.

The little microphones that you clip on your clothing are called **lavalier mics** (not "clip ons"). Most experienced speakers prefer to use lavaliers; and they're great until they're not. At their best, you won't even think about them and you can do whatever you want; but at their worst, they can pick up interference, the signal can drop out, or the microphone can just stop working if there is signal blockage.

Lavalier

Whatever kind of microphone you choose to use, you must practice with it (and plan how to get out of it if things go wrong – more on that later in this section).

Another important thing to know is from what direction your microphone picks up sound. Microphone heads are shaped so that they either pick up sound from one direction (only in front), two directions (front and back), or from all around.

Unidirectional (or cardioid) microphones are the most common type found

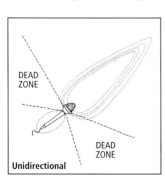

DEAD ZONE

DEAD ZONE

Unidirectional

on podiums or stands. To be heard in one, speak with your mouth pointed towards the front of it (though not directly at it – more on this below).

Bidirectional microphones are common in recording studios (think of two people singing a duet into a single microphone). Unless you are doing a live radio broadcast, you will rarely need one while presenting.

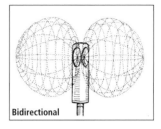

Bidirectional

Lavalier microphones are usually omnidirectional – or able to pick up sound from all directions. For this reason, you will occasionally see people with them clipped on upside down.

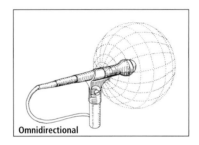

Omnidirectional

This is done to prevent an amplified breathing sound if they exhale from their nose. **Omnidirectional microphones** will also pick up noise from audience members near you.

Lastly, you will need to know the sensitivity of your microphone and its settings. This will tell you how far away you can be from it and still be heard. Think of sensitivity and directionality as two things that exist together like a "cloud" (or three-dimensional area) in front of the microphone. As long as you are speaking into the cloud, the audience will be able to hear you.

Do you need to use a microphone? The answer depends.

Yes, you need a microphone if the size of your audience is too large to hear you easily from the back row or if the acoustics in the room are bad. Even if you have a strong voice that can project in large spaces, remember that some of the people in your audience may have hearing disorders or may just not be able to hear as well as other people. Remember that your first obligation as a speaker is to make sure you can be heard! It's always a safe bet to use a microphone in a large space.

You also need to use a microphone if the speaker who presented before you used a microphone. Audiences grow accustomed to listening to a certain volume. It will be distracting if they're accustomed to hearing amplified sound and then all of a sudden, you begin speaking without amplification.

Use this simple list of Dos and Don'ts to maximize your overall speaking effectiveness when using a microphone

Do

■ **Do inquire in advance about what type of microphones are used in the space.** If you have the choice, choose the type that best serves your presentation.

■ **Do practice using it.** Use a substitute prop from the very start if you don't have the real thing.

■ **Do know the capabilities of your microphone.** Some are super-sensitive and can easily pick up your voice without you speaking too close to the microphone. Others require you to speak very close to them.

■ **Do speak in your normal range of vocal expressiveness.** Microphones amplify the volume of your voice but do not alter your expressiveness.

■ **Do speak across the microphone rather than directly into it.** You want your voice to be in the microphone's sensitivity cloud, but you don't want your breath to "explode" on it when you say "plosive" sounds like p, t, b, etc.

■ **If you are using a hand-held microphone, do decide which hand you will use to hold it for each and every chunk - and then practice doing that a lot.** It can be tricky to use a handheld microphone, especially if you are also using props and holding a remote unit to change your slides!

■ **If you are using a lavalier microphone, do wear clothing that will allow you to clip the microphone to it** (and/or to hide it underneath your blouse/shirt/dress/jacket if it is important that the microphone be unobtrusive).

■ **Do work with a sound technician to set the sound level for your voice in advance of your presentation.**

■ **Do have someone stand at the back of the room to make sure the sound levels are right for your voice and for the presentation.**

Don't

■ **Don't practice without a microphone or substitute prop.**

■ **Don't hide your face by holding the microphone too high.**

■ **Don't wait until you begin speaking into the microphone before turning it on.** Practice turning it on before you speak.

■ **Don't forget to turn off your microphone when you end.** Many embarrassing moments have derailed the career of a speaker when their microphone was left on. Some microphones have a "mute" button you can use if you need a moment to converse privately with someone.

■ **Don't blow into or tap the microphone to test if it's on** because it makes an unpleasant sound for your audience.

■ **Don't walk in front of the amplifiers or speakers -** otherwise it will produce a high-pitched and sustained unpleasant sound called feedback. Feedback happens when the sound from the speakers makes it back into the microphone and is re-amplified and sent through the speakers again. Your technician will work with you to lower the chance of that happening. She/he will also help you learn what to do if your microphone does produce feedback.

■ **Don't place your mouth too close to the microphone because it can pick up a variety of mouth noises.** These noises can occur when you inhale or exhale too close (we hear a gush of air) to the mic or when you open your lips and begin to speak (we hear a separating or smacking sound).

■ **Don't speak consonants like P, B and T directly into the microphone because they will produce sudden gusts of air that are picked up and amplified by the microphone.** These gusts of air are called "plosives" and like other types of mouth noises, they will irritate and annoy your audience.

■ **Don't shuffle the microphone in your hand.** The microphone is sensitive and will pick up and amplify this sound (called handling noise).

■ **Don't shout into a microphone.** It amplifies your voice sufficiently so there's no need to shout.

KEY TAKEAWAYS - HOW TO USE YOUR VOICE

■ Your voice is an instrument. Learn how to play it well.

■ Know how your voice works: air, resonance, and shaping the sound with your mouth, lips, teeth and tongue are the most important things to know about.

■ Increased volume is a function of air and direction. To speak louder, don't shout; simply use more air and point your mouth in the direction you want to be heard.

■ Variation in pitch or inflection can have a big impact on your message.

■ If you want to make sure your audience can understand you, pay attention to the way you articulate the separation between words. The beginnings and endings of words are often the most important parts to keep in mind.

■ Varying the speed of delivery in different parts of your presentation can help your delivery become more dynamic.

■ Pauses and silence can often convey meaning as well as or better than words.

■ There are many ways to increase the dynamics of your presentation. Vocal variety is one of the simplest and most effective ways to increase your audience's understanding and engagement with what you have to say.

■ "Uhs" and "ums" aren't really that big of a deal. The easiest way to get rid of their excessive use is to mean what you say and rehearse saying it.

■ Microphones can be tricky to use. If you need one, make sure to understand how it works and then practice with it (or a stand-in prop).

CHAPTER 11
HOW TO USE YOUR BODY

"Don't do gestures. They often come across as insincere. Instead just be expressive.
It is much more authentic."
- Darren LaCroix, 2001 Toastmasters World Champion of Public Speaking

Face First

Your face is the very first thing people notice when they see you. When you walk to the center of the room and greet your audience with a smile, it conveys confidence and professionalism. You look open and expressive and your audience immediately takes interest in you.

The only way you can learn to smile easily on stage is to practice in real life. Failure to smile during a presentation - even if you think there is nothing to smile about - can lead to a diminished "likeability" factor.

A word of caution (and another plea to practice): continuous smiling projects a lack of sincerity and comes off as rigid.

Learning to smile genuinely when you are nervous takes practice.

YOUR TURN

Because you may be nervous about your presentation, you should practice smiling when you walk up to begin your presentation, at strategic points throughout, and as you exit when you are finished.

We know it feels silly, so don't worry about doing this exercise all by itself.

Instead incorporate it into some of the other exercises that follow.

The point is not to practice the mechanics of smiling, but rather simply to build some muscle memory to remind your body to smile even if you become nervous later.

How to Stand

Everyone has their own distinct way of standing but there are a few universal guidelines that speakers use:

Formal

When you speak at a formal event, (whether or not you use a podium), stand with your weight distributed equally on both feet approximately shoulder-width apart. This stance makes you look confident. Bend your knees slightly. Don't lock them because it looks like you're tense and bracing yourself for something (plus, locking your knees restricts blood flow and can make you pass out!).

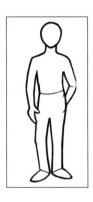

Casual

For events that are more casual in nature, you can stand as above but alternate it with one leg straight and the other one slightly bent. Either way is fine as long as you don't choose one and remain in that one position throughout your presentation. Repetitive shifting of your weight from one leg to another is also distracting.

Look around at the way people stand when they're in public. They usually stand with one leg straight and the other one slightly bent. Every now and then they shift their weight from one side to another, but they don't do so regularly or rhythmically.

Good posture is essential when speaking in public.

Posture is defined as your body position when standing. Your head, shoulders and chest should be aligned and comfortably resting on top of one another with your legs spread about shoulder-width apart and knees slightly bent. Do not lock your knees out because it makes you look rigid and tense.

Slight variations in "good" posture, if done too often or for too long, can become distracting. Leaning to one side, rocking back and forth, and slouching your shoulders are just a few examples of poor body language habits that can get in the way of your message.

YOUR TURN

In your daily life, practice standing with your weight placed equally on both feet.

Become conscious of the way you stand; particularly when you shift weight from one leg to the other.

Observe how other people stand. Notice when people look relaxed and comfortable and when they look tense and rigid.

Your posture is also directly affected by the way you hold your arms. The only rule is this: don't lock your arms in any one position for too long. At a minimum, learn to recognize when your body has become frozen. If you find yourself not moving anything for a long time, move something. Even mechanical movement is better than lifelessness.

Here are some other common bad habits to avoid:

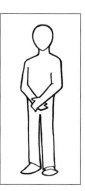

- Don't stand for any length of time with hands together behind your back.

- Don't stand for any length of time with hands locked together in front of hips.

- Don't stand for any length of time with arms crossed across chest.

- Don't stand for any length of time with one hand in pocket.

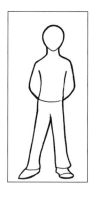

- Don't stand for any length of time with hands on waist.

Actually none of these postures are "bad." They only become problematic if you find yourself locked in one position or do any one thing too often.

The way you stand creates your brand.

Body Language, Gesture, and Movement

Did you know that your audience 'reads' more than just your posture when you present? They 'read' your body language whether you are still, moving, gesturing or not gesturing. For that reason, it's important for you to be aware of every part of your body when you practice and present.

You're probably wondering about the difference between gesture and movement. **Gesture** is the outward physical expression of an idea, opinion or emotion. Most people think that gestures are done only with the hands. They're not. Gestures are done with any and all parts of the body including your shoulders, arms, legs, and face, whether you are standing still or moving.

Most people focus only on what their feet and legs are doing when they are standing. Don't do that. Be aware of every part of your body and make sure they all work together to support your message.

Take a look at these figures and see if you can identify what their body language says.

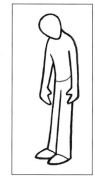

Figure 1 is standing shoulders slumped over and head hanging low, arms down by their side. Without words to say otherwise, the figure looks depressed or lonely.

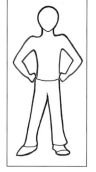

Figure 2 is standing with their feet shoulder-width apart, arms extended diagonally outward and upward, palms upward with their fingers extended, with their gaze slightly lifted. Without words to say otherwise, the figure looks confident and strong.

Figure 3 is standing with one hand on their waist. The other one arm is bent and their hand is scratching the back of their head while they gaze slightly downward. Without words, they look like they are perplexed and trying to figure something out.

How to Use Your Hands

"What do I do with my hands?" is one of the most common questions about presenting.

It's a funny question if you think about it. People rarely wonder what to do with their arms - but guess what? Your hands are attached to your arms! Your arms and your hands work together with the rest of your body! So the answer to the question is this: your hands (and arms) must work in tandem with your whole body. They are not just isolated parts!

Even though they've never had a problem in real life, for some reason when people need to speak in public, their brains freeze and suddenly they treat their hands like alien appendages. "Oh my god, I've just realized my arms are SOO long! Now, what am I supposed to do with my hands?"

You want the honest and easy answer? Are you ready? The answer is actually pretty simple: just leave them attached to the ends of your arms and use them like you always do.

Most people mistakenly think that there's a certain way that you're supposed to use your hands when speaking in public. But the only "right" way is your way.

As with movement, there are two golden rules about using your hands:

1. Vary the way you gesture. Avoid doing only one thing over and over. If you use your hands a lot in everyday conversation, you might want to "thin out" how much you use them when practicing your presentation. But usually the problem is the opposite.

2. Don't lock them up and freeze them in one place. Some people keep their hands in their pockets, folded across their chest, or clenched behind their back for long stretches of time. Unless you have unusual hand mannerisms, actively practice using your hands like you do normally in life.

YOUR TURN

Pair up and take turns telling your partner how to get to the nearest Starbucks coffee shop.

Give those directions without your hands (keep them in your pockets for example) and see how difficult it is.

Now, practice giving those same directions in front of an audience until you learn to use your hands expressively.

At first all of this may seem unnatural, but with enough practice, that unnaturalness will pass. The ultimate goal of practice is to make the effort invisible. When you focus on your message and simply let your voice and body support and enhance it, the vocal and physical tools we discussed in the last two chapters will become invisible to your audience.

You don't want your audience to notice anything about your presentation except the power of your message. Your ultimate goal is to make your presentation style effortless, authentic, and impactful. Ironically, the simplest way to do that is to practice and rehearse.

As with everything, the most important principle is just to behave naturally and let yourself be expressive.

If you are naturally expressive with your hands while talking to your friends, then allow yourself to be just as expressive in front of others. If you are naturally more reserved, then don't try to force yourself to gesture more than you normally would.

While it is possible to talk with your hands so much that it becomes distracting, the problem is usually the opposite. Everyone should recognize this: unless you are suffering from a neurological injury, **NO ONE** naturally stands with their hands and arms lifeless or ridged at their side.

When you are presenting, your goal is to focus on your audience and make sure that they are following what you are saying and understand your message. If you are wondering what to do with your hands, you're focused on yourself rather than your audience! Focus on them and let your hands do what they naturally want to do.

YOUR TURN

Go to a coffee shop or a park where people are talking to each other and notice that everyone gestures with their hands at least a little bit when they are speaking unselfconsciously.

Pay attention to the variety of things people do.

Observe how other people use their arms when they stand alone and when they communicate with others.

Notice how their entire body is connected to the gestures. Hand gestures rarely happen without the whole body being involved in some way.

How to Move

Movement is the transport of your body from one part of your speaking area to another. When you move, your body goes from one place to another. There are three basic guidelines about how to move when you're speaking in public:

1. Move only to make a point or communicate an idea. For example, if you want to point out an important statistic on a slide, you might walk close to the projection screen and gesture to the place on the screen. Avoid moving unless there is a good reason. We'll describe this in detail when you get on your feet and stage your presentation.

2. When you move, go there directly without pausing. It's distracting to your audience when they see you take a few steps, stop, take a few more steps, stop again, and then finally settle in one place.

3. The speed in which you move from one place to another has everything to do with the point you are trying to make. If your point is important and you want to create heightened interest, you might move fast with strong steps. On the other hand, if your point is more casual, you might move more slowly to make your point.

These guidelines will help you "block" – or design – the best movement for your own presentation.

Move it when you need to prove it.

How to Make Eye Contact

You build a strong connection to your audience when you make eye contact with them. When you do that, they feel like you have something important to say and in return, they'll give you more of their attention. And as an added bonus, **making eye contact with someone in the back of the room will also subconsciously enhance your vocal projection!**

Truthfully, there's no one right way to make eye contact, but there is at least one way to do it wrong: some people recommend that you make continual eye contact throughout. **Don't do that.** No one makes steady eye contact with another unless they are in a life and death struggle for dominance. Continuous eye contact is otherwise unnatural and makes it look like you are staring.

Soft Eye vs. Hard Eye Contact

There is a difference between "hard" eye contact and "soft" eye contact. Hard eye contact is a way to establish dominance and is the way you play the "who will blink first?" staring game. This kind of eye contact is inappropriate for most presentations (unless your presentation involves hypnosis or a personal challenge to join an elite military unit).

Soft eye contact on the other hand, involves not only focusing on the other person's eyes, but also using a wider focus that takes in their entire face and shoulders. Soft eye contact, while also allowing the muscles around your eyes to "smile," is usually the best approach for giving presentations (and as an added bonus will also "brighten" your voice)!

Let's look a couple of factors that affect where you look and how you make eye contact:

Who's in charge

There's no doubt where you should look when you present to senior leadership. **Make frequent (but NOT continuous) eye contact with the top executive in charge while including others.** After all, that's the person who needs to hear your message. But remember, don't look at them exclusively.

Even when you're speaking to a large group of people, if you know that senior leadership is in the room, start by making eye contact with them then work your way around the room. Try to include everyone. Go back and make eye contact with senior leadership when you deliver your key points.

Size matters

The size of your audience will affect how you make eye contact. **If you are sitting at a table with a small group, you'll make eye contact with whomever you are addressing,** just like in real life. You probably won't even think about it because you are used to talking in small groups. Just make sure you also include others as well.

But when you address a large group, it is sometimes not possible to make contact with a particular person. Instead shift your focus around the room with every point or two. But here's an important tip: **don't talk to the "room" as a generalized thing, instead, simply scan the room and try to make eye contact with people in certain places throughout the room.** If the light is in your eyes or if it's too dark to make out individuals, at least pretend that you are speaking to an individual from time to time. Make sure to include every quadrant of the room: If you look first at someone in the front, look next at someone in the back; if you make eye contact with someone on the left, try next to make eye contact with someone on the right, etc.

YOUR TURN

Scan your eyes slowly left to right or right to left when you give your opening or introduction.

This type of eye contact serves as a welcome to your audience. It invites them to lean in as you talk.

YOUR TURN

Look directly forward when introducing your main or big idea.

Speaking to an individual rather than to a generalized mass (even if only in your mind) is most important during your main points.

Remember, your goal is to do something specific for a specific audience, not to say words to a generalized crowd.

Your eye contact (whether real or imaginary) on each main point should be "soft" focus rather than a "hard" stare.

Scan your audience right to left or left to right during transitioning sentences.

Stop your scan and make eye contact with a person or group of people every time you deliver a new idea or want to make a point.

If you have three major points, make sure you make eye contact with three different parts of your audience. In your call to action, make eye contact with different parts of your audience.

Practice different ways to make eye contact:

Say this opening line as you **slowly look from right to left**:
> "What were you doing on the morning of September 11, 2001?"

Now, say the same sentence **looking at one section of the group**:
> "On this date, there was one event that forever changed the course of history."

Say this main idea line as you **slowly move your eyes forward to the front of the room**:
> "Unknown to most of us, there were five other major world-changing events that also took place on September 11.

Say this transitional line as you **look around the room**:
> "Raise your hands if you have seen or heard of the movie *Braveheart*."

Say this line as you **make eye contact with one part of the room**:
> "On September 11, 1287, William Wallace, (the man played by actor Mel Gibson) defeated the English in the Battle of Sterling Bridge."

Notice how these small differences in transitioning can have a big impact on the way the message might be delivered.

Pay attention to the way you use eye contact throughout your own presentation as well.

You keep them intact with good eye contact.

KEY TAKEAWAYS - HOW TO USE YOUR BODY

■ Smile when you enter and exit your speaking area.

■ Smile at strategic points in your presentation, if appropriate.

■ Be aware of your posture when presenting.

■ Avoid any one fixed position involving your legs, arms and hands when standing.

■ Make eye contact with all sections of your audience.

■ Move with purpose and to communicate an idea.

■ Movement should be direct and purposeful.

■ The speed in which you move relates to the point you are trying to make.

■ Vary the way you gesture - avoid repeating the same gesture over again.

CHAPTER 12
HOW TO USE THE STAGE

"… a Steve Jobs presentation is very much like a dramatic play – a finely crafted and well-rehearsed performance that informs, entertains, and inspires."
- Carmine Gallo, author, <u>The Presentation Secrets of Steve Jobs</u>

Before you begin to practice, it's important for you to know all about the stage and how to use it. For the purposes of this discussion, think of the word "stage" as ANY space from which you present (whether it is raised like a traditional stage or not). Knowing specifics about the size of the place from which you present, the seating arrangement, the placement of the projection screen, and whether or not there is a podium directly affects how you practice.

Parts of the Stage

All stages (in which the audience sits on the same side) are broken down into parts.

Make it a point to learn the names of each part because they'll help you remember your exact speaking location when you practice and present.

When you know the parts of a stage, you can be more specific (and therefore more helpful) when communicating with others. Saying "move down right when you change the slide" is easier to understand than saying "just go over there when you change the slide."

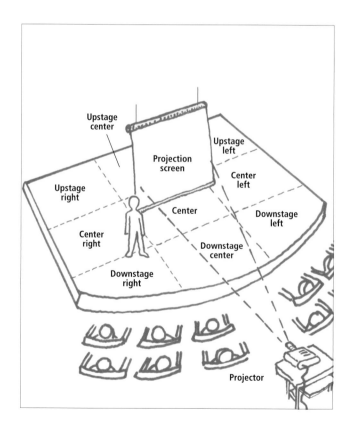

Stage Directions

Stage directions are always given from the point of view of the person standing on stage while facing the audience. So if you are standing center stage, when you move to the left, you will be moving stage left. If you move to the right, you will be moving stage right. If you stop just to the left of center stage, you will be standing center left.

The reason why it's called downstage and upstage is that when modern theatres first came into existence, the back of the stage was literally higher than the front and vice versa so when an actor moved away from the audience, they were literally moving upstage. When they moved closer to the audience, they were moving downstage. So if you stand downstage center near the audience and you move far away from them and to your right, you are moving upstage right. Make sense?

Three Types of Movement

There are three types of movement you can do on any given speaking area.

1. Horizontal movement from right to left or left to right.

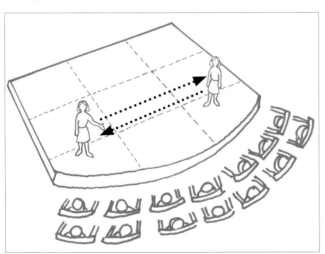

2. Vertical movement upstage to downstage or vice versa.

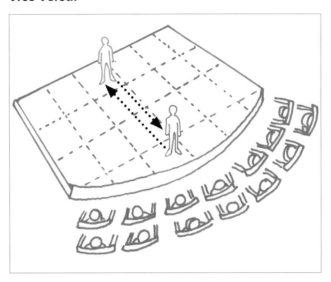

3. Diagonal movement from downright to upleft or upleft to downright.

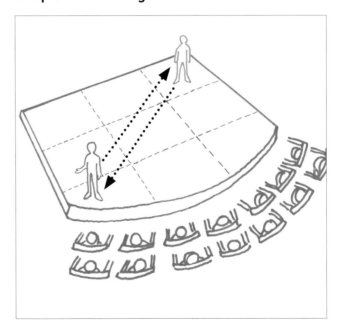

Just like in real estate, your location means everything. Here are a few examples of how location and movement can support and strengthen your message.

■ If you are close to your audience, it's easier to create influence than if you are farther away.

■ If you stand upstage (far away from your audience), and try to convince your listeners to buy into your idea, you've made your work harder.

■ If you are making a transitional point, you might want to move from stage right to left because you are figuratively moving from one idea to another.

■ If you want to shock your audience with a startling statistic, you might want to move directly toward your audience in order to set it up and make your point.

■ If you finish your point and want to show the statistic on a slide, you might want to move to the left or right of the screen to reveal the statistic.

■ For each and every chunk, decide the best place to stand and precisely when to move.

Where to Stand When You Start and End

Where you stand when you begin and end depends upon the type of presentation you're giving, the event itself, and the layout of the room. Unless you need a podium and plan to use slides, it's always best to deliver from the front of the stage/room in clear view of the audience.

No matter where you begin and end your presentation, be sure to practice walking to and from that location with confidence.

When you enter, start front and center.

Podium or No Podium

Most auditoriums and large event spaces will have a podium on the stage or at the front of the room. If you plan to use one, make sure you decide in advance where you want it placed and communicate that with your host or facilities coordinator before your arrival. In the next section, we'll talk more specifically about where to place the podium when you show slides on a projection screen.

When possible, avoid using a podium except during those times when you're speaking at a formal event. If you do use one, you'll need to practice with it to get comfortable. Check the height of it to make sure you can be clearly seen from the chest up. Never assume that the podium you practiced with is going to be the same height as the one you deliver from. You may need to ask for a step unit to stand on if you're not clearly seen from behind the podium.

Inexperienced speakers tend to hide behind the podium and clutch onto it hoping that it'll make them feel more comfortable. In the short run it may indeed make you feel more comfortable (after all it is a physical barrier), but such comfort comes at the expense of alienating yourself from the audience.

No matter how much pre-planning you've done, your request to have the podium moved may not have reached the right person. Or perhaps the person presenting just before or just after you needs the podium and your host decided that there's not enough time to move it back and forth.

When that sort of thing happens, you can stand and deliver your presentation beside the podium rather than behind it. This has the benefit of making you to "feel" anchored and potentially protected while also allowing your audience to see all of you. Some really nervous speakers find it comforting to keep one hand on the podium when they begin until their body realizes that the threat from the "big scary audience" is more imaginary than real. Then once they become more relaxed, they can let go of the podium.

Projection Screen

Knowing the size of the projection screen and how close or far away it hangs from the audience will help you when you practice and deliver. If you must use a podium, never place it on the same horizontal plane as the projection screen because you will be too far away from your audience.

In the United States, people read from left to right so many speakers like to place their podium on the audience's left (downstage right). This lets the audience "read" the room by looking first at the presenter and then at any slides he or she is using. Unless your slides are more important than you are, if you are forced to use a podium, consider trying to place the podium stage right. This allows you to be "read" as the primary element in your presentation.

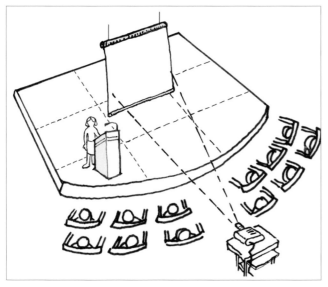

Even if you aren't forced behind a podium, if you will be using slides, the size of the screen and the placement of the projector will also determine how much playable space you can use. If the room is relatively small or the projector is placed on a cart in the middle of stage space, at a minimum the **CENTER** and **UPSTAGE CENTER** areas will be taken up by light and equipment. Give some thought as to how you will negotiate this limitation.

Projectors that hang down from a ceiling can give you a little bit more room, but the space **UPSTAGE CENTER** directly in front of the screen will still usually be filled with light from the projector. **The one thing you want to avoid if at all possible is becoming trapped in one spot far from the audience.** Note that if you are stuck **UPSTAGE LEFT** by a projector's light, then you will remain always far away from any audience **DOWN RIGHT** and vice versa. A little time spent planning out the logistics of moving in the space will help you in the long run.

Make sure the projection screen size is large enough for people sitting in the back row to clearly see the screen. If the screen is too small, ask the facilities coordinator (in advance) if it's possible to obtain a larger one to accommodate the room size. When you show your slides, go to the very back of the room and make sure your audience can see each and everything on your slides.

Regardless of your subject, your message, or the event, when you speak, you are the main attraction - not your slides on the projection screen.

How to Use Slides

When you reference an upcoming slide, stand on one side or the other so you don't block the screen. American audiences read from left to right, so if you stand on the right side of the screen (from your point of view), they will look at you first and then at your slide. If you stand on the left side of the screen (from your point of view), they will look at the slide first and then at you. Choose the side that best suits your purpose at the moment. But no matter which side you choose, don't stand too far away from the screen. If possible stand so the audience can see both you and the slide in the same visual field.

If you plan to use a projection screen, decide in advance and practice when to move to the location to reveal the slide. When you reference an upcoming slide, you should stand on one side or the other so you don't block the screen.

Reveal the slide only when you need it and not a moment before. If you bring it up before you finish making your point, your audience will look at it and might not listen as closely to what you're saying.

Conversely, when you are done talking about the content on the slide, get rid of it - otherwise your audience will keep looking at your slide and not at you. Many projection "remotes" have a button that lets you momentarily turn off your slides. Use it!

You don't need to look at every slide when you reveal them. If you're pointing out something important on the slide, by all means, point it out, but remember that your presentation is more about your connection to the audience than with your slides.

Whether or not you look at a slide when you change it depends upon the content of the slide and what you are saying at the time. In fact, making eye contact with your audience when you change the slide encourages them to look away from you before you look away from them. This subconsciously conveys a kind of dominance or mastery of the information relative to that of your audience and can subliminally make you seem in control of the moment. **Look at your slides only if you need to.**

Don't be a side show to your slide show.

Seating Arrangement

If possible, **find out the seating configuration of your audience and keep that in mind when you practice.** Knowing how close or far away and how wide your audience is relative to the stage will tell you how far you need to move and where to make eye contact throughout your practice sessions.

When possible, always set up your practice space with that arrangement. If you have the option to set the room up according to your needs, it's best to provide the facilities coordinator with a diagram of your preferred seating arrangement. In addition, plan to arrive early on the day of your presenta-

tion to make sure that everything is set up the way you originally asked (we'll discuss this more later).

How the chairs are arranged is very important to listener response. Ideally you want the front row of chairs as close to you as possible. The larger the chasm between you and your audience, the harder it is to connect with your listeners.

If you have a choice of rooms and you know the size of your audience, it's best to choose a room with just enough seats to accommodate the number of listeners you anticipate. It's better to have a medium-sized room full of people than a large room that seems empty. Again, the size of your room and the number of seats will directly affect your presentation.

Some presenters like to use the **ENTIRE** space when they present. That might mean walking down the center aisle or perhaps even moving to the back of the auditorium to purposefully include people sitting in the last few rows.

If you choose to use the entire auditorium, it's essential that every member of your audience see you at all times. If you disappear from view, even for a few moments, your presentation will come to an uncomfortable stop.

Look at the following seating arrangements and note how you can interact with your audience.

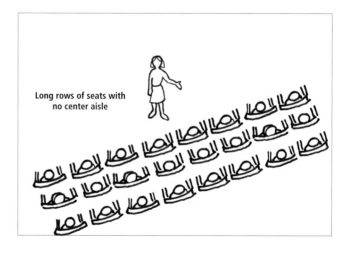

Long rows of seats with no center aisle

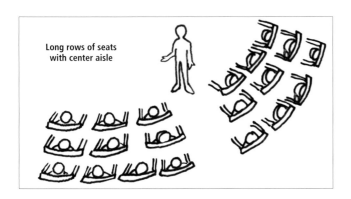

Long rows of seats with center aisle

If possible, it's also always good to have an aisle down the middle so that people can enter and exit from there in addition to the aisles on the far right or left sides of those seats.

Without a center aisle, people entering late will be forced to sit on the far right and left sides and can leave large gaps of empty seats in the middle. The center aisle also allows you to easily move out into the audience (if you choose to do so) to more easily connect with them.

Know the seating arrangement of your audience.

KEY TAKEAWAYS – HOW TO USE THE STAGE

■ Stage directions are always from the point of view of the speaker.

■ Stage directions include upstage, downstage, left and right.

■ There are three types of movement: horizontal, vertical, and diagonal.

■ Know the size and width of your seating arrangement and incorporate it into your practice.

■ Avoid using a podium when possible.

■ Set the podium off to the side but not too far away from the projection screen.

■ Practice with a podium if you plan to use it during your presentation.

■ Know how close or far away to stand from the projection screen.

■ Know how to reveal and remove the slide.

■ Know when to look at a slide.

CHAPTER 13
LEARN WHAT TO SAY

*"Rehearsing a speech is a balance between knowing it and yet, leaving room for inspiration.
In performing a speech, we are not going for perfect. We are going for authentic."*
- Judy Carter, author, <u>The Message of You: Turn Your Life Story into a Money-Making Speaking Career</u>

Now that you know all about your voice, your body, and the stage space, you've got to dig in and get to know what to say. That means you need to learn instead of memorizing your content.

Know Your Content

You might be surprised to find out that actors begin the process of learning their parts by first spending long hours digging into their script. We strongly encourage you **to do this sitting down before standing up and walking around**. So, what's the difference between learning and memorizing?

Memorization is the process of committing something to rote memory. Back in elementary school, you were probably required to memorize lists of states, rivers, cities and important people. But unless you used that information on a regular basis, those lists stayed with you only long enough to take the test.

For beginning presenters, even if you do memorize everything, there is a good chance you'll forget something the minute you get a small touch of stage fright. And if you've memorized everything by rote, one small mistake is all it takes to throw off everything. Have you ever seen anyone stumble on a word and have to start all over again from the beginning? It's painful to watch and even more painful to do. Worse, even if you do manage to memorize everything, you'll spend all of your time just reciting memorized words instead of honestly, authentically, communicating with your audience!

When you learn the contents and meaning of your presentation, you won't need to worry about forgetting what to say. **Instead of memorizing, learn.**

Learning is the process of acquiring knowledge by studying, practicing, and experiencing something. For presentations, it means connecting your words with the underlying meaning of

What do I say?
What do I say?
What do I say?
What do I say?

what you're saying. Learning doesn't happen immediately; it happens when you practice. When you practice and repeat, you learn.

For instance, when you hear one of your favorite songs from years ago, odds are you still remember all the words. You don't even have to think about them. They just come out automatically. As a matter of fact, you can probably drive, work out, or do lots of other unrelated things and still sing those words. All of them. You know the words so well that if you stood up in front of a large crowd of people you didn't know, you'd still remember them (you might not want to sing them out loud, but you'd remember them nevertheless).

You remember the songs you've heard over and over because of a thing called "muscle memory." **Muscle memory is the acquisition of a specific motor task through repetition.** When you sing those words over and over – no matter how good or badly you sing - the muscles of your mouth, tongue, and lips "record" certain pathways in your brain. After that, all it takes is a small trigger to activate those pathways again. Once you start to say the first few words, the rest of the words follow automatically.

That's how actors learn lines. They don't set out to memorize them. They learn them through muscle memory by repeating them over and over while hooking their lines to action, which helps them remember even more.

Don't memorize – learn.

Connect Your Lines to a Physical Action

How do actors remember their lines? Do they ever forget what to say? Yes, it's called "going up" on a line - and it's one of the worst feelings in the world. That's why actors always try to find something to do to help them remember. In addition to saying their lines out loud over and over, actors connect each line in the play to an action on stage. **This is called "blocking" and it is the most important step to learning any new play.**

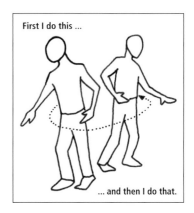

First I do this ...

... and then I do that.

In rehearsal you will often hear actors talking to themselves as they walk from one side of the stage to another, or perform simple tasks like sitting down or picking up a glass: "When I DO this, I SAY this." **Hooking each line to a specific action like this creates physical and neural pathways that make everything sink in that much deeper.** Likewise, the best speakers connect each part of their presentation to a different action or place on stage. That way, their bodies remember what to say even if their mind goes blank.

You don't need (or even want) to memorize your presentation. **Your goal isn't to get out all the words in the right order; your goal is to present your ideas simply, clearly, and with authenticity and for your audience to stay with you as you do it.**

One of the first mistakes people make when they start to practice is trying to memorize their entire presentation word for word. Don't do that. **As a matter of fact, don't worry about memorizing ANY of the words -** at least not yet. Later on, you might find it useful to memorize a few things word for word but we'll show you how to do that when and if it becomes important.

For now, concentrate on practicing a lot and carrying your notes in hand as you do so. Refer to them often when practicing. Remember, the more you practice, the easier it will be to deliver your message well. When you practice a lot, you'll eventually learn most of what you need to say and won't need to spend much time memorizing. Again, we'll show you how to memorize some key parts later on.

Connect each thought to a physical action.

Chunk It

Research demonstrates that when people are asked to remember things, they recall them better when they put things into categories or groups. This means it will be easier for you to remember what to say if you "chunk" information into smaller groups.

One of the biggest mistakes people make when they start to practice is that they work on the whole thing. They get up and try to learn their entire presentation from start to finish. Don't do that. Break it up and learn it one chunk at a time.

Some of you played a musical instrument when you were growing up. When you practiced, you broke the music down into a few bars at a time and played them over and over. This also allowed you to practice the more difficult sections out of order.

That's what you need to do when you practice your presentations as well. Break your presentation into small chunks and practice them one chunk at a time. Practicing your entire presentation is as useless as a new pianist sitting at the piano trying to play through an entire piece when you don't even know the notes to a single measure.

Earlier you learned that when you draft your presentation, you should create it in chunks. Many presentation chunks look something like this:

Hook
Introduction
Transition
Main point 1
Transition
Main point 2
Transition
Main point 3
Transition
Conclusion
Call to action

This outline has at least 11 different chunks to practice. If you want, you can break your chunks down into even smaller sections if it makes it easier for you to remember. It doesn't matter how many chunks you have when you practice as long as you chunk it at least a little.

You'll flunk it if you don't chunk it.

Say It Out Loud

A few years ago, we attended a presentation conference with some of the biggest corporations in the country. We were divided into groups and asked to draft our presentations. When each group was done preparing, we were told to practice our presentations out loud.

We then heard a group of vice presidents from a company say, "Practice out loud - we've never heard of that before!"

"Why do we need to do that?!"

"We'll be fine if we read it over a few times." But they weren't.

They were shocked to discover the impact speaking out loud had on their presentations. Those who practiced by speaking out loud were noticeably better than those who didn't.

Reading to yourself and speaking out loud are two completely different forms of communication. When you read, your brain interprets the words on the page and puts them together to form a coherent message. It's an elaborate **MENTAL** process that stays inside your head.

Reading silently and then getting up and trying to deliver a speech makes as much sense as reading a driver's manual silently to yourself and then getting in a car and trying to drive. Both can lead to disaster.

Say small chunks of your speech out loud until you feel that you know it. Again, don't worry about trying to memorize anything. Don't worry about getting on your feet yet, either. Just practice saying out loud each chunk until you get to know the flow of the words and the meaning of your ideas.

Don't worry about saying it the same way each time. In fact one of the next steps is paraphrasing – or learning to say it differently. We'll talk about that more later. For now, just say the basic words of each chunk over and over.

Here are some tools to keep in mind when practicing out loud:

■ Don't try to learn too much at once. Practice a lot but in short intervals.

■ Don't practice late at night. Your brain doesn't remember new information when you are tired.

■ Practice your vocal delivery until you sound conversational. Ultimately your audience wants to feel like you are talking directly to them as individuals.

We've already said this but it bears saying again: don't spend a single second trying to memorize. Yet.

You'll be proud when you say it out loud.

Say It a Lot

Practice saying each chunk a lot. Ironically it takes a lot of repetition to make it sound like you're saying it for the very first time.

Most of what you learn in life happens through repetition. There's not a single person on earth who learned to speak a language, play a sport, use a computer, or drive a car without repetition. If you accept the fact that repetition is the key to learning, why abandon that practice when getting ready to give a speech?

If you are new to the practice of speaking in public, you'll need more time to prepare. Be realistic about your delivery skills and don't kid yourself about how much rehearsal time you need to get ready. Everyone is different. But remember this: it always take longer than you think.

Remember this equation:

Practice Time = Importance of Message + Your Level of Skill

You won't be distraught when you say it a lot.

Say It Your Own Way – Paraphrase It

One of the best ways to help you remember your chunks is to say them in different ways. – or to paraphrase them.

The definition of "paraphrase" is a restatement of a text, passage, or work giving the meaning in another form. It means the act of using your own words to describe something. When you paraphrase it, you'll learn it rather than merely memorize it by rote. **Paraphrasing makes it easier to remember.**

Sometimes, people try to sound smart so they use large words throughout their presentation with the hopes of impressing their audience. But unless you are a Pulitzer Prize winning scientist talking to a group of well-educated professionals, stay away from the big words.

YOUR TURN

Look at the last sentence above and identify the key words. Then, without looking at the sentence, say the same idea in your own words. Now say it again, different from the first way. Don't try to memorize anything. Just say the idea in your own way and try to make it conversational.

Paraphrasing is one of the most effective ways to learn information quickly. We use this technique when we coach speakers. Many of them start out trying to recite memorized words and so when they stumble, they lose track of their message. Whenever this happens we say, "Just say it in your own words." **Then, when they do that, we say "Great! Now just say it just like that."**

Paraphrasing is how you converse with others. When a friend asks you what you did last night, you say it in your own words. You don't try to recite how you responded the last time someone asked you that question. You think the thoughts in your head and then convert them into words. You say it in your own way. Paraphrasing makes your ideas conversational rather than recited.

If you have trouble paraphrasing, it's because you don't know the meaning behind what you're trying to say. Memorize a few key words or phrases only and then focus on the thought behind what it is that you're trying to say.

You'll amaze when you can paraphrase.

YOUR TURN

Paraphrase your whole presentation in chunks. From the start of your presentation, paraphrase each chunk out loud at least three different ways until it's easy to remember.

Stage It on Paper

For each chunk, decide where to go and when you want to talk. As described in the last chapter, one of the first things you need to do is decide where to stand and when to move throughout your presentation. In the theatre we call this "blocking." The term comes from 19th century directors who used small actual wooden blocks to work out the staging of a play before they gave the directions to actors.

As mentioned earlier, actors learn their lines in part by connecting them to something physical. You'll do the same when you practice each chunk repeatedly and connect it to action.

You will always have an easier time remembering what to say if you connect your ideas to the simplest movement from one part of the stage to another. You don't need to choreograph specific hand gestures during your speech, but assigning a different location to each part of your presentation will help you remember what to say.

Decide Where to Stand and Where to Move for Each Chunk

Look at each part of your presentation and decide where to stand and when to move in order to get your audience to understand your message. For instance, you might decide on specific directions to walk.

To make things simple, use the following worksheet to initially block your presentation. As you practice, you might find that you need to change things, but this will give you a good place from which to begin. Remember to decide where you need to move for each section as well. Fill in these sticky note boxes as you go. It will be easier to remember each chunk when you assign a different location and different action to each one.

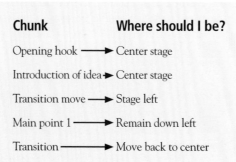

Chunk	Where should I be?
Opening hook	Center stage
Introduction of idea	Center stage
Transition move	Stage left
Main point 1	Remain down left
Transition	Move back to center

Blocking includes walking and talking.

BLOCKING YOUR PRESENTATION

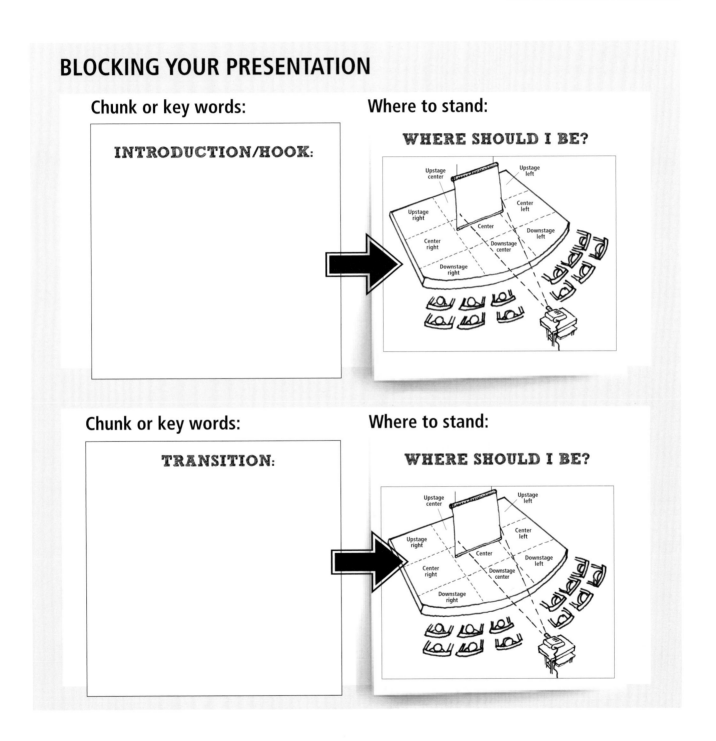

Chunk or key words:

INTRODUCTION/HOOK:

Where to stand:

WHERE SHOULD I BE?

Chunk or key words:

TRANSITION:

Where to stand:

WHERE SHOULD I BE?

BLOCKING YOUR PRESENTATION

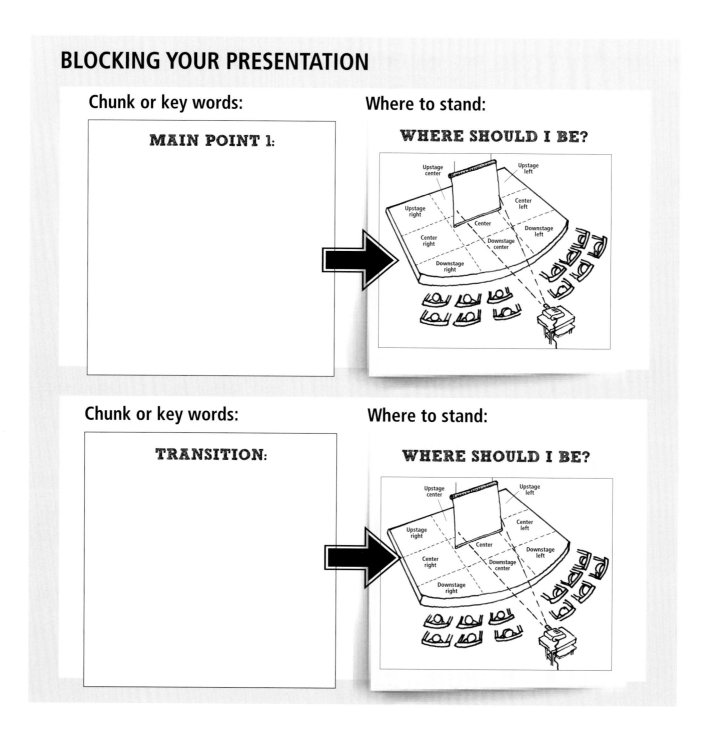

Chunk or key words:

MAIN POINT 1:

Where to stand:

WHERE SHOULD I BE?

Chunk or key words:

TRANSITION:

Where to stand:

WHERE SHOULD I BE?

BLOCKING YOUR PRESENTATION

Chunk or key words:

MAIN POINT 2:

Where to stand:

WHERE SHOULD I BE?

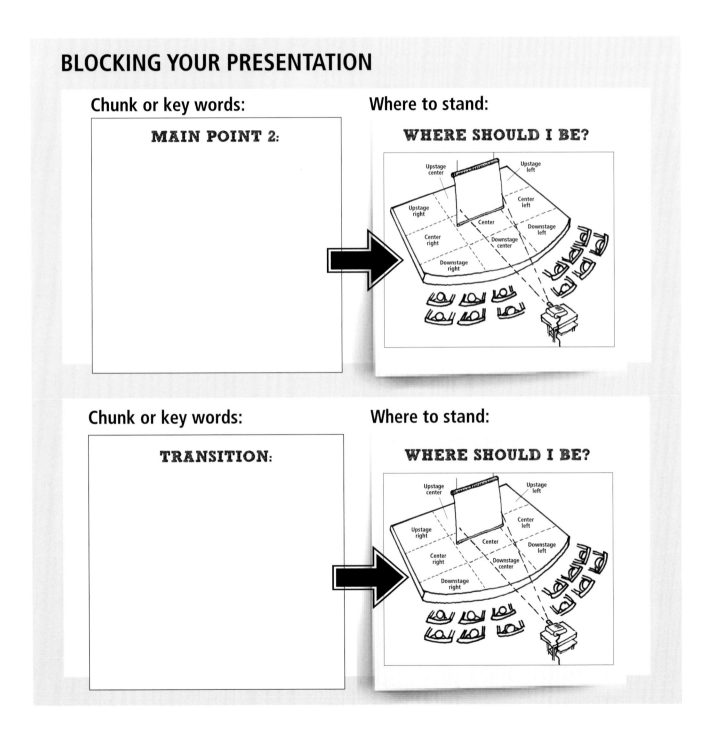

Chunk or key words:

TRANSITION:

Where to stand:

WHERE SHOULD I BE?

BLOCKING YOUR PRESENTATION

Chunk or key words:

> MAIN POINT 3:

Where to stand:

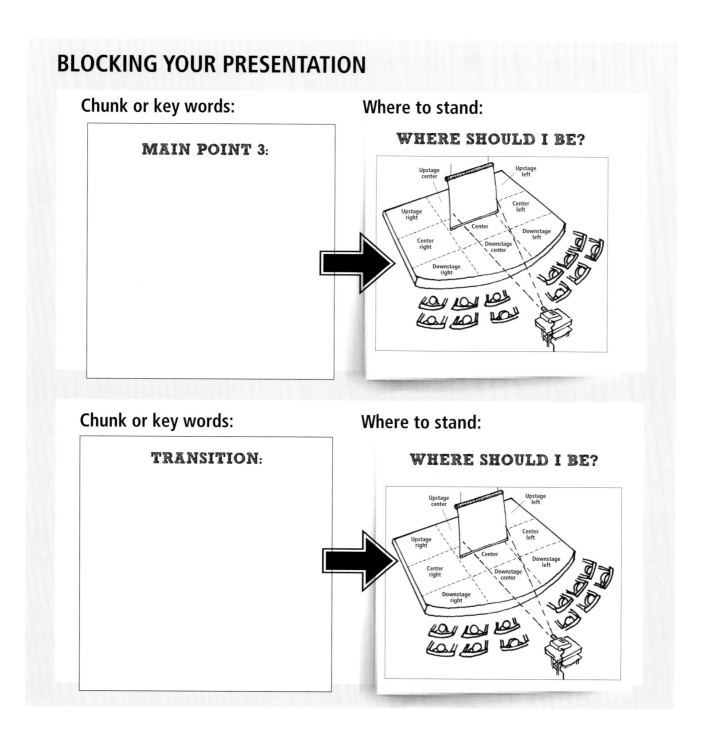

WHERE SHOULD I BE?

Chunk or key words:

> TRANSITION:

Where to stand:

WHERE SHOULD I BE?

BLOCKING YOUR PRESENTATION

Chunk or key words:

CONCLUSION -
CALL TO ACTION:

Where to stand:

WHERE SHOULD I BE?

Chunk or key words:

TRANSITION:

Where to stand:

WHERE SHOULD I BE?

BLOCKING YOUR PRESENTATION

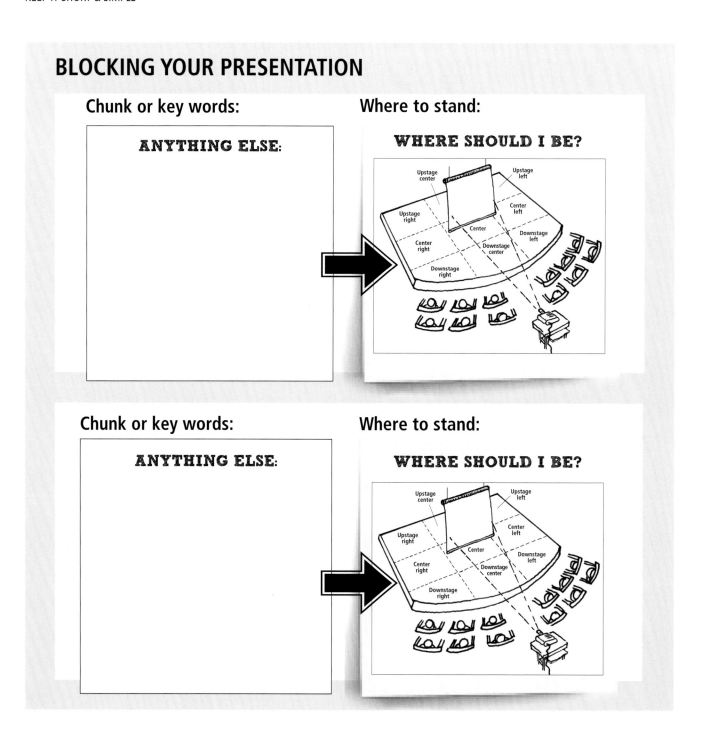

Chunk or key words:

ANYTHING ELSE:

Where to stand:

WHERE SHOULD I BE?

Chunk or key words:

ANYTHING ELSE:

Where to stand:

WHERE SHOULD I BE?

KEY TAKEAWAYS – LEARN WHAT TO SAY

- Chunk each section and learn them one at a time.

- Say them out loud. A lot.

- Say it a lot. In fact, say it so many times.

- Paraphrase it. Say it a lot.

- Block it. Decide where you go and when you talk for each chunk.

CHAPTER 14
BRING IT TO LIFE

"The purpose is to make your audience see what you saw, hear what you heard, feel what you felt."
-Dale Carnegie, author, <u>How to Win Friends and Influence People</u>

Your First Moment

Pause. Look at your audience and take a short moment to simply "be present." Use this pause to help set the tone for your presentation or speech.

If your presentation is good news, fill this pause with a smile. Your smile will let your audience know that you have something exciting to share with them.

If your message is more serious in nature, simply focus on the purpose of your message.

If you choose to stand behind a podium, place your hands on the sides. Rest them comfortably and use them for gesture or emphasis when and where necessary. Even if you are nervous, avoid grasping the podium tightly (or you will broadcast your fear to the audience).

If you are brave enough to stand beside the podium or abandon it completely, good for you! Practice will make your fearlessness even more rewarding for both you and your audience.

Your audience needs this moment to ready themselves and take you in. While you're walking up to your speaking area, they're saying to themselves "So what, who cares, and what's in it for me?" Your pause answers their questions with a resounding "Wait until you hear what I'm gonna say to you!"

YOUR TURN

When you start to practice, as soon as you get to your speaking location, turn toward your imaginary audience, take a breath in, and exhale. If you are holding your breath, your audience will be as well. When you breathe out, it gives your audience permission to breathe out as well.

Get on Your Feet One Chunk at a Time

Interestingly, by this stage, you might notice that you don't even need to say your entire presentation to remember it. If you've worked through all the steps in order, you may find that you are able to work like the actors mentioned earlier who rehearse by talking quietly to themselves: "When I move here, I say this, and when I make this point, I do this," etc. If you find that this is true, congratulations; you are well on your way to having learned your presentation!

At this point, since you are physically practicing and learning your presentation, it's important at this stage to incorporate the use of any props, handouts, and/or cue cards if you plan to use them during your presentation.

Practice with Props and Handouts

A prop is any object used in a presentation or speech to anchor your message and help your audience remember your ideas. Using props shifts focus away from you and onto something else to make your points more understandable and more memorable. When used effectively, props can transform a good presentation into a great one by creating a "wow" factor.

Use these practice guidelines if you decide to use a prop:

■ **Select props that enhance and support your ideas.** Avoid using any props that detract from your message.

■ **Keep your prop hidden from the view of the audience until such time as you need to unveil it;** otherwise it will "steal" focus away from you.

■ **Create anticipation by verbally introducing it just prior to revealing it to your audience.** Carefully craft your words so that it builds excitement.

■ **Make sure the prop is large enough to be seen by everyone in the audience.** Using a prop that is too small will frustrate your audience unless it's visible to everyone.

■ **Practice handling your prop, including how you reveal it,** how many hands it takes to make it visible, the exact position of the prop when it's resting in your hand or on table, etc. If the prop is mechanical in that it "does" something, make sure it works before you use it.

■ **Decide the best location for your prop.** Place it near the area where you want to reveal it to your audience.

YOUR TURN

Now that you have some rough blocking in mind, work through each chunk, practicing where to stand, when to move, and when to reveal and remove your slides.

Repeat these movements over and over until you feel that you really know it well.

Try to find something physical to help you connect to the main idea of that chunk.

Props, handouts or slides can both support your idea and help you remember what to say.

When you've repeated each section a few times, go onto the next section only when you know that section well.

Keep working your way through until you've gone through each and every section.

■ **If you hold it in your hand/s while you speak, make sure it doesn't cover your face.**

■ **Remove the prop from sight when you've finished making your point.** Leaving it in plain view of your audience will keep their attention on the prop and not on you.

■ **Do not pass the prop around after you use it.** If you pass it around, your audience will focus on the prop and not listen to you.

■ **When using handouts in your presentation, be selective about WHEN you decide to hand them out.** When we present, we usually place any handouts facedown on the table in front of our audience and ask them NOT to turn them over until we tell them to do so. For a larger group, we sometimes place the handouts under chairs and, again, ask them to leave them there until we instruct them to reach under and pick them up. Timing is important. **An audience that is reading a handout is one that is not listening to you.**

Remember, a prop or a handout will enhance and clarify your presentation only if you use them to your advantage. Handing them too early, taking too long to pass them out, or leaving them on display once you are finished with that point will take focus away from you and your message.

If You Need Cue Cards or Notes

If you need to use cue cards/note cards for some reason, you must practice with them. **Do not use them as a substitution for practice.**

Whether or not you use them depends upon the presentation. If the event is rather informal and you were a late addition to the presentation, it will most likely be acceptable.

However, if you write out and read your entire presentation on cue cards, you will drive yourself crazy trying to read them word for word. More importantly, you will look unprepared and your audience will stop listening to you the moment you begin to read.

The most important suggestion we can give you about using note cards is this: **glance at them quickly and look back at your audience before you begin to speak.** Do not read from the cards while looking down.

Here are a few suggestions when rehearsing with cue cards.

■ **Practice, practice, practice.** You must practice with your cue cards, otherwise they'll watch you fumble about and your message will be lost.

■ **Don't try to hide them from the audience.** It will be distracting to see you take a "sneak" peak at your cards. If you use them well, they won't be distracting and they'll soon forget that you have cue cards in your hand. If you're OK, your audience won't even think about it.

■ **Use your cue cards early but not at your opening.** If you use them for your opening, you'll look unprepared. Don't wait too long or it will look like you suddenly got nervous and forgot what to say.

■ **Don't look apologetic.** Again, your audience will accept it if you accept it.

Most people use 3x5 unlined index cards. You can also use 5x7 although they may be too distracting because of their size.

Also in the event of stage fright, larger cue cards or cards written on paper rather than card stock can exaggerate any shaking in your hands.

Write in large letters so that your notes are easy to follow and leave plenty of white space. Only write one idea per card and keep the words or phrases to a minimum.

Good example:

LINDA JAMES, PRES 09

2M - 6 MOS.

Bad example:

Linda James, president
since 2009

She raised $2,000,000 in
the past six months.

Put Down Your Notes / Script and Put It All Together

In the theatre, actors rehearse scene by scene, often out of order – and only when they are ready do they put the scenes together and run them in order. This is also good a good way for you to practice your presentation.

Work slowly through large chunks, stopping only if you need to fix something. If you do encounter any problems, make sure to stop and fix it as you go - otherwise you'll be building muscle memory for bad habits - and they'll be harder to get rid of later on. Once you have worked through each part in order, go ahead and run the whole presentation from beginning to end without stopping.

Rehearse in Front of Others

After you have practiced putting the entire presentation together, it's now time to invite a few people to watch you give it. Now, your practice time turns into rehearsal.

Rehearsal is where you work with others to make your presentation better. If your rehearsal partners have knowledge of public speaking skills, they can give you a few critical suggestions. But even if not, you can use their presence to help you get used to presenting in front of people.

YOUR TURN

After you've practiced each chunk repeatedly, put several chunks together and practice them in order to get a sense of flow.

Begin working through chunks of your presentation without your notes or script.

If you need, ask someone to carry your script with them and cue you if you need help remembering what to say (actors do this by staying in character and calling out "line" – this is a good way for you to rehearse as well).

How to Memorize Key Words and Phrases

We mentioned earlier that we didn't want you to try to memorize your presentation word for word. And by now, through muscle memory and sheer repetition, you probably know most of what you need to say by this point anyway.

However, if there are some powerful or compelling key words and phrases that you want to be sure to include, you will want to build specific muscle memory for saying them – your opening hook, a few key points, and your call to action, for example.

There are a few simple ways you can memorize key words or phrases.

■ **Have someone carry a script and cue you as you quickly run through your presentation.** Say those key phrases quickly and automatically without even thinking about them. Repeat them over and over again.

■ **Practice them while doing other things.** Actors practice their lines while driving their car, washing dishes, working out, jogging, walking to work, etc.

■ **When you repeat something over and over, you hardwire those patterns in your brain.** When you practice out loud, chunk by chunk, while doing something else, you make it automatic.

Get in the habit of saying any key words or phrases out loud everywhere possible in many different environments. That way, you'll know it so well that even if you get stage fright, your mouth will keep on saying the words it learned. We'll cover more about how to deal with stage fright later in this book.

Practice out loud everywhere while doing other things.

Dress Rehearsal and What to Wear

Practice in the clothes you plan to wear during your presentation. Jackets, dresses, suits and shoes affect your posture, the way you move and your overall comfort level and so it's important that you get used to presenting in those clothes. If possible, go through your dress rehearsal in the actual space including all technology, props, and handouts you plan to use.

Think of presenting as performing a role in which you've been cast to play yourself - the best version of yourself for the occasion. Always dress authentically but not casually. Dressing more casually than your audience projects a lack of seriousness about your subject. However if you have never worn a tie or high heels before, you will look uncomfortable and awkward wearing them (in fact if you've never worn high heels before, you might even fall down!).

If you are presenting in an office building, a suit might be appropriate, but that same suit might alienate an audience of factory workers. If it is a formal event, dress formally. If everyone else is wearing Hawaiian shirts, consider wearing the best Hawaiian shirt you can find.

Take note that the temperature inside an establishment can range from very warm to very cool. Some medical or high tech buildings are kept unusually cool because of special equipment needs and in some instances, rooms can run from very hot to very cold. Air conditioners can break and heating systems can shut down so always give thought to not only what you wear but also what clothing you bring with you.

If you present outside, check the weather forecast and be prepared for the unexpected.

A good rule of thumb is to always dress one step better than your audience.

KEY TAKEAWAYS – BRING IT TO LIFE

■ Get on your feet, one chunk at a time.

■ Practice with props and handouts.

■ Put down your notes and put it all together.

■ Rehearse it in front of others.

■ Memorize key phrases.

■ Do a dress rehearsal.

■ Exit the stage with as much confidence as you entered.

CHAPTER 15
ON THE DAY YOU PRESENT:
PREPARATIONS AND ROUTINES

"The relationship with your audience starts before you walk on stage."
- Nick Morgan, contributor, Forbes Magazine

This chapter is short but in many cases you will find the information in it just as important to creating a successful presentation as everything else in this section.

Eventually, when you've presented a lot, you'll develop your own list of rituals for everything you do related to your practice and presentation habits. What we describe for you in the next few pages is a suggestion. You should also observe other people's routines and habits and then develop your own. There is no one right way to get yourself ready to present; however, there is a wrong way. If you do nothing in preparation, you can be assured that you've learned the wrong way of prepping.

Create Some Moments Before

A long time ago, on the television show called *Seinfeld*, there was a character named Kramer who always burst into rooms full of energy. Audiences never saw the actor warming up before that moment, but in order for the entrance to be explosive, the actor had to be fully energized in character before anyone saw him. Presentations are like this as well.

The moment before your audience sees you is as important to your performance as is your first impression.

There are several moments before that all great performers (whether presenters, actors, or athletes) use to their advantage:

THE NIGHT BEFORE OR THE MORNING OF

All great performers do something the night before or the morning of their presentation to make themselves feel **CONFIDENT** that they have fully prepared. This can be anything from a pragmatic ritual (like shining your shoes, or eating something specific for dinner or breakfast), to a superstition (like making sure all the money in your wallet is facing the same way), to making sure to get in a light workout the morning before a big presentation. These things are not - strictly speaking - NECESSARY for a good performance, but almost all great performers use them as a way to feel more relaxed and in control of events.

If you want to seem confident, you have to be confident. A "pre-flight" ritual can help.

ONE TO TWO HOURS BEFORE

Closer to the event, all great performers orient themselves in the space (for instance, think of a professional sports team warming up in the stadium before the game). One or two hours before your presentation, take a moment to stand in the space you will be presenting in later. Review your opening and closing lines and any other important "must-remember" things you need to say. Walk through where you stand during certain sections of your speech. Consider this a physical version of your 60-second fly-over. Then, forget about everything and just relax. You are as prepared as you are ever going to be. Letting your mind relax before presenting is nearly as important as rehearsal (for instance many professional athletes wear headphones and listen to music before a big game. The headphones allow them to shut out distractions and mentally and physically relax before having to focus intently). You should do something similar.

Pro athletes walk through the stadium and then relax before the game. You should too.

JUST BEFORE

All great performers do something to **REFOCUS** just before they have to perform to align their body, voice, and mind to concentrate on the task at hand. This can be anything as simple as deliberately breathing deeply, to doing a "power pose" (straightening up and rolling your shoulders back) in the restroom before the meeting. Although you audience should not see you do these things, you should consider the moment of refocusing as PART of your presentation.

To increase your presence, do something to refocus your mind and body just before you speak.

How to Begin

For the audience, **your presentation begins the moment they FIRST see you.** This can be as soon as when you are greeting people as they enter the room, or as late as when you leave your seat to get up to speak. The important thing to keep in mind is that long before you say a word - in fact by the time you have taken your first three steps - your audience has already developed an impression of you.

If you are a guest speaker and a newcomer, your presentation always begins as soon as you enter the room. You make a first impression when you introduce yourself. The very first chapter of this book has tips to help you do this well.

Breathe Out!

When we become stressed, our bodies automatically breathe in. However we do not always automatically breathe out. This can be a problem for nervous presenters because of something called the sympathetic nervous system. Part of your body is attuned to actually "feel" the sensations you imagine others are feeling. Your audience is wired this way as well. That means if they see that you are obviously nervous, their bodies will experience some degree of something similar. Therefore when you don't breathe out and relax, your audience won't either.

Before You Speak

As soon as you get to your speaking location, turn toward your audience, take a breath in, and exhale (you don't have to do so obviously). If you are holding your breath, your audience will as well. When you breathe out, it gives your audience permission to breathe out as well. They don't need to hear you exhale (in fact if they do, they will think you are nervous) – simply breathing out fully is enough; their bodies will recognize the micro-gestures your body makes when you relax.

Pause. Look at your audience and take a short moment to simply "be present." Use this pause to help set the tone for your presentation or speech.

If your presentation is good news, fill this pause with a smile. Your smile will let your audience know that you have something exciting to share with them. If your message is more serious in nature, simply focus on the purpose of your message.

This is the point where preparation becomes delivery. If you've done it right, your practice and rehearsal will transition seamlessly into actually doing your presentation.

How to End

A lot of speakers spend their time practicing their content and the way they start but they don't spend any time on how they end. Your presentation isn't over until you exit the stage so it's important for you to practice how you exit. After all, **the way you exit the stage will either support or contradict your message.**

If you don't remember how to write a closing statement, quickly review the **Section 3: "Write It."** With that in mind, here are a couple other pointers to help you craft your ending:

When your audience applauds, stand wherever you stood when you finished for a brief moment and receive their applause. You don't necessarily have to thank your audience (unless that is the part of the closing you want to leave them with). If anything, they should be thanking you for the clarity with which you've conveyed complex information, or your words of wisdom or inspirational message.

If you wish, of course you can gesture to them and say "thank you." Some speakers like to clap their hands to thank the audience for being such receptive listeners. Again, it all depends on the final image or thought you want to leave them with.

Even if you didn't feel you did your best, **receive their applause graciously and exit your speaking area as gracefully as you entered it. Never apologize or show frustration when you exit the stage.** No matter what, **make sure your body language reflects confidence and positive energy.** Even if you made a mistake, if your overall message was short and simple, clear and strong, no one will notice or care that you made any mistakes.

In **Chapter 7: "Transform Your Outline,"** you learned how to write a final sentence that will linger with your audience. The way you exit the stage, the expression on your face, and your overall demeanor will be the last thing they remember. A smile on your face and a confident stride will put the cap on your short and simple, clear and strong message.

Don't diminish your finish. Exit with confidence.

KEY TAKEAWAYS – LAST MINUTE PREPARATIONS AND ROUTINES

■ Deliberately create useful moments before to help you begin your presentation fully energized and present.

■ For maximum effect, begin your routines the night before and / or the morning of your presentation.

■ One to two hours before your presentation, go over it one last time and then RELAX – do something to take your mind off of presenting.

■ Refocus just before your presentation to bring yourself fully into the present moment.

■ Breathe. Air is free and good for you. Breathing out is as important as breathing in.

■ Allow your body to be as expressive as it needs to be to convey the emotional import of what you need to say.

■ Exit the stage as gracefully as you entered it.

■ If you do it right, practice and preparation will blend seamlessly into successful delivery.

CHAPTER 16
DEALING WITH STAGE FRIGHT

"The human brain starts working the moment you are born and never
stops until you stand up to speak in public."
- George Jessel, comedian and public speaker

Whether you're a beginner or experienced professional speaker, everyone gets nervous before they speak in public. Some people experience it as a minor case of butterflies in the stomach and others might feel it as an overwhelming sense of fear.

The first step in learning how to deal with it is to recognize what it is and why it occurs so that you can stop it from becoming as big a problem as it feels like.

Stage fright can feel like a matter of life or death because biologically at one time, it kind of was.

What It Is

Physically, the anxiety you feel about giving a presentation is the same type of anxiety a caveman might have felt when running from a bear. Your body reacts to the stress of presenting in the same way it does for any perceived potential threat. Knowing how this works can help you avoid panic if you start to feel the beginnings of stage fright.

■ When you stand in front of an audience, a part of your brain responds to the new sensation by **signaling your adrenal glands to release chemicals,** which then act upon your body to prepare you to face a possible threat (you will feel this as general nervousness and/or as "butterflies" in the pit of your stomach).

■ Your **heart rate and breathing change** to focus on that threat (which you may experiences as a shortness of breath, sweating and/or flushing in your face and neck).

■ **Blood flows from your extremities to your core** to help you survive in case your limbs are ripped off (which you might experience as a shaking of the knees, a trembling of the hands, and/or a feeling of lightheadedness).

■ **Your mind becomes hyper-focused on the danger** (which you might experience as tunnel vision and an inability to remember what you were going to say).

Many people have heard of the natural "fight or flight" response to stress, but not as many people know that the reaction is actually "freeze, fight, or flight." Stage fright occurs when your brain senses a potential threat in seeing people watching you and then "freezes" so as not to do anything that might get you killed. **This is why stage fright feels a lot like paralysis - because it is a type of paralysis.**

The good news is that it is only temporary; those stress chemicals pass through your system relatively quickly. So unless you're actually being attacked by a bear, the sensation of fear you feel will soon pass. Your nerves usually go away after you've presented for a few minutes – unless you continue to focus on your fear!

If you continue to focus only on the fear you're feeling, you can think yourself right into a tailspin. You have probably seen someone "melt down" when overcome by nerves. The reason this happened is that the speaker continued to feed their own fear. Don't do that!

When you feel yourself getting nervous, just remember that those sensations are natural and temporary. Think to yourself: "It's okay. This will pass soon. All I have to do is get through the next few seconds and my body will start to relax." This can be hard to do when you are nervous, but with a little bit of practice in front of people, your body will begin to relax sooner and sooner.

Public speaking is like any other skill: the more you do it, the easier it gets.

Why Stage Fright Happens

There are several reasons why you might experience stage fright before giving a presentation:

■ **You feel nervous because you want to do well.** This is natural and can be a good thing. Some speakers say that this initial flutter helps sharpen their focus just before they go onstage.

■ **You feel nervous because you're not prepared.** On a subconscious level you know you haven't put in the time and aren't fully prepared. There is no excuse for this type of nervousness.

■ **You fear that the audience won't like you and/or your presentation because of either your content or how you present it.** If you've done your homework and prepared as described in this book, your anxiety will most likely go away shortly after you begin.

■ **You fear that something will go wrong and you won't know how to recover.** This is one of the biggest reasons that stage fright happens and fortunately, there are ways you can deal with this.

What You Can Do About It

Some degree of stage fright is natural. Don't compound your problems by focusing on your fear. Dealing with stage fright simply requires knowing how to focus your energy. Professional speakers, athletes, actors, and musicians use one or a combination of the following methods to help them harness the power of temporary nervousness. If you are worried about feeling nervous, do some or all of the following:

■ **Put your focus on your audience and not on you.** Remind yourself of your purpose, premise or big idea by saying it out loud. **Stage fright happens when you focus on YOURSELF rather than YOUR AUDIENCE.**

■ **Breathe.** You can do this standing up or sitting down. Place your feet flat on the floor and bend your knees slightly so you can feel the full weight of your body connecting to the floor. Close your eyes. Place your hands on your abdomen and inhale deeply while you count silently to a slow count of 10. Inhale all the way down until you feel your lower abdomen push your hands outward. When you reach 10, exhale while counting to 10. Do this for a few minutes.

■ **Exercise.** Many people find it helpful to do a light workout prior to their presentation. Then they shower and get ready. Exercise releases chemicals in your body called endorphins, which in turn trigger a positive feeling in your body.

If you don't have time to do a full workout, simply place your hands against a wall and bend your knees. Then take a breath in, and as you exhale, push hard into the wall. This exercise engages the rectus abdominis muscles, which in turn prevents the production of fear-producing chemicals in your body such as noradrenaline or epinephrine.

■ **Accept it so that you can let it go.** In other words, it's pointless to try to tell yourself to **NOT** be nervous. When you try to block your feelings, they don't go away. If anything, they get more intense. But if you simply accept that some nervousness is inevitable and just let yourself "ride it out," almost always, your nervousness will subside on its own.

Think of a child who cries intensely one minute and the next, is running around laughing. They can do this because they were willing to accept rather than try to block the feelings. What happens to a bubble if you hold it underneath the water? At best, it just stays beneath the water or at worst, it breaks up into lots and lots of tiny bubbles but either way, it doesn't change unless you let it rise to the surface.

■ **Adjust your attitude - focus on what you can DO.** Replace your negative thoughts with positive ones such as "I'm ready to go" or "I'm excited to share this news with you" or "I can't wait to see your excitement when…" Again, the bad stage fright is a result of focusing on yourself rather than your audience. To combat it, focus on the **GOOD** things your presentation will do for **YOUR AUDIENCE**.

Some degree of nervousness is GOOD for you. Learn to focus it.

The Best Cure

The best way to deal with stage fright is to **practice and present**. We're going to say this again.

The best cure for stage fright is to practice and present. The more experience you get, the less you'll be afraid of speaking in public. Some TED Talk speakers are known to practice up to 300 times for one presentation. The more important your presentation, the more you need to practice. Most people in the professional world are busy people. They have a work days overfilled with stuff to do. They don't want to waste their time listening to someone who's not prepared.

The more you speak your presentation out loud, the less your body will recognize your speaking as anything unusual and therefore potentially threatening. Speaking in public is a skill like any other: the more you do it, the better you get at it. It's not magic. Preparation and practice are the keys.

Expect the Unexpected

As we mentioned earlier, one of the biggest reasons why people get stage fright is that they fear they'll freeze up and look stupid if things go wrong. First of all, it's imperative that you know that **there's no such thing as a perfect presentation.** Well prepared speakers anticipate most of the things that can go wrong and practice how to recover when the unexpected happens.

Mistakes happen all the time. Even TV broadcasters make mistakes - and they're reading from a teleprompter! They mispronounce names, skip over important facts and then go back to correct themselves. When they do, they don't apologize or send any kind of non-verbal cue that they made a mistake. The truth is that usually your audience hardly notices when things go wrong unless you point it out. They'll only notice it if they see you struggling or scrambling to recover.

Unexpected things happen, too. A microphone battery dies, the lights suddenly dim, a siren blares from the street. Just acknowledge it casually without nervousness and proceed accordingly.

Here's a little secret that "newbies" to the world of public speaking don't know. Audiences sort of like it when things go wrong because it makes them look human.

If it's OK with you, it'll be OK with them. **"Don't apologize" is one of the golden rules of public speaking.** Learn it well and learn it now.

If Things Go Wrong

The best way to deal with things that go wrong is to **practice your recovery.** Out loud. **Plan out what to do and say when things go wrong and then get on your feet and practice it.** A lot.

Gymnasts perform complex routines that include double and triple somersaults. Sometimes, we see them fall off their apparatus. Ever wonder why they rarely get hurt when they fall?

Because when they're learning a new trick, they learn how to fall correctly. They practiced how to "bail out" safely so if they fall, they won't get hurt.

You can do the same with your presentation. When you practice how to recover, you'll feel confident that you can address it easily if it happens. With that in mind, make a list of all the things that can go wrong in your presentation and decide what to do when it happens. **Here's a sample list:**

- I'll forget what I'm supposed to say.
- Tech fails and I have no slides to show.
- I'll forget what I'm supposed to say.
- I won't know how to answer a question.
- I'll lose my place.
- I'll drop the prop I'm supposed to show.
- I'll forget what I'm supposed to say.

YOUR TURN

For everything that can go wrong, plan out what to say and how to recover.

Don't just think through your recovery.

Get on your feet, do and say out loud what you need to do.

Practice, practice and practice how to recover from each of these things. The more you practice, the better off you are.

DISASTER RECOVERY
What could go wrong?
EXAMPLE: Here are a few common things that can go wrong and how to recover from them.

Disaster:

WHAT COULD GO WRONG:

I forget what to say next.

Recovery:

HOW TO RECOVER:

Option A: Remind myself what I just said. Doing this might remind me of what I need to say next.

Option B: Look at my outline, notes, or cue cards.

Disaster:

WHAT COULD GO WRONG:

My tech stops working.

Recovery:

HOW TO RECOVER:

Option A: Take a moment to fix it. Everyone understands these things happen.

Option B: If fixing it is taking too long, say "That's okay, here's what's even more important than my slides ..." and then just tell them my presentation simply.

DISASTER RECOVERY
What could go wrong?
YOUR TURN: List things that could go wrong and practice recovering from them. **PRACTICE OUT LOUD.**

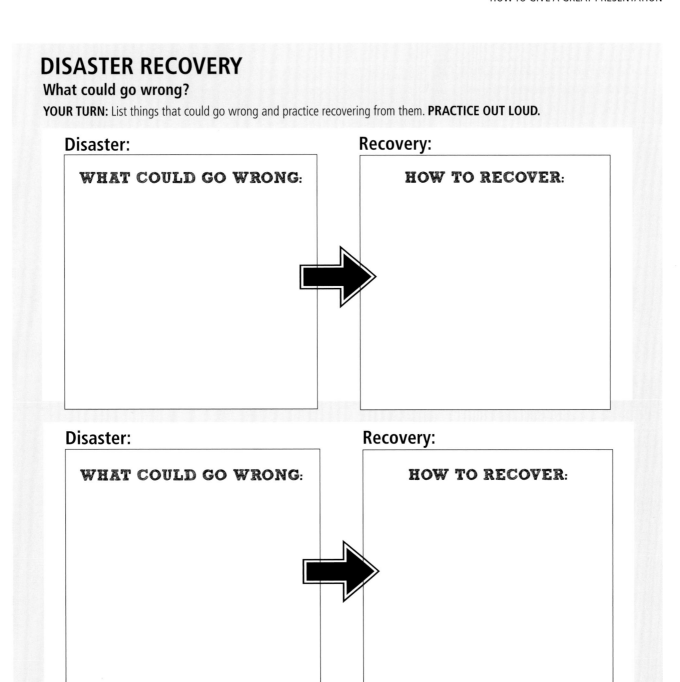

Disaster:

WHAT COULD GO WRONG:

Recovery:

HOW TO RECOVER:

Disaster:

WHAT COULD GO WRONG:

Recovery:

HOW TO RECOVER:

DISASTER RECOVERY
What could go wrong?

YOUR TURN: List things that could go wrong and practice recovering from them. **PRACTICE OUT LOUD.**

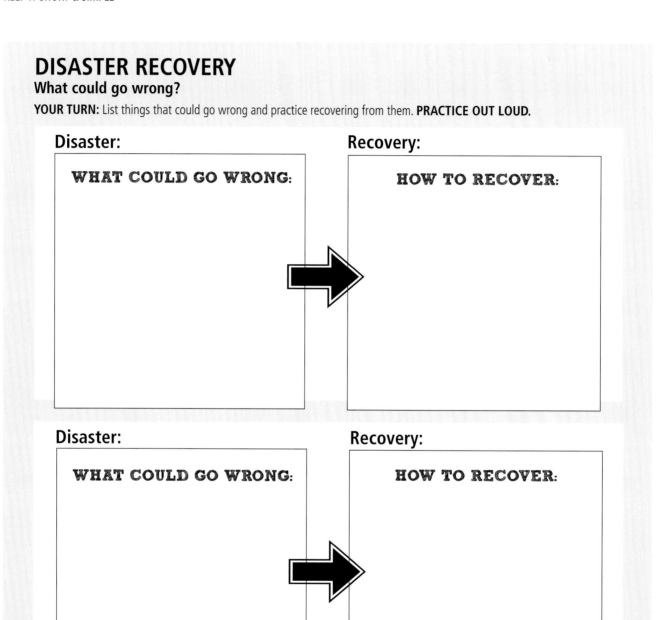

Disaster:

WHAT COULD GO WRONG:

Recovery:

HOW TO RECOVER:

Disaster:

WHAT COULD GO WRONG:

Recovery:

HOW TO RECOVER:

KEY TAKEAWAYS – DEALING WITH STAGE FRIGHT

■ Some degree of stage fright is natural and useful. Don't freak out if you feel it beginning.

■ The best way to deal with stage fright is to focus on something other than your own fear.

■ If you begin to feel nervous, put your focus on your audience and not on you.

■ Breathe.

■ Exercise beforehand.

■ Accept your nerves so you can let them go.

■ Focus on what you can do rather than on the things you can't control.

■ The best cure for stage fright is preparation and practice.

■ Mistakes will happen.

■ The goal is not perfection, it's authenticity.

■ Audiences do not mind when you make mistakes unless you draw attention to them.

■ Don't apologize.

■ Take a few moments to plan what you will do if something goes wrong.

■ Practice your recovery out loud.

PART 2

REAL WORLD PRESENTATIONS

PART 2   SECTION 1
STANDARD BUSINESS PRESENTATIONS

YOU GIVE THEM EVERY DAY

It's just after 8 a.m. and you're next in line at Starbucks. A familiar voice catches your ear. You turn around and see it's your boss, Xavier Rodriguez. He says "Good morning, Joy."

After you return the greeting he says "I see that you're on my calendar for 10 a.m. today. What's that about?"

After a brief moment you reply "I know you're looking for ways to reduce inventory but still keep our customers happy. I have an idea that'll just take a few minutes of your time."

He says "Great! I look forward to hearing more. See you at 10."

You just gave the pre-pitch for an elevator pitch. At 10 a.m. you do the real thing.

After that, your friend Bob says "Hey, I see you got a new phone; what kind did you get?" You respond by informing him about its features and why it was worth the money.

At 11 a.m. your friend Shannon turns to you and says "I'm going to meet my sister for lunch and I'm tired of the same old places. You got any suggestions?" You spend the next two minutes persuading her to go to this fabulous new Asian bistro that just opened down the street.

Later in the afternoon you call a meeting to brainstorm with your team on how to deal with the temporary loss of a coworker who's out on maternity leave.

On your drive home from work your mother calls and asks if you know when her computer will be fixed. You give her a status report on what the Apple technician told you over the phone.

It's the end of a typical day. All in all, you gave 11 presentations – real-world presentations. In life and at work you give lots of them every day. In fact, you give hundreds and even thousands every year.

Since you give so many, how do you know the difference between one type of presentation and another? In many ways, they're the same. All presentations need a clear beginning, middle and end and all presentations would be better if they were kept short and simple.

However, there are differences as well. The main difference is in their purpose. Each one is designed to accomplish a specific task for a specific audience. Simply put, there aren't really different "types" of presentations so much as there are just different purposes for presentations.

HOW TO USE
THIS SECTION

"A successful presentation needs to be both buttoned up (orderly) and free-flowing (a conversation.)
The tension between the two, the fact that both things are happening at once, defines the process."
- Dale Ludwig and Greg Owen-Bolger, authors, <u>The Orderly Conversation: Business Presentations Redefined</u>

Section 1 includes examples of the different types of presentations that you'll give throughout your career. Each type of presentation or skill has its own chapter.

For clarity and ease of use, the act is divided into two parts. The first part includes examples of the types of things everyone recognizes as "presentations." These are the talks, reports or trainings you will be asked to give throughout your career.

On the first page of every chapter is a blank template designed specifically for that type of presentation. Just fill in the blanks to create your own when you need it.

Within the chapter, we'll walk you through the thought process behind creating a presentation of that type and build it for you slowly so you can see how to create one from start to finish.

Finally, we'll show you a detailed outline of the example presentation fleshed out more completely – sometimes including things you might say or images that you might use.

Because the purpose for each type of presentation is different, you'll notice that each one requires a slightly different thought process.

SECTION 1 INCLUDES:
How to Give an Informative Presentation
How to Give a Status Report
How to Give a Persuasive Presentation
How to Give an Elevator Pitch
How to Give a Training Session
How to Give a Pitch Book Presentation
How to Give Other Types of Presentations
How to Title Your Talk

CHAPTER 17
HOW TO GIVE AN INFORMATIVE PRESENTATION

"The two words 'information' and 'communication' are often used interchangeably,
but they signify different things. Information is giving out; communication is getting through."
- Sydney J. Harris, author and journalist

Informative Presentation

A type of presentation designed to explain a specific topic to an audience.

Most books on public speaking make a distinction between informative presentations and persuasive ones. It is important to know the difference, but it's even more important to recognize that the distinction has more to do with degree than type.

There is a fine line between an informative presentation and a persuasive one. In fact, most informative presentations contain an element of persuasion in them, and all persuasive presentations inform.

Know Your Purpose
Informative vs. Persuasive Presentation

If the thing you want them to DO involves personal change, then you have to put together a presentation **persuasive enough to convince them to change their behavior.** But if your audience doesn't really have much choice in the matter (for instance if you are in the military and the presentation is about a new set of orders coming down the chain of command) or if your audience's choices are very limited (for instance if you are a human resources instructor explaining how to fill out an online form), then persuasion isn't as important. **The difference between an informative and a persuasive one is what you want your audience to DO at the end of the presentation.**

Using the Template

Each chapter in this section includes a blank template to help you visualize your next presentation of that type.

The templates are divided into two sections:

1. Stuff you will keep in mind but not necessarily say out loud includes questions you'll want to keep in mind about the **PURPOSE** of your presentation. Staying focused on the **PURPOSE** of your presentation will help you stay on task regardless of any problems you encounter.

2. Stuff you will say out loud and/or otherwise include in your presentation includes questions or places to keep notes about the presentation outline you devised while doing the exercises in this book. The templates in each chapter differ slightly in the suggestions for things to keep in mind while crafting the body or main points of your presentation.

TEMPLATE - INFORMATIVE PRESENTATION

BACKGROUND NOTES: Stuff you will keep in mind but not necessarily say out loud:

    TITLE:_____

    PURPOSE

        Audience should FEEL:_____

        Audience should DO:_____

        Audience should THINK:_____

    IN ONE SENTENCE:_____

PRESENTATION: Stuff you will say out loud and/or otherwise include in your presentation:

    BEGINNING / INTRODUCTION

        Hook:_____

        Desire / Problem:_____

        Solution:_____

        Name / Credibility:_____

    MIDDLE / BODY: Prioritize main points - no more than five - biographically, thematically, cause and effect, or another way

        Point 1:_____

            Hook or evidence:_____

        Point 2:_____

            Hook or evidence:_____

        Point 3:_____

            Hook or evidence:_____

        Points 4 & 5: (Only if necessary)_____

            Hook or evidence:_____

    END / CONCLUSION

        Question and answer:_____

        Call to action:_____

        Last thing they leave with:_____

Know Your Audience
What do you want them to feel, do, and think?

The trick to putting together an informative presentation is figuring out what information **needs** to go into the presentation (and what doesn't) and what's the best **order** for that information for a particular audience.

As always, the easiest way to do that is to recognize that your presentation is always about more than just the information. Remember to keep the **focus on your audience**. The things you want them to FEEL, DO, and THINK are just as important as facts. The world is full of informative presentations. The worst are nothing more than information dumps. The best presentations do more than merely inform.

> If the primary goal of your presentation is to clarify, correct, educate, explain, enlighten, inform, instruct, remind, remediate, or train, then your **presentation is primarily informative.**

An Illustrative Example
Gettysburg National Battlefield Park

If you were visiting the Gettysburg Battlefield National Park, **how beneficial would it be if the information presented to you when you entered the park was merely a list of facts?** Let's take a look at a list of some facts that could be included in this presentation:

The Facts
- The park covers 9.358 square miles.
- The park was acquired in 1895.
- The park has 43,000 artifacts from the Civil War.
- There are 12 museums within the park.
- There are more than 14,000 monuments, markers, and tablets in the park.
- In 1863, a battle between two armies fighting in the Civil War was fought for three days on some of the grounds now controlled by the park.
- There were around 82,289 Union solders at that battle.
- There were around 75,000 Confederate soldiers at that battle.
- The battle resulted in around 23,049 casualties for the Union Army and around 28,063 casualties for the Confederate Army.
- The battle was fought during some of the hottest days of the summer.
- President Lincoln made some famous remarks while dedicating the cemetery on a Thursday afternoon four-and-a-half months after the battle.
- The battle marked an important turning point in the American Civil War. It was the last time the Confederate Army invaded Union territory.

These are facts. All of them are true and all of them are informative. But not all of them are necessary or even all that useful to a first-time visitor to the park. So if facts alone aren't good enough, how exactly should you go about putting together an informative presentation about Gettysburg?

The same way you would begin putting together ANY presentation: **by clarifying your message and focusing on your audience!**

Figure out what you want them to FEEL, DO, and THINK (in that order)! Here's what to do first:

CLARIFY YOUR MESSAGE
Know your audience

Who are they?
> People from all over the world. Some of them have been here before, but there are many first-time visitors.

Where are they?
> In the Visitor's Center at the entrance to the park.

Why are they there?
> To stand on the ground where the battle took place, look around and imagine what it must have been like to have been there while the battle was being fought.

What do they want?
> To learn more about the Battle of Gettysburg and to experience the sensation of standing on the ground where the battle was fought.

When do they want it?
> Right now (as soon as possible after this presentation).

How familiar are they with your topic?
> Some of them will be very familiar, some of them not familiar at all.

Just by answering these basic questions, you already know a great deal about how to put together an informative presentation. **Your goal should be to orient people to the park and to provide them with an overview of the battle and what traces of that battle remain within the park.**

Your audience is looking for more than just information. They have travelled here to physically interact with that history. The sensory experiences of this place - the visceral nature of the place itself - is also important.

The more specific you can be about your audience, the better.

Segment your audience
Never try to create a single presentation that is all things to all people! Some people have already been to the park while others have not. The same presentation will not work for both groups. Begin by identifying the group within the group that most needs your information. Concentrate on them first. If necessary, you can put together other presentations for other audiences later.

Your audience determines your content – the body of your presentation
For instance, the park sometimes hosts reenactment groups who know as much about the battle as many of the tour guides. Your presentation to them might focus more on "backstage" information about how the park operates on a day-to-day basis. Many advanced Civil War enthusiasts would appreciate being able to see some of the more obscure items in the collection, but these same obscure items wouldn't necessarily help first-time visitors understand a broader overview of the battle.

Because most people coming to the park will be first-time visitors, keep answering some basic questions about that audience:

What will they like?
> The things they will like most are easy-to-understand facts that put the battle into context, paint an evocative image, or help them visualize the battle.

What will they not like?
> Most of them will not care much about the park's management structure. Many of them will be afraid of being overwhelmed with too many dates and details.

Now that you know this information, your presentation is already beginning to take shape. For instance:

What will you want them to feel?
> Welcomed and not overwhelmed. Oriented to the landscape in relationship to the battle. Confident that their visit will be pleasant and educational.

What do you want them to do?
> Choose between one of several options for exploring the park (either on their own or with a guided tour). Visit the sites that personally interest them the most.

As you can see, **by taking just a moment to figure out what you want them to FEEL and to DO, it becomes much easier to organize the information you want them to THINK about.**

What do you want them to think?
Identifying what you want your audience to think for informative presentations is straightforward. You want them to think "I understand." But how exactly do you get them to think that? Simple: by organizing your information clearly.

Prioritize your main points
After you gather facts you think will be important for this audience, the next step is to prioritize how you will present the information to them. One of the simplest ways to organize this information is chronologically in the order it occurred. If you were to organize the facts in this way, it would look something like the sticky notes on the next page.

GETTYSBURG BATTLEFIELD FACTS
Chronological order

BEFORE THE BATTLE

DURING THE BATTLE

AFTER THE BATTLE

A general named Meade was in command of the Union Army.

A general named Lee was in command of the Confederate Army.

Unlike most other battles in the same campaign, the Confederates attacked from the north, while the Union Army fought coming from the south.

The battle resulted in around 23,049 casualties for the Union Army and 28,063 casualties for the Confederate Army.

The battle lasted three days.

It did not rain during the battle, but a heavy downpour soaked the battlefield the day after.

There were around 82,289 Union solders at the beginning of the battle.

There were around 75,000 Confederate soldiers at the beginning of the battle.

The battle began without the knowledge or consent of either commander.

The battle was fought during some of the hottest days of the summer.
It was nearly 90 degrees during Pickett's Charge on the third day, July 3, 1863.

The number of casualties on the Confederate side included more than a third of General Lee's entire army.

President Lincoln made some famous remarks while dedicating the cemetery on a Thursday afternoon four-and-a-half months after the battle.

Of course there are many other ways you could organize your information.

For instance, **you could also organize it biographically** - for instance, around the experiences of a particular person who was at the battle; **or thematically** - by focusing on the impact the battle had on solidifying national arguments about slavery; **or in terms of cause and effect** - exploring more deeply the idea that the battle began without the knowledge or consent of either commander, or that it began as a series of small engagements that eventually added up to one of the largest battles in the war.

In fact, there are many, many ways that you can organize any information. There is no one right way. The simplest way to figure out the best option is just to play around with the information to see what seems like it will work best for your particular audience.

Remember, **the first step to putting together any presentation is getting clear about your message.** You begin to do this by answering some questions about your audience. Then you try to hone your message down to its simplest form. Then get all of your information in order and check again to be sure your points are as simple as possible.

Getting Clearer: Zooming Out

The easiest way to make sure your message is clear is to first **zoom out** and try to put everything you've learned in simple terms (no more than will fit on a sticky note). In our example, this step would look like this:

Who is your AUDIENCE?
> First-time visitors to the park.

What is their DESIRE or PROBLEM?
> They want to understand the battle and explore the park. But there is a lot of information within the park and it can get confusing.

What is your SOLUTION?
> I will give them a short chronological overview of the battle and its aftermath.

After that, the next step is simply making sure you have your message as clear as possible.

Getting Clearest: Short Description

The easiest way you do this is to try to say it in ONE SENTENCE or as close to that ideal as possible.

For example, at this point, your presentation for general first-time visitors to Gettysburg National Battlefield Park is pretty broad and so your sentence will be too. Indeed, this step is almost always the hardest one to do for informative presentations - after all it's hard to cram a whole lot of information into a single sentence!

But the goal of this step isn't to force you to do linguistic gymnastics. The goal is simply to make sure you have honed your initial idea down to something clear and manageable.

So for now, to keep things simple, cut yourself some slack and allow yourself two sentences that include most of the ideas you need to present.

> Over the course of three days in 1863, here on this ground, over 157,000 Americans fought one of the most important battles in the nation's history.
>
> There is more to see, learn, and experience here than you can do in a single visit, so you'll need to make some choices about how you want to explore the park.

STRUCTURE YOUR PRESENTATION

Start with a Hook

The first step in that process is to figure out how to begin your presentation with impact. **Even an informative presentation needs to start with a hook - with something that grabs the audience's attention.** Here is a list of possible ways to hook your audience:

A physical object

The battlefield itself: "You are standing on some of the most hallowed ground in the world."

A visible image

"This is a topographical map of the battlefield. As we talk through the events of the battle, lights and arrows will demonstrate how the various armies maneuvered against each other."

Striking facts or statistics

"On July 1-3, 1863, here - and in the fields around you as far as you can see - over 157,000 men fought with everything they had for the very soul of this great nation. At the end of those three days, rain began to fall on the 7,058 men who lay dead or dying; on another 33,264 who had been wounded, and somewhere over another 10,790 who were missing in action. This ground marks both the high point and the beginning of the end for the Confederacy - and the beginnings of the nation we live in today."

A personal story

"Ordinary soldiers had no idea how bloody and important this battle would turn out to be. In a letter to his family after the battle, William Wheeler, a lieutenant in the 13th New York Independent Battery, writes: *'Early on the 1st of July we started for Gettysburg, about eleven miles distant … We were marching along, thinking of anything but an approaching fight, when suddenly one of General Howard's aids came galloping up and ordered me forward at double-quick. The roads were very stony, and my wheels were in very bad condition, but ahead I went; the gun-carriages rattling and bouncing in the air; feed, rations, kettles and everything else breaking loose from the caissons, the cannoneers running with all their might to keep up, for the road was so very rough, that I was afraid to have them mount. For at least four miles the race continued, and I brought my whole Battery safely into position on the right of Gettysburg . . . my breathless cannoneers made their appearance one by one, and soon each detachment was full.'"*

The actual presentation / exhibit at Gettysburg National Park uses a combination of all of these hooks. It is an outstanding example of an informational presentation done right.

You don't have to use all the hooks you can imagine, but you do need to **think through at least a few dynamic ways to grab your audience's attention.**

Once you have some ideas about how to start, the next most important thing you need to figure out is how you can end your presentation with just as much or more impact. The worksheets in Chapter 2 will help you do this.

For now, to keep things simple, it's important to recognize that you can easily come up with a strong ending by just answering these questions:

End with a Bang

How can you REINCORPORATE some of the information from the rest of your presentation (especially your initial hook)?

You can highlight the fact that because the Confederates lost over a third of their entire army in the battle, they never recovered enough strength to invade the North again. You can also highlight the fact that if the South had won the battle, many people believe the Union government would have sued for peace - in effect winning the war for the South. Thus even though it began almost on accident, the Battle of Gettysburg turned out to be the key turning point in the entire war!

What is your CALL TO ACTION?

> After this introductory presentation, visitors to the park should choose the way they would like to continue exploring the park on their own. I can provide them with a list of possible options.

What is the LAST THING you will leave with them?

> This answer is easy: a map of the park and a list of places/times for guided tours.

The actual presentation/exhibit at Gettysburg National Park uses a combination of all of these things, but, again, you don't have to incorporate everything you can think of. The point is simply that you need an actual ending rather than just finishing by saying "well that's all I've got." A little bit of thought upfront will go a long way toward making your presentation both more entertaining and more memorable.

The last step before outlining your presentation is simply figuring out how you will introduce yourself. The easiest way to figure out how to do that is to answer the question "Why should they listen to you?" (Remember, even though you are introducing yourself, the presentation is about THEM, so even your introduction needs to focus on why THEY should care).

In our presentation example, the information is best delivered by a park ranger so for the sake of illustration, let's make you a park ranger named Frank. Then the answer to the question would look like this:

What is your name / What is your CREDIBILITY?

> "My name is Frank Rogers. I'm a ranger here in the park and I'll be your guide for the next 20 minutes as we explore the monumental events that changed this great nation."

That's it. That's all there is to it. Once you have done all of these steps, it is a simple matter to fill in the blanks and put together a clear, concise outline of your presentation. For your convenience, a detailed outline of what our example presentation would look like is included at the end of this section (this example is deliberately long to demonstrate how even complex presentations can be made simple).

Visual Aids and Rehearsal

Once you have your outline completed, you will want to design any visual aids by using the list of tools in **Section 4: "Design It;"** and rehearse and deliver your presentation according to the list of suggestions in the **Section 5: "Practice and Present."**

As you can see, putting together an informative presentation is not really all that different from putting together ANY presentation. The trick is simply in figuring out what information is most important for your audience based on how you want them to feel and what you want them to do and then figuring out a good way to organize that information.

Help Them Remember

Some books on public speaking also take a lot of time to point out that it is important to make informative presentations memorable. In other words, if your audience needs the information, then they probably also need to remember it! It's your job to find a way to do just that.

One of the most effective ways to help your audience stay engaged throughout your presentation is to **include different modalities of learning.**

There are three basic learning modalities:

some people learn best **VISUALLY**
(by seeing something),

some learn best **AUDITORILY**
(by hearing something),

and some learn best **KINESTHETICALLY**
(by physically touching or doing something).

Most people remember best when a combination of all of these is included in a presentation.

If you put together your presentation as we suggest from the very beginning: by thinking about the types of **HOOKS** you might use - by asking questions about what physical objects, visual images, striking facts or statistics, or personal stories you might include - and by using only the information your audience really **NEEDS** - then you have already been making your presentation as memorable as possible at every step of the way!

Final Thoughts

Informative presentations are often harder to put together than persuasive ones because it's not always clear what information you need to include or what order it needs to go in. However, the exercises in this book will go a long way toward helping you recognize the best information and best order for any particular audience. As always, keeping it short, simple, and focused on your audience is the key.

The three most important rules for you to remember once you're done drafting your presentation are:

1. Prepare
2. Practice what your prepare
3. Present what you practiced

KEY TAKEAWAYS - HOW TO GIVE AN INFORMATIVE PRESENTATION

■ Most informative presentations also need to include some persuasive elements.

■ Consider your audience when you begin.

■ Segment your audience. Never try to create a single presentation that is all things to all people!

■ Decide what you want your audience to do, feel, and think by the end of your presentation. That will help you decide what **INFORMATION** needs to go into your presentation and what information can - and should - be left out.

■ Experiment with different orders for the information you need to present. Try it chronologically, thematically, biographically or any other way.

■ Make every section as dynamic as possible (what we call "hooks:" stories, examples, illustrations, props etc.) so it'll be easier for your audience to understand and remember all the information.

■ End with a bang. Make your ending as strong as your opening hook.

■ Make sure your **CALL TO ACTION** is doable and not complicated. For example: "If you need help deciding, look for the guides dressed in …"

■ Use different learning modalities to present the information to keep them engaged and make it memorable (let them see, hear, and do things).

DETAILED OUTLINE - INFORMATIVE PRESENTATION
Gettysburg National Battlefield Park

BACKGROUND NOTES: Stuff you will keep in mind but not necessarily say out loud:

TITLE: *Overview of Gettysburg National Battlefield Park.*

PURPOSE

Audience should FEEL: *Welcomed, oriented, confident, and empathetic with the soldiers.*

Audience should DO: *Choose one of several options for exploring the park.*

Audience should THINK: *How all the facts about the park fit into a cohesive story.*

IN ONE SENTENCE: *"On this ground in 1863, over 157,000 Americans fought one of the most important battles in the nation's history. There is more to see, learn, and experience here than you can do in a single visit, so you'll need to make some choices about how you want to explore the park."* (Yes, that's actually two sentences; read the chapter.)

PRESENTATION: Stuff you will say out loud and/or otherwise include in your presentation:

BEGINNING / INTRODUCTION

Hook: *The battlefield itself, a topographical map, striking statistics, and a personal story.*

Desire/Problem: *To understand the battle. I could say: "If not for the things that happened here over 150 years ago, the United States of America as we know it now might not exist. The transition from old to new was complex and painful. The information in this park reflects that complexity."*

Solution: *An overview of the three days of battle and aftermath. I'll say: "For those who are interested, a short presentation will provide an overview of the battle to help orient you to the park and make your time here as enjoyable and educational as possible."*

Name / Credibility: *"My name is Frank Rogers. I'm a ranger and I'll be your guide as we explore the monumental events that changed this great nation."*

MIDDLE / BODY

Point 1: *Background: Quick overview of what happed in the Civil War before the battle.*

Hooks or evidence: *"Fresh off a decisive victory at Chancellorsville, General Lee invades the North"* (show map and pictures of Southern soldiers, play sounds of marching boots).

"General Meade positions Union Army between Lee and Washington" (show map and pictures of Northern soldiers, play sounds of marching boots).

Point 2: *The first day of the battle.*

Hooks or evidence: *"The battle began with short skirmishes as each side felt out the strength of the other"* (show interactive map).

Hooks or evidence: *"The South won the first day. Northern forces retreated to the south of town" (show interactive map, plus excerpts from soldiers' diaries).*

Point 3: *The second day of the battle.*

Hooks or evidence: *" Lee attacked the Union's left flank" (provide startling statistics and story about the defense of Little Round Top).*

"Lee attacked the Union's right flank" (show images of the aftermath of the fighting on Culp's Hill and Cemetery Hill).

"The day ended in a stalemate" (show map of battle, plus startling statistics and excerpts from soldier diaries describing the carnage).

Point 4: *The third day of the battle.*

Hooks or evidence: *" General Longstreet suggested withdrawal, but Lee resolved to attack anyway" (show excerpts from diary entries and quotes attributed to both generals).*

" General Armistead's failed advance and Pickett's Charge mark' the high water mark of the Confederacy'" (give startling statistics about the carnage and excerpts from soldiers' diaries about hand-to-hand fighting and the decimation of Pickett's soldiers).

Point 5: *The aftermath.*

Hooks or evidence: *" The Confederate Army withdrew" (show maps detailing positions of each army during the retreat and quotations attributed to Lee about his regret).*

" Casualties on both sides were staggering" (startling statistics about losses in both armies and images of the aftermath of the battle).

" Never again would the South be able to wage war in the North. The end of the Civil War began with this battle" (show images of newspaper articles from the day and a note about how much longer the war would go on anyway).

END / CONCLUSION:

End with a bang: *A reintegration of the initial hook explaining why this battle was so important (show images of President Lincoln at Gettysburg and play a recording of an actor reading the " Gettysburg Address").*

Call to action: *Tell them to choose one of several paths / suggested itineraries for exploring the park.*

Question and answer: *Place the Q&A at the very end so that those who want to leave can do so. Announce where the rangers will be if visitors have other questions later.*

Last thing they leave with: *A map of the park and places times to meet for guided tours.*

CHAPTER 18
HOW TO GIVE A STATUS REPORT

"This report, by its very length, defends itself against the risk of being read."
- Winston Churchill, prime minister of Great Britain (1940-45, 1951-55)

Status Report

A report that summarizes a particular situation at a stated period of time.

Status reports are really just short informative presentations. They are the most common types of presentations given in business today. Unless you work for yourself or own your own company, at one point in your working life you will be asked to update your boss or coworkers about a project you are working on. Often, several of these reports are given back to back at regularly scheduled meetings. This can be a problem if any of the presentations before yours go longer than scheduled (which unfortunately happens too often).

The Purpose

As the name suggests, status reports are just that: "reports." They are verbal updates used to present information about a project to a group of coworkers. There are specific things that go into a status report. Unfortunately, most people don't know how to deliver them succinctly.

The main problem with most status reports as used in business today is that there is usually very little information that

NEEDS to be delivered to an audience in real time. Usually, most of the information you'll be asked to deliver could be laid out effectively in a written memo or email - which would allow your audience to go over the information at their own pace when it is most convenient for them.

Consequently, one of the reasons why so many status report meetings are held is this: management requires face-to-face meetings to update each other because they say employees don't read their emails. On the other hand, employees complain that upper management's emails are too frequent and too long and they don't have time to read all of them. This problem is widespread and most likely won't go away anytime soon. However, you can do your part by making your status report presentations as effective and painless as possible

CLARIFY YOUR MESSAGE
Know Your Audience

Though your audience usually consists of coworkers who know something about your project, you still need to gear your status report for your specific audience. Sometimes you will need to deliver a status report to a specialized audience

TEMPLATE - STATUS REPORT

BACKGROUND NOTES: Stuff you will keep in mind but not necessarily say out loud:

    TITLE:_____

    PURPOSE

        Audience should FEEL:_____

        Audience should DO:_____

        Audience should THINK:_____

    IN ONE SENTENCE:_____

PRESENTATION: Stuff you will say out loud and/or otherwise include in your presentation:

    BEGINNING / INTRODUCTION

        Desire/Problem: (the task you were assigned)_____

        Solution: _____

        Name / Credibility: (only if needed) _____

    MIDDLE / BODY

        Point 1 - Past: (accomplishments to date)_____

        Point 2 - Present: (challenges, unresolved tasks and problems)_____

        Point 3 - Future: (goals, milestones, and deadlines)_____

    END / CONCLUSION

        Call to action: (anything needing to be assigned)_____

        Question and answer: (more of a discussion than formal Q&A)_____

        Last thing:_____

or people who do not know you. It's always important to gear the report to the audience.

A status report is just a specific type of informative presentation that doesn't (usually) need an opening hook or to end with a bang. For instance, putting together a common status report presentation might look something like this:

Who is your audience?
My boss and/or coworkers.

Where are they?
The same conference room we always present in.

Why are they there?
Because they have to be. The purpose of the regular meeting is so that everyone can keep up with what everyone else is doing.

What do they want?
To know what my team is doing so they can determine if anything we are doing will affect any of the projects they are working on.

When do they want it?
At our regularly scheduled meeting in the slot assigned for my presentation.

How familiar are they with your topic?
Everyone is familiar with the goals of the company but they might not know exactly how my particular project fits in with the larger strategy.

What will they like about the information?
Some of them will be happy that my team has already accomplished a lot.

What will they not like about the information?
Some of them will be unhappy we have not yet accomplished everything.

Prioritize Your Main Points

Since you will be updating your coworkers about things they're already familiar with, the purpose of your report is to provide everyone with relevant information about the past, present, and future of the project.

The simplest way of laying out that information is called the "PPP" approach. Different companies sometimes name each "P" differently, but the result is always the same:

The first "P" has to do with the PAST (the words used in the acronym might be "Progress" or "Planning" or something similar).

The second "P" has to do with the PRESENT (the words used in the acronym might be "Problems" or "Productivity" or something similar).

The last "P" has to do with the FUTURE (the words used in the acronym might be "Plans" or "Priorities").

Obviously, if you use the PPP approach, your main talking points will be presented chronologically. Like all types of presentations, the way you prioritize your main points is going to depend upon your specific audience and the purpose of your presentation.

Whatever the specifics of the acronym used, it is important to know that at the core, all of the elements in PPP systems have to do with time:

- What has happened up to this point?
- What's happening now?
- What can we expect to happen next?

The easiest way to put together your own status report is to simply answer those basic questions. This format is so simple that it's used by many of the fastest growing companies in the world.

Older companies or those with slower growth (and therefore more tolerance for wasted time) sometimes use other systems (or longer acronyms), but no matter what the specifics of the preferred approach, every company in the world wants their status reports to include at least some version of what we just described.

Feel, Do, Think
What do you want them to FEEL?

confident that my team is on the ball and capable of finishing the project on time and on budget;

reassured that their projects will not be negatively impacted.

What do you want them to DO?

say "That's fine" and let me get back to work so I can finish the project!

What do you want them to THINK?

since I will just be updating everyone about things they already familiar with, the simplest way to do that is just to provide everyone with a little bit of relevant information about the past, present, and future of the project.

Let's dig a little deeper into this last thing. If there are people present who may not be familiar with the details of the project, you might want to fill them in with a few more details such as what were you asked to do and why you were you asked to do it.

This is sometimes called a background statement, and the simplest way to explain how to use it is just to put it into context.

An Illustrative Example

Imagine that you had been asked to give a status report on a project you had been working on. The clearest way to start is just by introducing yourself and mentioning the task you were given.

"Hi I'm Bob. I think everyone here already knows me."

"As part of the 'Reach Out to the Customer' initiative, our team was asked to put together a list of new high value potential customers."

That's it. That's all that you need for the introduction of your presentation. Everyone is now on the same page and has some context for what you are going to say next. So now you can jump right in to the main body of your presentation:

Main point 1: The PAST
What have you done thus far?

"We've spent the last two months gathering data from similar companies and other known sources of information. We have also sent out surveys to all existing customer distribution centers to help us identify any untapped demographics we might have missed."

Main point 2: The PRESENT
What challenges or difficulties have you encountered? What unresolved tasks remain?

"The biggest hurdles we've had up to this point are simply time and cooperation from our distributors: not everyone has gotten back to us as quickly as we might have liked. As a result, we have only 87% of the information we hoped to have at this point."

Main point 3: The FUTURE
What specifically will you be doing to accomplish this task in the future? What are your goals, milestones, deadlines, etc.?

"To meet this challenge, we are going to temporarily rearrange staffing to increase the number of contact hours our researchers can devote to running down the information. We hope to be back on track by December to meet the January deadline that marketing has asked for."

The end of your presentation is just as simple to put together: just let people know if there are any **action items** they need to take and **invite questions** or discussion.

In our example, that can be accomplished as simply as saying: "Let me know if you have any concerns" and then engaging in any discussion that follows.

Some companies might also have you add some additional information to this; but otherwise basically **that's all there is to it. It's just that simple.** A status report does not need to be any more complicated than this.

Before you present, it is sometimes useful to mentally zoom out and remind yourself of your purpose in presenting.

Getting Clearer: Zooming Out

Who is your audience?
My co-workers.

What is their desire or problem?
To know how the timeline of my project will affect them.

What is your solution?
Reassure them that we've got everything handled and the results will be on time.

What is your short description?
"Despite some minor setbacks, we are on track and will be ready by the deadline."

STRUCTURE YOUR PRESENTATION

Since the format is already predetermined by corporate culture, there is no need to worry about organizing your presentation for maximum impact.

In other words, you usually don't need to worry about starting with a hook or ending with a bang. In essence, **a status report is just the middle part of an informative presentation delivered without worrying about grabbing your audience's attention.**

Visual Aids and Rehearsal

Since some corporate cultures encourage the use of slides in these types of presentations, you might also need to make at least one slide for each of these points. If you are used to giving these reports, rehearsal can be kept to a minimum. However if you suffer from stage fright, rehearsal can help reduce that considerably. Nothing makes you feel more confident than knowing you are prepared.

Final Thoughts on Status Reports

Crafting your status report according to simple PPP content has the added bonus of making it possible for you to shorten your presentation down to its bare essentials at a moment's notice if time runs short because those who presented before you run long.

As your career advances, there may come a time when you're the person in charge of scheduling meetings and setting agendas. If and when this happens, consider whether or not a "presentation" is actually the best way to get status update information to all your teams.

Many of the fastest growing companies have begun switching away from regularly scheduled meetings back to written - or online - "reports" to distribute this kind of information widely. In fact, all of the information in the example above could easily, quickly, and cheaply be disseminated via email or other online documents. Doing so could potentially save the company a lot of time and manpower in lost productivity and endless meetings. For now, just remember that if you're asked to give a progress report, you'll make everyone's life much better by keeping it short and simple.

KEY TAKEAWAYS - HOW TO GIVE A STATUS REPORT

■ Status reports aren't really presentations; they're just really short informative reports.

■ If you have to give a status report as a presentation, keep it short and simple.

■ As always, begin by considering your audience.

■ One of the easiest parts of putting together a status report presentation is figuring out what information needs to go in it. Usually the format or required content is already standardized. Simply follow the blueprint or outline of your company culture.

■ In the absence of clearly defined corporate blueprints or outlines, simply include information about the timeline of your project: What has happened up to this point? What is happening now? And what you want to happen in future?

■ Only invite people to the meeting who need to hear the information in person. That includes people who are directly affected by progress or can influence the outcome.

■ When you are put in charge of scheduling meetings for status reports ask yourself this: Is this best or most cost-effective way to get all that information to the people who need it?

DETAILED OUTLINE - STATUS REPORT
Update the management

<u>**BACKGROUND NOTES:**</u> Stuff you will keep in mind but not necessarily say out loud:

TITLE: *Update on customer initiative*

PURPOSE

Audience should FEEL: *I want them to feel confident that my team is on the ball and capable of finishing the project on time and on budget; reassured that their projects will not be negatively impacted.*

Audience should DO: *I want them to say "That's fine" and let me get back to work so I can finish the project!*

Audience should THINK: *I want them to know about the past, present, and future of the project.*

IN ONE SENTENCE: *"Despite minor setbacks, we are on track and will be ready by the deadline."*

<u>**PRESENTATION:**</u> Stuff you will say out loud and/or otherwise include in your presentation:

BEGINNING / INTRODUCTION

Hook: *Not needed for this particular status report.*

Desire / Problem: *" As part of the customer initiative, our team was asked to put together a list of new high value potential customers."*

Solution: *Reassure them that we've got everything handled and the results will be on time.*

Name / Credibility: *" Hi I'm Bob. I think everyone here already knows me."*

MIDDLE / BODY

Point 1 - Past: *" We've spent the last two months gathering data from similar companies and other known sources of information. We have also sent out surveys to all existing customer distribution centers to help us identify any untapped demographics we might have missed."*

Point 2 - Present: *" The biggest hurdles we've had up to this point are simply time and co-operation from our distributors: not everyone has gotten back to us as quickly as we might have liked. As a result we have only 87% of the information we hoped to have at this point."*

Point 3 - Future: *" To meet this challenge, we are going to temporarily rearrange staffing to increase the number of contact hours our researchers can devote to running down the information. We hope to be back on track by December to meet the January deadline that marketing is asking for."*

END / CONCLUSION

End with a bang: *The biggest bang for this group will be giving them time back from the meeting. So keep it short and simple and don't waste any more of their time than necessary.*

Call to action: *List of any action items I want members of the other teams to do.*

Question and answer: *" Let me know if you have any questions or concerns"*

Last thing: *Present in under the time limit so that they can get on with the rest of their day – give them some time back!*

CHAPTER 19
HOW TO GIVE A PERSUASIVE PRESENTATION

"In making a speech, one must first study three points; first, the means of producing persuasion;
second, the language; third, the proper arrangement of the various parts of speech."
- Aristotle, dead Greek guy

Persuasive Presentation
A specific type of presentation in which the speaker has a goal of convincing the audience to understand and agree with their point of view.

If you read the chapter on **"How to Give an Informative Presentation"** then you already know that there is a fine line between an informative presentation and a persuasive one. Most informative presentations contain an element of persuasion in them, and all persuasive presentations also inform.

Know Your Purpose
Persuasive vs. informative presentation

The main difference between an informative presentation and a persuasive one is what you want your audience to DO at the end of the presentation. If the thing you want them to DO involves changing a behavior or doing something that they don't have to do or are not already doing, then you need to put together a presentation persuasive enough to convince them to change their behavior.

In many ways, putting together a persuasive presentation is easier than putting together an informative one because with informative presentations it is not always clear how to organize your information or filter out the stuff that doesn't NEED to go into it. But persuasive presentations always give you a clear starting point for how to begin organizing your information.

Simply start by answering this question:

If what you are asking your audience to do makes so much sense, why aren't they already doing it?

TEMPLATE - PERSUASIVE PRESENTATION

BACKGROUND NOTES: Stuff you will keep in mind but not necessarily say out loud:

TITLE:_____

PURPOSE

    Audience should FEEL:_____

    Audience should DO:_____

    Audience should THINK:_____

IN ONE SENTENCE:_____

PRESENTATION: Stuff you will say out loud and/or otherwise include in your presentation:

BEGINNING / INTRODUCTION

    Hook:_____

    Desire / Problem:_____

    Solution:_____

    Name / Credibility:_____

MIDDLE / BODY: State your suggestion directly, inoculate against fears, and remember that emotional and/or moral reasons usually work better than facts alone.

    Point 1:_____

        Hook or evidence:_____

    Point 2:_____

        Hook or evidence:_____

    Point 3:_____

        Hook or evidence:_____

    Points 4 & 5: (only if necessary)_____

        Hook or evidence:_____

END / CONCLUSION

    End with a bang:_____

    Call to action:_____

    Question and answer:_____

    Last thing:_____

If the answer is "they don't know about it," then your persuasive presentation will need to include a lot of informative parts. See for example the hypothetical Bonko Egg Scrambler presentation from Chapter 3. Note how much information it contains: "it slices, dices, scrambles in seconds; similar products cost hundreds of dollars; supplies are limited; buy now and get a second one free." Those are not just facts for facts' sake. They are in the presentation to persuade the audience about the value of the product.

On the other hand, if the reason your audience isn't already doing the thing you want them to do because there is some **resistance** to the idea or previous **habits** that are getting in the way, then your presentation must **be persuasive enough to get them to DO the thing you want them to do**; and it also has to be persuasive enough to get them **to STOP doing whatever they're doing instead** (for instance, lying on the couch instead of exercising).

If the primary goal of your presentation is to do something they don't HAVE to do - to buy, change, establish, fund, hire, invest, modernize, obtain, participate, purchase, reward, travel, upgrade, use, write, or anything similar – **then your presentation is primarily persuasive.**

Information Is Not Enough

The biggest mistake people make when putting together a persuasive presentation is assuming that information alone will persuade anyone to do anything. If this were true then no one in the world would smoke. It's true that in the past cigarettes were marketed for their health benefits (it may be hard for us to believe today, but there was a time when cigarettes were advertised as "Doctor approved!").

Today, no one smokes because they think it is a healthy thing to do! Everyone who smokes already knows that it is a terrible thing to do. Trying to "persuade" someone not to smoke by "informing" them about the dangers of smoking is an enormous waste of time.

Even before they become addicted, people start smoking for physical reasons (it is pleasurable), for emotional reasons (it is comforting and sometimes social), and for habitual reasons (because it is part of a routine). You're almost guaranteed to fail in your attempt to persuade a smoker to stop smoking if you present only logical facts about the health risks of smoking. In fact, recent neurological research suggests that almost ALL of our decisions are influenced more by emotions than by logic - or at least that emotions and logic are very hard to separate. In particular, people don't make strictly logical decisions about things that touch on what they already believe.

For instance, in any political discussion there are always contradictory facts bandied about by people on either side of a debate. Research shows that nearly everyone in these situations filters the facts they choose to believe through an emotional prism: they disproportionately seek out facts that agree with how they already **FEEL** about an issue and only then begin to intellectually weigh the evidence.

In other words, people don't think about all the facts before deciding how to feel. Instead, they feel first and then their thoughts are influenced by those feelings. This is true not only with politics but with many other things as well.

Know Your Audience
What do you want them to feel, do, and think?

It is beyond the scope of this book to argue this point at any length. If the topic interests you, we invite you to do more research on the science of how people make decisions. But for now - to keep things short and simple - just recognize that of the three things that form the purpose of your presentation - what you want your audience to **FEEL**, what you want them to **DO**, and what you want them to **THINK** - relying on information alone is always the least effective way to persuade anyone to do anything.

So how exactly do you go about putting together a persuasive argument? You already know the answer: start with your audience and how they FEEL about the topic.

An Illustrative Example
Persuading Rachel

Let's pretend that you want to persuade someone who is not in this class to use this book to help them with an upcoming presentation. Imagine for instance that you have a friend who is in a panic because she needs to give a presentation the next day. She, of course, has not started to work on the project yet and so is buying coffee to help her stay up late enough to do the whole project before class in the morning.

> She sees this book sitting next to me and asks, "Hey, is that book any good?"
>
> "Yes," I say. "It's awesome."
>
> "Do you think it could it help me with my presentation?" she asks.
>
> "Yeah, it'd definitely help," I say.
>
> "I don't know," she says. "I took a different public speaking course and the book we used had a lot of boring stuff in it that we got tested on. I don't have time to read another book. I'm going to have to stay up all night just putting together slides for this stupid presentation as it is."

CLARIFY YOUR MESSAGE

You know exactly what to do to help her out. She's a good friend and you don't want to see her stay up all night. And because you are brilliant - because you have internalized every lesson in this book – you're able to instantly put together a persuasive presentation on the spot in your head, just by mentally going through all the questions you know you should ask. These are the thoughts that flash though your mind in an instant:

Know Your Audience

Who is she?
> Rachel, a fellow university student who is not in my public speaking class.

Where is she?
> In a coffee shop.

Why is she there?
> Getting coffee to help her stay up late so she can put together the stupid presentation that is due tomorrow.

What does she want?
> Help putting together her presentation (actually she doesn't want to give the presentation at all - but since she HAS to, she wants to do as little work as possible).

When does she want it?
> Right now (or at least before the coffee wears off).

How familiar is she with your topic?
> Not much. She had a different public speaking class that used a different book.

Your Audience Determines Your Content
The body of your presentation

Because you've already read the book, you realize that the next steps are most important parts of putting together a persuasive presentation. In particular, you remember that emotions - **FEELINGS** - are often the most important parts of influencing someone to do something. So you quickly answer the following questions in your head:

What will she like?
> The steps in *Keep It Short & Simple* are simple, easy, straightforward, time-saving, and effective.

What will she not like?
> She has already read a different book on public speaking and isn't convinced that another book will help her - and more importantly, she is so short on

time that she's afraid that any time she spends looking at this book will be time away from putting together the stupid slide show for the stupid presentation that is due tomorrow.

You realize that these two pieces of information - the things that will tend to predispose Rachel TOWARD what you want her to do, and the things that will prejudice her AWAY from what you want her to do - are the keys points you need to address when trying to convince her to use the book.

In particular, you realize that not only does your presentation need to address reasons why she should use this book, it must also address the reasons she is not already using it.

Answering questions about what she will like and not like also helps you instantly clarify the most important emotional and action based parts of your persuasive presentation:

> **What do you want her to feel?**
> Reassured that her time will not be wasted and excited by the possibility that the book can help her.

> **What do you want her to do?**
> Borrow my book for the night and give it a try.

> **What do you want her to think?**
> I want her to think "I am persuaded. I will do what you suggest." But how exactly do I get her to think that? Simple: by organizing my information as persuasively as possible.

Prioritize Your Main Points
Inoculation and emotion

Persuasive presentations are easier to prioritize than informative ones. This is because the first part of your presentation needs to **do something to specifically address your audience's resistance to your suggestion** (the things they will **NOT LIKE** about your suggestion). The earlier in your presentation you do this the better; otherwise as your audience listens to you, they will be thinking "yeah, but … [their fears or concerns]" thus limiting the impact of anything else you have to say.

This principle is sometimes called **INOCULATION** – a term taken from the way that people are inoculated against disease by giving them a small dose of the thing they want to protect against. For your next persuasive presentation, after you hook your audience, **include a small dose of the thing they are resisting in order to help them move past it.**

The most famous example of this principle is the "Friends, Romans, countrymen" speech from the play *Julius Caesar* by William Shakespeare.

In the play, after a group of men stab Julius Caesar to death on the floor of the Roman Senate (a true historical event), Caesar's friend, Marc Antony, speaks to an angry mob to persuade them to riot against the murderers. Antony's first and most important point is to address the crowd's fears about Caesar, especially the point just made by the lead murderer, Brutus, that Caesar would have made himself a dictator if they had not killed him.

First, Marc Antony grabs his audience's attention:
> "Friends, Romans, countrymen, lend me your ears;"
> (*Everyone listen to me!*)

Then, he immediately addresses his audience's fears and concerns:
> "I come to bury Caesar, not to praise him.
> "The evil that men do lives after them;
> The good is oft interred with their bones;
> So let it be with Caesar."
> (*I'm only here to bury my friend, not to make you like him*).

When this play is staged, Antony has to yell these lines over the voices of the angry mob (in the script they are yelling things like "Caesar was a tyrant!" and "We are blest that Rome is rid of him!"). Since the crowd is so angry, Antony's goal at this point is just to get his audience to let their guard down enough to listen to him.

He continues to inoculate the audience against the things that Brutus said by including a small part of them into his

own speech in a way that dispels the audience's fears:

> "The noble Brutus
> Hath told you Caesar was ambitious:
> If it were so, it was a grievous fault,
> And grievously hath Caesar answer'd it."

> (*Even if what Brutus said was true, Caesar has more than paid for anything he might have done wrong*)

This **inoculation against fears** is often the most important part of any persuasive presentation. The only way you can know how to do this is if you have already asked yourself the question "What will they NOT like?" The answer to this question needs to be part of your presentation.

One of the most important things you should do early in any persuasive presentation is address the things that your audience might NOT LIKE about your idea.

Because you have already read the book, you realize that the best way for you to organize your instant presentation for Rachel is to say something to alleviate any fears she might already have (although you don't have to do it in iambic pentameter).

For instance, after you hook Rachel's attention, you might say something like:

> "*Keep It Short & Simple* isn't like other textbooks. It isn't heavy on theory or stuff you get tested on. Using it will save you lots of time. If you just start putting slides together you won't even know where to start or what you don't need to include – and you'll end up wasting much more time than it will take you to use this book."

Simple, right? Persuasive, right? (See? We said persuasive presentations were easier to organize than informative ones).

The next chunk of information is just as simple to prioritize.

Because you know that emotion plays a large part in the way people make decisions, you also know that you need to address Rachel's emotions early on and/or demonstrate your own emotions or feelings about your idea.

The most famous classic example of this principle also comes from the play *Julius Caesar*.

In the play, after Marc Antony has hooked his audience's attention and begun to inoculate their fears, he continues by presenting a logical back-and-forth between what "Brutus said" and what "Caesar was" (a thesis - antithesis argument for those interested in rhetoric), but the MOST powerful moment in Antony's speech is when he emotionally breaks down and begins to weep:

> "You all did love him once, not without cause:
> What cause withholds you then, to mourn for him?
> O judgment! thou art fled to brutish beasts,
> And men have lost their reason. Bear with me;
> My heart is in the coffin there with Caesar,
> And I must pause till it come back to me."
> (He pauses to cry)

In the play, this is the moment that finally persuades the crowd that Antony is right (in the script the crowd says things like: "There is much reason in his sayings!" and "There's not a nobler man in Rome than Antony!"). And even though this is just a play, it is also an accurate representation of the power of emotion to persuade.

Rhetoricians as far back as Aristotle have recognized that **emotion often moves people to action much better than logic does.**

For those interested in the study of rhetoric, the Greeks recognized three distinct ways of trying to persuade an audience.

In order of persuasiveness they are: **pathos** - an appeal to emotion; **ethos** – an appeal to morals; and **logos** – an appeal to logic. The most persuasive arguments contain all three.

Because you know that emotion is powerfully persuasive, you realize that addressing Rachel's emotional concerns and/or describing some of your own can also be the tipping point in persuading her to follow your suggestion.

Because of this, you might say:

> "I know you're worried that you don't have enough time to use this book. I would be too. But trust me, using this is going to make you feel a lot better tomorrow, especially when your presentation is really good instead of really bad; and when you've had a good night's sleep instead of being really tired because you stayed up all night putting together slides you're not happy with. Knowing exactly what to do step by step always makes me feel better."

At this point, you are almost finished. The last chunk of the main body of any persuasive presentation is usually just a simple statement of what you want them to DO.

In the case of your presentation to Rachel, you might simply say something like:

> "Just try a few of the sticky note worksheets from the beginning. If they don't instantly help you organize your thoughts, you can always stop and go back to putting together a bunch of wordy, boring slides."

As always, **the first step to putting together any presentation is getting clear about your message.** So before you go further, it's important to remind yourself about your main message - otherwise, you might get carried away thinking of reasons why Rachel should or shouldn't use this book. So just to check that your thoughts are clear, you quickly run the following list through your head:

Getting Clearer: Zooming Out

Who is your audience?
> Rachel.

What is their desire or problem?
> Help with her stupid presentation.

What is your solution?
> Let her borrow my book.

Getting Clearest: Shortest Possible Description

Not all persuasive presentations are going to be as simple and easy to figure out as this one, but all of them share the same basic parts. The structure of most persuasive presentations is so straightforward that honing your presentation down to a single sentence is easy; with most persuasive presentations, your single sentence is usually simply a statement of the thing you are trying to convince them to DO. For instance, if you had to, you could easily present the key ideas of your presentation to Rachel in a single sentence.

Your persuasive presentation in a really short sentence:
> Here, borrow my book and give it a try.

Your persuasive presentation in a compound sentence:
> Here, borrow my book and give it a try because the simple, easy, and effective exercises in it will save you a lot of time and make your presentation much better.

At this point you are ready to put together an outline of your presentation in your head. In fact, you've already done it. Because you have thought things through so well, the presentation basically writes itself:

STRUCTURE YOUR PRESENTATION

You quickly answer the following questions in your head:

How can you start with a hook? Could you use a physical object, a visible image, a shocking statistic or a personal story?

Yes, I can use all of them. The physical object is the book and my visible image is flipping through the book to show her how easy the exercises are. My shocking statistic and personal story is the fact that I personally use the book to put together my own presentations.

How can you end with a bang? Can you reintegrate the opening hook?

Yes. Just say something simple like "I'm telling you, the stuff in this book is simple and easy to use and will end up saving you a whole lot of time and headache and will make your presentation much, much better."

What is your call to action?

"Here, borrow it for the night."

What is the LAST THING You will leave with them?

I'll lend her my book.

What is your credibility on this issue?

"I've used this book to put together dozens of presentations. I use it for every presentation I have to give in every class I have and I've gotten an "A" on every one."

That's it. That's all there is to it. You just put together an entire persuasive presentation in your head on the spot. For your convenience, a detailed outline of what this example presentation would look like is included at the end of this section.

Visual Aids and Rehearsal

Because you are putting together this presentation on the spot (what some other presentation books call "impromptu"), you don't need to put together any visual aids or to rehearse (that's what makes it impromptu). But for other presentations you might put together in the future, you might want to use some visual aids and will almost certainly want to rehearse. The tools in **Section 4: "Design It;"** and the steps in **Section 5: "How to Practice and Present"** will help you do that.

The Role of Body Language and Tone of Voice

There is one more very important point to keep in mind when you're giving any kind of persuasive presentation. Your body language (55%) and tone of voice (38%) constitute up to 93% of the impact you make upon your audience! What this means is that having a good outline for your presentation is not nearly enough to persuade anyone.

For instance, say the words "Borrow my book and give it a try" with uninterested body language (sitting back, no eye contact, checking the messages on your phone while you say it) and with a sigh and a disaffected, dropping vocal tone.

Go ahead, we'll wait. How persuasive do you think that was? How much do you suppose anyone believes your advice?

On the other hand, what if you said those same words with body language that was congruent with your message (friendly smile, open body, eyes focused on the listener)? And what if, at the same time, you spoke with enough passion in your voice for the listener to really believe that your idea will help them? How much more convincing would that be?

The level of energy and passion in your body language and tone of voice is essential when you deliver any persuasive presentation. Ultimately, persuasion rests almost entirely on commitment and conviction, on congruency between the words you say and your body language and tone of voice.

So how exactly do you go about doing that? Practice and rehearsal with feedback is almost always the best way. However, if you ever find yourself with little time for practice or rehearsal, at the very least, take a moment before you speak. Then take a breath and focus on conveying your message with conviction and authenticity. Your presentation will be much more persuasive if your words, body, and voice are all working together to demonstrate your belief in what you are saying.

Final Thoughts

As you can see, putting together a persuasive presentation is not really all that different from putting together ANY presentation. In fact, persuasive presentations are usually easier to organize than other types of presentations.

When you put together your next persuasive presentation, simply follow the same steps you would when putting together any presentation, but also ask yourself this one additional question: why aren't they already doing this?

The answer to that question will help guide you to finding the most persuasive words to say. Then simply recognize that your body language and tone of voice will be far more useful to you than those words. To persuade them, you must persuade yourself first (or if you haven't had an ethics class yet, - at least learn how to fake it convincingly).

The three most important rules for you to remember once you're done drafting your presentation are:

1. Prepare

2. Practice what your prepare

3. Present what you practiced

KEY TAKEAWAYS - HOW TO GIVE A PERSUASIVE PRESENTATION

■ Most persuasive presentations also need to include informative elements.

■ Never assume that logical arguments alone will help you persuade your audience. Emotion is often a much more effective tool for persuasion than facts alone.

■ Because logic alone won't persuade anyone, you should also include emotional,ethical and/or moral elements in your presentation (the Greeks thought that the three most persuasive types of arguments were – in order – pathos [emotion-based arguments]; ethos [morally-based arguments]; and logos [logical-based arguments]. The most persuasive arguments include all three elements).

■ Always begin by considering your audience.

■ In particular, ask yourself why they are not already doing the thing you are trying to persuade them to do. If the reason is because they don't know about it, then your persuasive presentation will need to have a lot of informative or educational elements in it.

■ Very early on, address their resistance to the idea or the habits that are getting in the way (to INOCULATE against the thought "Yeah but…").

■ Other than that, you should put together your persuasive presentations just like you would any other presentation:

- by asking questions about your audience;
- by defining your purpose (feel, do, think);
- by prioritizing the points you want to include.

■ Focus on making every section as dynamic as possible (use what we call "hooks:" stories, examples, illustrations, props, etc.). This will make it easier to persuade your audience.

■ Your body language and tone of voice are the most important tools you have for persuading others.

■ To persuade others, first persuade yourself. The most persuasive presenters believe what they are saying.

DETAILED OUTLINE - PERSUASIVE PRESENTATION

Persuade Rachel to use the *Keep It Short & Simple* book

<u>**BACKGROUND NOTES:**</u> Stuff you will keep in mind but not necessarily say out loud:

TITLE: *Keep It Short & Simple is awesome!*

PURPOSE

Audience should FEEL: *Reassured that her time will not be wasted and excited by the possibility that the book can help her.*

Audience should DO: *Borrow my book for the night and give it a try.*

Audience should THINK: *" I am persuaded. I will do what you suggest."*

IN ONE SENTENCE: *"Here, borrow my book and give it a try."*

<u>**PRESENTATION:**</u> Stuff you will say out loud and/or otherwise include in your presentation:

BEGINNING / INTRODUCTION

Hook: *Show her the book. Flip through it. Say: " This book is awesome! Look how easy the exercises are."*

Desire / Problem: *" I know you don't want to stay up all night putting together a presentation that isn't any good."*

Solution: *"Why don't you borrow this for the night and use it to help you put together your presentation in way less time with way less stress?"*

Name / Credibility: *" I've used this book to put together dozens of presentations. I use it for every presentation I have to give in every class I have and I've gotten an A on every one."*

MIDDLE / BODY

Point 1: *Inoculate against Rachel's fears.*

Hook or evidence: *Other textbooks didn't help her. Say:" It isn't like other textbooks. It isn't heavy on theory or stuff you get tested on."*

Fear of not having enough time." Using it will save you lots of time. If you just start putting slides together, you won't even know where to start or what you don't need to include – and you'll end up wasting much more time than it will take you to use this book."

Point 2: *Address emotion.*

Hook or evidence: *Acknowledge her fears and show empathy. Say:" I know you're worried that you don't have enough time to use this book. I would be too."*

Dig deeper into those fears. "But trust me, using this is going to make you feel a lot better tomorrow, especially when your presentation is really good instead of really bad; and when you've had a good night's sleep instead of being really tired because you stayed up all night putting together slides you're not happy with."

Share some of my own emotion. "Knowing exactly what to do step by step always makes me feel better."

Point 3: Simply state my suggestion.

Hook or evidence: "Seriously. Just try a few of the sticky note worksheets from the beginning. If they don't instantly help you organize your thoughts, you can always stop and go back to putting together a bunch of wordy, boring slides."

END / CONCLUSION

End with a bang: Reintegrate the initial hook. Say: "I'm telling you, the stuff in this book is simple and easy to use and will end up saving you a whole lot of time and headache and will make your presentation much, much better."

Call to action: "Go ahead and borrow it for the night."

Question and answer: "After all, what do you have to lose? So what do you say?"

She'll reply: "Gosh, golly-gee. That's really groovy of you!"

I'll pause. "Why are you talking like that?"

She'll say: "I figured that since we're being used as an example in a textbook, I'd use some wholesome 1950s language."

Please don't do that," I'll say. "That's just weird. Besides, I think 'groovy' was from the 60s."

"Really?" she'll ask.

"70s maybe. I dunno. Just please stop it. So do you want to borrow the book or not?"

"Sure," she'll say. "Thanks."

Last thing: I'll lend her this book.

CHAPTER 20
HOW TO GIVE AN ELEVATOR PITCH

"The average attention span of a modern human being is about half as long as whatever you're trying to tell them."
- Meg Rosoff, author, <u>How I Live Now</u>

Elevator Pitch

A brief persuasive speech used to spark interest in a process, product, service, organization, or event and its value proposition.

Elevator pitches are short persuasive presentations. The concept behind the name is that you find yourself in an elevator with a potential investor and have only the amount of time it takes the elevator to go up to the top floor to make your pitch. Believe it or not, things like this do indeed happen in real life. However, **the goal of a real elevator pitch is usually just to pique the investor's interest enough to get another, longer meeting** (successful pitches usually end with an exchange of business cards or something similar). We highly recommend that you read the previous chapter on **"How to Give a Persuasive Presentation"** if you haven't already done so. It covers the details about how to convince your audience to buy into your ideas.

Business Schools and Public Speaking Classes

In many business schools and public speaking classes, the idea of an elevator pitch has morphed into a more codified type of presentation with the following "rules." Elevator pitches should be:

- no longer than 90 seconds long (some are assigned to be as short as 30 seconds);

- done without the use of any slides or projected media (however props are often allowed);

- delivered without the presenter moving around too much (as if standing in an elevator);

Different departments or classes might also impose certain other restrictions (like what specific information needs to be included in the pitch).

Real Life Application

The original idea of an elevator pitch was precisely what it sounds like - it was designed to persuade (or "pitch") someone to invest in a company, but the idea has a wider application as well. In real life, "elevator-length" presentations are also useful for:

- introducing an individual, or group to someone who might be interested in what they do;

- generating interest in a product on the street or at a

TEMPLATE - HOW TO GIVE AN ELEVATOR PITCH

BACKGROUND NOTES: Stuff you will keep in mind but not necessarily say out loud:

    TITLE: _____

    PURPOSE

        Audience should FEEL: _____

        Audience should DO: _____

        Audience should THINK: _____

    IN ONE SENTENCE: _____

PRESENTATION: Stuff you will say out loud and/or otherwise include in your presentation:

    BEGINNING / INTRODUCTION

        Hook: _____

        Desire / Problem: _____

        Solution: _____

        Name / Credibility: _____

    MIDDLE / BODY: State your suggestion directly, inoculate against fears, and remember that emotional and/or moral reasons usually work better than facts alone.

        Point 1: _____

            Hook or evidence: _____

        Point 2: _____

            Hook or evidence: _____

        Point 3: _____

            Hook or evidence: _____

        Points 4 & 5: (only if necessary) _____

            Hook or evidence: _____

    END / CONCLUSION

        End with a bang: _____

        Call to action: _____

        Question and answer: _____

        Last thing: _____

trade show (where potential customers are walking by);

- striking up a conversation at a bar, buffet line, or any other place that people congregate;

- any other time you need to give a short, succinct summary of a product or service you offer;

The major benefit of an elevator pitch is that it is designed to be as short and impactful as possible and is designed to be deliverable without slides or other visual aids (usually). In public speaking classes, the other goal of assigning an elevator pitch is that it forces you to learn how to create presentations that are short and simple - but of course, if you are using this book, you are already doing that!

In other words, an elevator pitch is absolutely no different than any other presentation you might give, except for the fact that you can't use any slides (not just shouldn't) and that you need to keep the entire presentation under a certain length.

So how do you begin? Of course you know the answer by now - everyone repeat together: **start with your audience!**

An Illustrative Example
Clean and Green

Let's use a traditional elevator pitch designed to persuade a venture capitalist to invest in a start-up company. A pitch that was given in class by a master of business administration student will serve as a good example.

The student's name was Sarah and her company's name was "Clean and Green" (not the real name). The company's product was a new dry cleaning method that was cheap, effective, and environmentally friendly. Sarah didn't need money for her business so much as she needed access to certain business markets. The audience for the pitch was a venture capital investor in town.

CLARIFY YOUR MESSAGE
Know your audience
Who are they?
Steve, a venture capital investor in town.

Where are they?
Visiting the MBA class to judge several elevator pitches (If this were in the real world rather than class, my pitch might actually be done in an elevator, or in any place that allows me to take a moment of the investor's time).

Why are they there?
It is part of a class setup; the investor will come to class and will be free to choose or not choose to invest in any business opportunities that pique his interest (If this were the real world rather than class, I might have specifically targeted him for the pitch and used this step as a way to try to think about where a good opportunity to meet him might be).

What do they want?
Good, undiscovered businesses to invest in.

When do they want it?
The investor is a savvy businessman who is always looking for good investments; however, he is unlikely to invest on the spot. He will perform due diligence on any potential investment.

How familiar are they?
A little. He owns several other businesses in town but does not own anything like a laundromat. This is a fundamental weakness my pitch. (If this were a real-world pitch, I would be better off targeting a potential investor who was more familiar with the dry cleaning business, particularly one who already owned at least one dry cleaning company.)

A Most Important Question
Remember the most important follow-up question for all persuasive presentations (including elevator pitches) involves why the idea is not already in place. In particular:

> "If Clean and Green is such a good investment, **why isn't the investor already invested in it?"**

The answer in this case is that Steve was previously unaware of the opportunity. This is both good news and bad news. The good news is that there is not necessarily a great deal of resistance to the idea (and therefore less need to spend a lot of time on an inoculation section early in the presentation). But the bad news, of course, is that this means that your persuasive presentation will need to include a lot of information and you do not necessarily have a clear way to organize it yet.

Your Audience Determines Your Content

The body of your presentation

In order to decide what goes into the content of your elevator pitch, you've got to dig a little deeper to understand more about your audience. So let's continue with our simple steps:

What will they LIKE about investing?

It is a good product that saves money over traditional methods and is better for the environment. He might like that the investment request is not just about money but also about getting access to wider markets.

What will they NOT LIKE about investing?

He might not like having to spend time learning about this industry.

He also might not like that I don't already have access to wider markets.

He'll probably ask why he should spend time investing in something that will possibly only provide a small return (although the industry itself is large, it is also fragmented - owned mostly by families or small business owners).

Certainly he'll ask if it is such a good idea, why everyone in the dry cleaning business isn't already using it, and he will ask why I don't simply finance the entire thing with a small business loan.

What do you want them to FEEL?

Intrigued by the possibility of investing; confident that I know what I am doing; reassured that any investment will generate a good return.

What do you want them to DO?

It is unrealistic to ask for an investment on the spot.

A better ask would be for a follow-up meeting or for an introduction to a business partner who might be more familiar with the dry cleaning business.

Because of the weakness of this particular pitch for this particular audience, Sarah decided to pitch both possibilities at once: Steve could either further investigate investing on his own, or take a "finder's fee" (to be negotiated later) for an introduction to someone who might be more willing to invest without having to take time to learn more about the dry cleaning industry.

What do you want them to think?

At the end of most persuasive presentations (elevator pitches are short persuasive presentations), I would want my audience to think "I am persuaded; I will do what you suggest." And if this were only a class assignment (and not a pitch to a real investor), I'd aim for an investment on the spot. But in the real world, the actual goal of an elevator pitch is usually just to get the other person to think "I am intrigued. Let's schedule a meeting so you can tell me more."

Sarah decided to design her class pitch as a real world pitch (after all, she was delivering it to a real potential investor), so what she wanted Steve to think at the end of her pitch was "I am intrigued. I will either pursue this further myself, or introduce you to someone else who can help you." In order to do this, she first had to figure out what things might intrigue Steve.

She started by making a list of possible information. Her first list included important financial details about her business such as:

- the company's current financial situation
- revenue model
- management structure
- marketing strategy, etc.

However Sarah soon realized that for this pitch to this audience, those details would only detract from the overall impact she wanted to achieve. If she were pitching to a different audience with more detailed knowledge of the industry, then these details might be particularly useful. But since this investor did not have such specialized knowledge, Sarah decided that these details would be less useful for this particular pitch (she thought of it as "getting too far in the weeds"). Nevertheless, she prepared to answer detailed questions about each of these subjects. She simply did not include that information in her formal pitch.

Prioritize Your Main Points

In the end Sarah was able to hone her list down to the following five points. This was not the exact order she eventually went with, but prioritizing in this way gave her a good place to start when designing her ultimate pitch.

Structure Your Presentation

The following sticky notes contain five points that Sarah had accumulated up to this point in her preparation.

1. The problem Clean and Green solves: better cleaning with less environmental impact than tradition dry cleaning solutions.

2. Story of how I arrived at the solution and the history of my company.

3. My unique sales proposition: what sets Clean and Green apart from other, similar, compa[nies] (i.e. my competitive advanta[ge])

4. My proof of concept: returns and revenue so far in the three stores that currently use prototypes of my product, plus my application towards a patent.

5. The future value of the company relative to its current earnings (i.e. the product is poised to take off).

Getting Clearer: Zooming Out

Next, Sarah needed to zoom out just to make sure her message was clear:

Who is your audience?

Steve, a venture capital investor in town.

What is their desire or problem?

He is looking for good, undiscovered businesses to invest in.

What is your solution?

Offer him an option to either look into investing in the company or to take a finder's fee for an introduction to someone who knows more about the dry cleaning industry.

Getting Clearest: Shortest Possible Description

Sarah knew that the next step was honing her message down to the shortest possible description. She also knew that for elevator pitches, it was important to get that description down to as close to **ONE SENTENCE** as possible. Any longer and it would be too easy to spend more time than necessary for a 90-second pitch! With this in mind, her **ONE SENTENCE** began to take shape:

> Clean and Green is a unique way to modify existing dry cleaning services in a way that is both more effective and more environmentally friendly than existing methods –
>
> and so it is a fantastic investment opportunity for you because the product is well positioned to take off within the next few months!

Sarah did not worry about writing a run-on sentence - or about getting the sentence "right" in any way - because she knew that the whole point of this step was simply to make sure she knew what the main focus of her presentation should be (See? even that was close to a run-on sentence - and everything is still fine).

STRUCTURE YOUR PRESENTATION

Start with a Hook

The next thing Sarah needed to do was to figure out how to start strong and end with a bang. Because this was an elevator pitch, she knew she couldn't use any visual images or handouts to grab her audience's attention, but she did briefly consider using a prop (an interesting-looking mechanism associated with her process). Ultimately though, she settled on combining two tried and true methods of grabbing an audience's attention: providing a shocking statistic and asking questions directly to her audience.

Shocking statistic and direct question

"Did you know that the dry cleaning is a $9-billion-a-year industry but that as of yet, there aren't that many big players who sell to everyone?

That's a nice shirt, suit and tie. Do you ever have any of it dry cleaned? Wouldn't you like to earn even a tiny profit from every shirt, suit, tie, dress or anything and everything that's been dry cleaned in this room?

What about in this city? Country? The world? You would? I would too, and I'm building a company that can grab a big piece of that enormous pie."

End with a Bang

Sarah knew she needed to end as strongly as she had begun. She also realized that one of the secrets to selling is to give your audience something easy to agree with. One "yes" often leads to another. So she searched for a way to reincorporate her original hook and to clarify her original ask to make it easy for Steve to say yes. This is what she came up with:

What is your call to action / conclusion?

"I started by asking if you would be interested in owning a small piece of every dry cleaning transaction in this room and in this city. Clean and Green is already well on its way to that goal. With your help, we can expand to other cities and regions and eventually to the nation and the world."

What is the LAST THING you will leave with them?

"I am so sure that Clean and Green will succeed that I further ask that if you are not already personally interested in investing (though of course you are), that I will pay any finder's fee (subject to negotiation) if you will introduce me to any other potential investor who is as wise and well-dressed as you are. Thank you for your consideration."

Finally, Sarah knew she had to find a way to introduce herself and establish her credibility for delivering the pitch. To keep things as short and simple as possible, she decided to combine introducing herself with a quick overview of her big idea (the problem her company solved).

Credibility and big idea (problem / solution)

"Hi I'm Sarah Johnson, CEO of Clean and Green, a company that's poised to revolutionize the way that dry cleaning is done. Clean and Green is a patent-pending process that makes dry cleaning both more efficient and more environmentally friendly."

Visual Aids and Rehearsal

Because this was an elevator pitch, Sarah knew she couldn't put together any slides. However, she also knew that because she had only 90 seconds in which to deliver her pitch, that she needed to rehearse it even MORE than she would have for a longer presentation. Longer presentations give you more buffer room, but in an elevator pitch, every second and every word counts!

She rehearsed it and timed it and then rehearsed it again until she knew that she could consistently deliver her entire pitch in well UNDER 90 seconds. In fact, she worked until she eas-ily could do the entire thing in 60 seconds - because she knew that then she could RELAX and focus on connecting with her audience instead of worrying about talking fast!

Did She Succeed?

Sarah's final ask was unusual in that she offered two options. Her professor wasn't entirely convinced that such a bold final ask was a good idea. In fact he later remarked that her small jokes at the end ("subject to negotiation" and "wise and well dressed") added to the sense that Sarah was merely hedging her bets (which of course she was). It's beyond the scope of this book to comment on the soundness of Sarah's business plan or even to suggest a better way for her to have ended (indeed, the question and answer session revealed that Sarah's initial valuation of her company at $500,000 was highly ambitious given her current earnings).

Nevertheless, in the end Sarah got most of the investment she was seeking. Steve agreed to introduce Sarah to an acquaintance of his who had more experience in the industry. He did not ask for a finder's fee. He pointed out that it did not require much effort on his part to make the introduction and that he was happy to be able to play a part in helping someone as industrious as Sarah try to grow a business.

The point in using this pitch as an example is to **demonstrate how straightforward the process is for developing ANY elevator pitch**. It doesn't matter whether or not it was a perfect pitch: it did everything it needed to – in this case, that included getting to "yes!"

Final Thoughts

Elevator pitches are short, persuasive presentations. Because your goal is persuasion, early in your pitch you need to make sure to **INOCULATE** your audience against some of their fears. However, you do not want to spend too much time doing this (after all, you only have a few seconds to convince them – you don't want to spend the majority of that time talking about reasons they might NOT want to invest!).

The good news is that for most elevator pitches, the audience already knows that you are going to ask them to do something. Placing your ask up front is a great way to prevent your audience from listening to you while also having to think "fine, but what are you asking for?" Placing your ask up front can also help clarify the first part of the main body of your presentation (after you hook them and introduce yourself, go ahead and let them know what you are asking of them). An example of how this works can be found in the detailed breakdown of Sarah's presentation on the next few pages.

People Invest in You

Even more importantly, because elevator pitches are intended to **PERSUADE** in a short period of time, there is much more to delivering a good one than just figuring out what to say.

In the end, Sarah succeeded not because her business plan was strong, but because she was able to demonstrate passion about the potential of her idea. Investors do not merely invest in companies, they also invest in people. **Sarah's body language and paralanguage (the way she held herself and the con-** **viction that came through in her voice) were the MOST important parts of making her pitch ultimately successful.**

This is the same for any elevator pitch you will give. There is a cliché in sales that **the first pitch you make is to yourself.** Your audience will have a much easier time being convinced if you, the presenter, are convinced. If you do not honestly and passionately believe in your ideas, then why should anyone else? In this sense, practicing and rehearsing are simply ways to make sure that you give your ideas the full respect they deserve.

Before you pitch to anyone, make yourself your first audience and give your ideas the respect and passion they deserve.

The three most important rules for you to remember once you're done drafting your elevator pitch are:

1. **Prepare**
2. **Practice what your prepare**
3. **Present what you practiced**

KEY TAKEAWAYS - HOW TO GIVE AN ELEVATOR PITCH

◼ Elevator pitches often need to include short sections that inoculate your audience against having their mind wander during the pitch. For elevator pitches and other presentations that will obviously end with an ask, one of the easiest ways to do part of this is to include your ask up front.

◼ Other than the need for inoculation, put together your persuasive presentations just like you would any presentation:
  • ask questions about your audience
  • define your purpose (feel, do, think)
  • then organize the other points you want to include

◼ Experiment with different ways to organize your content. Try it every way you can think of to see which way seems best for that particular audience.

◼ Focus on making every section as dynamic as possible (what we call "hooks:" stories, examples, illustrations, props, etc.). This will make it easier to persuade your audience.

◼ Your body language and tone of voice are the most important tools you have for persuading others, especially when delivering a short presentation.

◼ Practice being authentic and likable.

DETAILED OUTLINE - ELEVATOR PITCH
For Clean and Green

BACKGROUND NOTES: Stuff you will keep in mind but not necessarily say out loud:

TITLE: Clean and Green

PURPOSE

Audience should FEEL: *Intrigued by the possibility of investing. Confident that the owner knows what she is doing. Reassured that any investment will generate a good return.*

Audience should DO: *Look into investing in the company or take a finder's fee for an introduction to someone who knows more about the dry cleaning industry.*

Audience should THINK: *" I am intrigued. I will either pursue this further myself, or introduce you to someone else who can help you."*

IN ONE SENTENCE: *"Clean and Green is a unique way to modify existing dry cleaning services in a way that is both more effective and more environmentally friendly than existing methods - and so it is a fantastic investment opportunity for you because the product is well positioned to take off within the next few months!"*

PRESENTATION: Stuff you will say out loud and/or otherwise include in your presentation:

BEGINNING / INTRODUCTION

Hook: *" Did you know that dry cleaning is a $9-billion-a-year industry but that as of yet, there aren't that many big players who sell to everyone? That's a nice shirt, suit and tie. Do you ever have any of it dry cleaned?"*

Desire / Problem: *" Wouldn't you like to earn even a tiny profit from every shirt, suit, tie, dress or anything and everything that's been dry cleaned in this room? What about in this city? Country? The world? You would?"*

Solution: *"I would too, and I'm building a company that can grab a big piece of that enormous pie."*

Name / Credibility: *"Hi, I'm Sarah Johnson, CEO of Clean and Green, a company that's poised to revolutionize the way that dry cleaning is done. Clean and Green is a patent-pending process that makes dry cleaning both more efficient and more environmentally friendly."*

MIDDLE / BODY

Point 1: *I'm already in business (inoculate against skepticism).*

    Hook or evidence: *" In return for 10% of my company, I'm asking for a small investment of $50,000 to streamline manufacturing costs and give me a strong partner in accessing wider regional markets across the country."*

Point 2: *Point out pending patent and proof of concept (more inoculation).*

    Hook or evidence: *"A prototype of this process is already being used by three companies in town with great success. It has cut down on the amount of chemicals needed for dry cleaning and increased their profits accordingly, as a result we have filed for and been given a provisional process patent."*

Point 3: *Tell him how the company started.*

    Hook or evidence: *"I began to develop this process while I was deployed with the U.S. Army in Afghanistan and noticed local women mixing a particular mineral in with their soap while washing clothes."*

Point 4: *Discuss my unique perspective.*

    Hook or evidence: *"Over the next three years, I worked with chemists and engineers to create a unique patent-pending process that reduces the number of harmful chemicals, water, and steps needed to dry clean clothes of any type."*

Point 5: *Potential future earnings*

    Hook or evidence: *"The cost of the chemicals traditionally used for dry cleaning has been steadily rising. This, combined with the strong potential for future environmental restrictions on many of the processes used today makes this an ideal time to invest in new processes with the potential to revolutionize the industry by saving money and reducing environmental impact."*

END / CONCLUSION

End with a bang: *Reintegrate opening hook:" I started by asking if you would be interested in owning a small piece of every dry cleaning transaction in this room and in this city. Clean and Green is already well on its way to that goal."*

Call to action: *"With your help, we can expand to other cities and regions and eventually to the nation and the world."*

Last thing: *"I am so sure that Clean and Green will succeed that I further ask that if you are not already personally interested in investing (though of course you are), that I will pay any finder's fee (subject to negotiation) if you will introduce me to any other potential investor who is as wise and well dressed as you are. Thank you for your consideration."*

Question and answer: *For elevator pitch presentations, the Q&A always goes at the very end, so I can control how long it takes to give my presentation.*

CHAPTER 21
HOW TO GIVE A TRAINING SESSION

"The secret of getting successful work out of your trained men lies in one nutshell -
in the clearness of the instructions they receive."
– Robert Baden Powell, journalist, military leader

Training Session
An organized activity given for the purpose of imparting information to improve the recipients' knowledge or level or skill.

Companies all over the world present training sessions for their employees in order to inform them about products, policies, procedures, potential customers, pricing, and presentation. At one point or another in your career, you'll most likely be asked to give a training session.

Start with Your Audience
The first thing you need to know about a training session is that it's simply another type of informative presentation. And like all presentations, the main starting place should be on the audience rather than the information.

Unfortunately, far too many training sessions are put together using ALL of the information that could be included regardless of audience. In other words, they are presented as "information dumps" in which a presenter puts together a slide show and "downloads" everything that could be covered on a particular subject to an audience who may or may not care.

In fact, most of the bad presentations you've seen in your life were probably training sessions designed like that. What also made them bad is the fact that you might have been required to attend them even though the content had little to do with your line of work.

Think of all the boring classes and training sessions you've sat through in your life. One of the reasons those were so bad is that they were poorly organized and poorly presented, and they were not geared for a specific audience.

So how do you make a training session interesting? The same way you make any presentation interesting: by focusing on your audience.

An Illustrative Example
Increasing patient satisfaction scores

A few years ago, I was hired by a large company to provide training to physicians to help increase patient satisfaction scores at hospitals after patients are discharged from the hospital. These scores are important because companies with high patient satisfaction scores get financial bonuses from the government, while companies with low scores are finan-

TEMPLATE - A TRAINING SESSION

<u>**BACKGROUND NOTES:**</u> Stuff you will keep in mind but not necessarily say out loud:

    TITLE:_____

    PURPOSE

        Audience should FEEL:_____

        Audience should DO:_____

        Audience should THINK:_____

    IN ONE SENTENCE:_____

<u>**PRESENTATION:**</u> Stuff you will say out loud and/or otherwise include in your presentation:

    BEGINNING / INTRODUCTION

        Hook:_____

        Desire / Problem:_____

        Solution:_____

        Name / Credibility:_____

    MIDDLE / BODY: State your suggestion directly, inoculate against fears. Are there things for them to do physically (for kinesthetic learners)? Are there things for them to see - other than words on slides (for visual learners)? Are there things for them to hear (for auditory learners)?

        Point 1:_____

            Hook or evidence:_____

        Point 2:_____

            Hook or evidence:_____

        Point 3:_____

            Hook or evidence:_____

        Points 4 & 5: (only if necessary)_____

            Hook or evidence:_____

    END / CONCLUSION

        End with a bang:_____

        Call to action:_____

        Question and answer:_____

        Last thing:_____

cially penalized. The difference can mean millions of dollars annually.

You might never have to give a training session to doctors, but this example will demonstrate how easy it is to design training even for skeptical audiences - and also show that training sessions do not need to be long to be effective (in fact, the opposite is usually true).

Each week, I would fly out to a different hospital being managed by the company and meet with the doctors in the company's group. Every meeting began in the same way: with a room full of unhappy looking doctors. Some of them were at the end of their shifts and some were even there on their day off. None of them wanted to be there.

This could be a trainer's worst nightmare - but strong emotion can also be a gift if you know how to leverage it to help design your presentation.

I put together the outline for this training in exactly the same way that you should put together any presentation: by first answering a few simple questions about my audience and how they might respond to my information. The answers to the questions looked like this:

CLARIFY YOUR MESSAGE

Know your audience

Who is my audience?

Hospitalists (doctors of internal medicine who take care of the patients who have been admitted to the hospital).

Where are they?

I will meet them in their main office in the hospital. Sometimes these rooms have conference or meeting furniture set up but more often they do not. Most of the time, the hospitalist office is a smallish room with chairs and a few desks (and usually piles of papers or boxes stacked in corners). In short, it's not an ideal room in which to give a formal presentation, so using slides would be a bad idea.

Why are they there?

They have been told to attend a mandatory meeting.

What do they want?

To get out of this meeting and get back to work helping patients get well.

When do they want it?

Even before they meet me they will be ready for the meeting to be over.

How familiar are they with your topic?

After the implementation of the Patient Protection and Affordable Care Act (commonly called "Obamacare"), all hospitals were required by law to track patient satisfaction scores, so all the doctors will know about the topic at least generally.

What will they LIKE?

They will like anything that makes their jobs easier or helps their patients get well.

What will they NOT LIKE?

They will not like the fact that this presentation is focused on patient "satisfaction" rather than patient care. Most physicians are skeptical that patient "satisfaction" is a good measure for care or wellness. So this is something that I have to address or inoculate against.

What do want them to FEEL?

Disarmed, relaxed and at ease.

What do I want them to DO?

Listen to the whole thing and engage with the training.

The next part was figuring out what I wanted them to THINK. Note: there is always an element of persuasion in training. I wanted them to think: "Those are good ideas; I'll try them." But this would be difficult to do because they were coming to the meeting already skeptical of my message. So I needed to **PRIORITIZE** the information in a way that was persuasive. Because I already knew a great deal about my audience and how they might feel about the information I could present, the thought process for prioritizing was pretty simple. It went like this:

How should I prioritize the information?

Because they're already unhappy about having to attend a mandatory meeting, I will need to keep the information as short as possible!

I need absolutely no more than three main points! Also, since most physicians are pressed for time, most of what I present needs to be focused on things that save time or things that can be done simply without adding to their time-load. And finally – and most importantly – I need to focus not only on things that will improve patient "satisfaction" (something they might not care about) but also on things that will improve patient "care."

The most obvious overlap of these two things is in the area of medical compliance (getting patients to follow a doctor's advice): some of the things proven to improve medical compliance are also things that will improve patient satisfaction scores. **THAT is what I know I should focus on!**

The simplest way to do that would be to explain:

- how patient satisfaction works, and then
- point out things that they can do with body language and tone of voice, and finally
- a few things about the words they use when talking to patients (or more precisely, about the order of the words they use).

That kept the entire presentation as short and simple as possible. With these priorities in mind I could now zoom out and make sure my idea was as clear and simple as possible, which should always be your goal:

Getting Clearer: Zooming Out

Who is my audience?
Hospitalists.

What is their desire or problem?
They want this meeting to be as short as possible, but they also need ways to improve their patient satisfaction scores.

What is your solution?
Give them three simple tools they can use to improve patient satisfaction scores and also improve overall patient care and help save time.

In one sentence:
"You can build better rapport with your patients in less time by using a few simple strategies."

Once I had done all of that (which took only a few minutes), I was able to structure the outline of the presentation.

STRUCTURE YOUR PRESENTATION
Start with a Hook

Because I knew they would be coming to the meeting with preconceptions about "mandatory training" - and because I had gone through the exercises in this book - I devised a **HOOK** that would flip their idea (as well as amuse them) about why I was there in a way that put us all on the same side. I began the same way every time:

"So, before I begin, what were you told about the reason for this meeting?"

"Mandatory meeting from corporate," they would say sourly. "About increasing patient satisfaction scores."

"Wow, that's the best way to start any presentation ever!" I would say with sarcasm. "Well, you're in luck because I honestly don't care about patient satisfaction scores."

At this point they would all look up (most of them hadn't even bothered looking at me up until this point). The reason this worked as a hook is because I knew THEY didn't really care about patient satisfaction scores.

Most doctors want to HEAL patients, not sell them something. **By deliberately going against their expectations, I had their attention**. A second ago, they were sure they were about to sit through another boring training session. Now they didn't know what to expect.

Once I had them hooked, I knew I had to stay ahead of them by immediately addressing some of their concerns. So I built on my hook by inoculating against their fears even further.

> "In fact, there is some evidence that patient satisfaction scores have absolutely nothing to do with positive health outcomes," I would go on. "If you want better patient satisfaction scores from a drug-seeker, just give him Dilaudid!" (Drug-seeking behavior by addicts is common in hospitals - and Dilaudid is a morphine-like drug highly prized by heroin addicts.)

By this point, every physician in the room was looking at me in complete agreement. Some were nodding, some were actively leaning forward, but NONE of them was indifferent at this point. So I continued to get them on my side by laying out my credentials.

> "Your corporate office sent me, but I don't work for them. I'm a medical educator at Virginia Commonwealth University. I run the standardized patient program at our medical school and teach communication to students, residents and fellows across the health system. I'm also a researcher and at the moment I'm traveling around explaining some of the simple ways we've found to improve medical compliance in patients."

This was the kicker: EVERY physician cares about medical compliance (whether or not a patient follows a doctor's advice). Patient satisfaction might not save lives, but medical compliance absolutely does.

Now I had EVERYONE'S attention. How did I do it? Simple: by **doing something to grab their attention and beginning the conversation with something that mattered to THEM!**

Your training session is not only about the information, it's also about what that information means to your audience!

The final thing I had to do to hook them was make them realize that they wanted to hear what I had to say. So I went on:

> "I know you've all got other things you could be doing right now, so I won't waste your time. Feel free to leave anytime. If you want to stay, I can give you the highlights in 10 or 15 minutes. I'll stop talking no matter what in 20 minutes. I'll stay longer afterwards for anyone who wants me to go into more detail or if there are any particular questions."
>
> "Please stay," they would always say. "Tell us what you've got."

Content: The Main Points

At that point I would launch into the main body of my presentation – the actual training I was hired to provide. If I had tried to just begin the training without first convincing my audience of doctors that the information was important and useful for them, few of them would have listened to me and everyone's time would have been wasted. But because I had hooked them – because I had convinced them that the training was directly relevant to them and inoculated against some of their fears about how much of their time it was going to take – the physicians always engaged fully in the training.

Unless there was an emergency (which happens in hospitals from time to time), no one ever left (even though I told them they could). The training was designed to be as interactive as possible. I said things for the doctors to **hear** (to engage **AUDITORY** learning). I drew things on a board for them to **see** (to engage **VISUAL** learning), and I led very short exercises for them to **do** (to engage **KINESTHETIC** learning).

By the end of the training session, I had given the physicians three specific tools to use and told three stories - or provided data or other visual aids - for each of these three main points. There were no slides. When I needed visual aids, I simply drew rough charts on a white-board (using slides would have reinforced their fear that I was from "Corporate" – but drawing on a board reinforced that I was an individual who merely wanted to share useful information). There were also business cards and some other literature (handouts) designed to be used by the physicians when admitting patients to the hospital.

End with a Bang

Since doctors are always crunched for time, the biggest bang would be if I could summarize all of the training in a few simple easy-to-do steps. So that is exactly what I did. I concluded with a very quick summary of those tools (as repetition to help them remember) and provided one specific call to action.

Call to Action

My call to action was designed to emphasize the simplicity of the final bang: I simply challenged them to try those three tools in the clinic for a week to see if they could discern a difference in their patients' behavior.

The Last Thing

The corporate office had provided new business cards and some other literature for the physicians to hand out to patients upon being admitted to the hospital. I integrated these tools into the exercises in the training session and then left those tools with them as a way to help anchor some of the ideas we had talked about during training.

Visual Aids and Rehearsal

I practiced and rehearsed incorporating these visual aids into my presentation. After several times of presenting, I found that I no longer needed to rehearse out loud every time, but I always found it useful to go through my entire presentation once the night before and then to remind myself of my purpose and main points before entering the room.

That was it. The training was always well received by the physicians, the corporate office got the dissemination of standardized information they needed, and no one felt their time was wasted. If you ever have to give a training session, you can do much the same thing if you simply focus on your audience.

Remember, the key is starting with your audience, not the information!

A detailed outline of the presentation is included later.

Final Thoughts
The art and science of training

It is beyond the scope of this book to provide a comprehensive account of pedagogical practice (pedagogy is the science of learning); however, there are some things that are important for you to do when presenting a training session.

The first thing to keep in mind is that the **maximum adult attention span is about 20 minutes.** In other words, it's difficult to keep your audience's attention on a single task for longer than 20 minutes. If your training needs to last longer than that, you'll need to break your information up into several different chunks and present it in a different way. **A good rule of thumb is to switch up the things you're doing every 10 to 15 minutes.** Long informative presentations are not only boring, they are ineffective. **Break the rhythm. Do some unexpected things.**

Keep yourself on track and make sure you start and end on time. While planning time, figure out how long it's going to take you to present a particular unit and stick to that time. Know that **a training session always takes longer than a regular informative presentation because you must allow time for the training to sink in.**

Most people learn best when you use a combination of these three basic learning modalities:

■ **Visual** - Make sure your audience can see what you are describing.

■ **Auditory** - Make sure your audience can actually hear what points you're trying to make.

■ **Kinesthetic** – Make sure your audience can physically touch or do something.

From the start, be sure to **identify the goals of the training session and the best way to communicate them** to the trainees. Because the purpose of a training session is for your audience to **LEARN**, it's important that you include as many learning **MODALITIES** as possible in the way you present information. You might engage in a discussion, show a video, or have them pair up and break them into small groups. It is not enough to simply lecture and show slides. In order for the learning to sink in as deeply as possible, your audience must also be able to physically move or interact with something during the training.

You can include more than three pieces of information, **but if you include more than five chunks, it'll be very difficult for your audience to remember.** If you end up including more than that, make sure you leave them with written information so they can learn it on their own.

Also, you can't cram too much information into a short period of time. **A good rule of thumb is that one new piece of information takes about 10 minutes to present** (the example with the doctors was very fast paced because they are generally very fast paced people - but notice that even for them, I covered only three main points in 20 minutes).

Although most training sessions are done in large groups, people don't always learn as well in large groups (it becomes too easy to disappear into the crowd). So when you design the learning experiences you want to use, give some thought to occasionally **dividing the large group into smaller groups or pairs**. This has the added benefit of also changing up the rhythm of your presentation and thus keeping your audience engaged. Again, when you break the rhythm of your presentation, you increase your audience's chances to remember what they heard.

The main goal of any training session is to have your audience put into practice what they learned. In order to do that, you'll need to make the training as hands-on as possible. In other words, if you want them to learn a new way to close the deal on a sales pitch, you must design the training session so that they have the opportunity to get on their feet and practice out loud what you want them to do.

Involve your audience as much as possible. Ask them to share their experiences with the topic because some of them might have a great deal of experience with what you have been asked to present.

Double check that your audience understands the information. Check in frequently by asking them what you just covered, along with the details. Their responses will tell you whether or not they're absorbing your information.

Your job as a trainer is to figure out ways to **excite and engage** them while presenting information that will hopefully impact their careers in meaningful ways. Throughout your life ,you have occasionally learned from poor teachers and failed to learn from good ones. Effective training has as much to do with the learner as it does the teacher. If your audience is engaged and trying to learn, they'll learn.

**If they're bored, they will not learn.
Simple as that.**

KEY TAKEAWAYS - HOW TO GIVE A TRAINING SESSION

■ Training sessions are informative presentations.

■ Focus on your audience rather than the information. The goal is not to deliver the information, but to deliver the information in a way that matters to your audience.

■ Start and end on time.

■ The key to effective training is to make sure your audience is engaged and interested in what you are teaching.

■ Change up the things you are doing with your audience every 10 to 15 minutes.

■ Break the rhythm. Do some unexpected things.

■ Include as many different learning modalities as possible. This will help you to keep your audience engaged and help them retain the information (let them see, hear and do things).

■ Do activities and exercises that include different group sizes (do some things with the whole audience and some with smaller groups or pairs).

■ Make every section as dynamic as possible (use what we call "hooks:" stories, examples, illustrations, props, etc.) so it'll easier for your audience to understand and remember all the information.

■ Make it hands-on – include your audience as much as possible.

■ End with a bang. Pull it all together in a way that engages your audience.

■ Make sure your call to action is straightforward and easily actionable. For example: "Try this for a week and see how it works . . ."

DETAILED OUTLINE - TRAINING SESSION
Increasing patient satisfaction scores

<u>BACKGROUND NOTES:</u> Stuff you will keep in mind but not necessarily say out loud:
> **PURPOSE**
>> **Audience should FEEL**: *Disarmed and at ease.*
>>
>> **Audience should DO**: *Listen to the whole thing and engage with the training.*
>>
>> **Audience should THINK**:*"Those are good ideas; I'll try them."*
>
> **IN ONE SENTENCE:***"You can build better rapport with your patients in less time by using a few simple strategies."*

<u>PRESENTATION:</u> Stuff you will say out loud and/or otherwise include in your presentation:

BEGINNING / INTRODUCTION

Hook: *Direct question:" Before I begin, what were you told about the reason for this meeting?" And statement:" I honestly don't care about patient satisfaction scores. "Inoculation: " In fact there is some evidence that patient satisfaction scores have absolutely nothing to do with positive health outcomes. If you want better patient satisfaction scores from a drug-seeker, just give him Dilaudid!"*

Name / Credibility:*" Your corporate office sent me, but I don't work for them. I'm a medical educator at Virginia Commonwealth University. I run the standardized patient program at our medical school and teach communication to students, residents and fellows across the health system. I'm also a researcher and at the moment, I'm traveling around explaining some of the simple ways we've found to improve medical compliance in patients."*

Desire / Problem: *Building better rapport with patients in less time." I know you've all got other things you could be doing right now, so I won't waste your time. Feel free to leave anytime. If you want to stay, I can give you the highlights in 10 or 15 minutes. I'll stop talking no matter what in 20 minutes. I'll stay longer afterwards for anyone who wants me to go into more detail or if there are any particular questions."*

Solution:*" There are three easy strategies for interacting with patients that can increase patient compliance AND increase patient satisfaction scores AND save you time."*

MIDDLE / BODY
Point 1: *Patient satisfaction is a remembered event; measured after the fact.*
> **Hook or evidence:** *Story of going on anniversary date and doing most things wrong, but getting one romantic moment right.*

Contrast with story of going on anniversary date and doing everything right, but then fighting at the end of the evening.

Give data showing the same thing happens with patient satisfaction scores.

Point 2: *Body language and tone of voice are key elements.*

　Hook or evidence: *Short, entertaining exercise about proxemics around a desk.*

Contrast with story about proxemics in an elevator.

Story about how the exact same ideas play out in the hospital.

Point 3: *Patient centered conversations involve asking before you tell.*

　Hook or evidence: *Story of a patient hearing he is positive for HIV.*

Contrast with story of a patient with the same diagnosis who lives with an HIV-positive partner.

Tell story of how these same ideas play out with a patient admitted through the emergency department with a broken hip.

Point 4: *None (Even three main points is pushing it for this presentation).*

END / CONCLUSION

End with a bang: *Quick list of three simple activities that will increase both compliance and patient satisfaction - listed quickly to show how simple it can be:*

- *A strategy for streamlining patients' intake at admission to hospital*
- *A strategy for increasing positive anchor points with patients throughout the day*
- *A strategy for communicating with patients during discharge*

Call to action: *" Just try these three strategies for a week and see how it goes. If they don't immediately make your life easier, forget them and go back to doing things the way you always have."*

Question and answer: *The Q&A is at the very end, so those who want to leave can do so.*

Last thing: *Give them business cards and handouts.*

CHAPTER 22
HOW TO GIVE A PITCH BOOK PRESENTATION

"One of the biggest mistakes entrepreneurs make when pitching to angel investors is bombarding them with data and boring PowerPoint slides instead of inspiring and engaging them."
- Carmine Gallo, contributor, Forbes magazine

Pitch Book Presentation
Marketing document compiled by an investment bank for use in client presentations to win new business or for attracting new clients.

Historically, a pitch book (or pitch deck) was a marketing presentation used by investment banks to generate discussion about the potential of investing in a particular company. As the name suggests, many of them were (and still are) printed out in multiple pages, bound, distributed, and read through line by line. Originally, they were reports rather than presentations. It was only after PowerPoint became widely used as a way to create and share documents that pitch books came to be referred to as "pitch decks" and the presentation became the preferred method of review.

Business School vs. Real-Life

Eventually, business schools began to make students give pitch book presentations in class because the format requires detailed data-driven analysis of a company's financial, management, and marketing structure in relation to wider industry trends and financial markets. As a result, class-assigned pitch book presentations have less to do with generating discussion about potential investment than with making sure that students know how to choose, analyze and interpret relevant data. In other words, an **in-class pitch book presentation usually has less to do with the presentation itself than with demonstrating you can do all the work that goes into putting one together.**

In a previous chapter on elevator pitches, the presenter, Sarah, decided against including financial details about her company (its current financial situation, its revenue structure, management structure, marketing strategy, etc.) because she thought those details were too far in the weeds for an elevator pitch. However, if we follow this same metaphor, the goal of a pitch book presentation is to burrow as deeply into the weeds as possible.

If you are assigned to give a pitch book presentation, you might feel that you need to go against the suggestions in this book (keep it short and simple; only include information that your audience actually needs; make your presentations as dynamic as possible; don't use slides unless you absolutely have to, etc.). But all the same guidelines still apply. There is no reason to make your presentation long or boring. A pitch book presentation is simply a very specific presentation for a very specific audience for a very specific reason.

TEMPLATE - HOW TO GIVE AN PITCH BOOK PRESENTATION

BACKGROUND NOTES: Stuff you will keep in mind but not necessarily say out loud:

    TITLE:_____

    PURPOSE

        Audience should FEEL:_____

        Audience should DO:_____

        Audience should THINK:_____

    IN ONE SENTENCE:_____

PRESENTATION: Stuff you will say out loud and/or otherwise include in your presentation:

    BEGINNING / INTRODUCTION

        Hook:_____

        Desire / Problem:_____

        Solution:_____

        Name / Credibility:_____

    MIDDLE / BODY: Main Points - As many as they ask for (most require only five.)

        Point 1: Your unique value_____

        Point 2: Your business model_____

        Point 3: Your marketing plan_____

        Point 4: Competition analysis_____

        Point 5: Your management team_____

    END / CONCLUSION

        End with a bang:_____

        Call to action:_____

        Question and answer:_____

        Last thing:_____

Keep in mind the suggestion from Chapter 1 about always trying to create a presentation for an "actual" audience, rather than merely to fulfill a class assignment. To save you the time of having to flip back through the book, we'll repeat the suggestion here:

> Here's a tip: Next time you are assigned a "presentation" that is really a report, do yourself a favor and **create a second, different audience for your talk besides your teacher!**
>
> **IMAGINE** a person or group who could **BENEFIT** from knowing the information you have been asked to report!
>
> This will let you filter your information and prioritize what you need to say - which will in turn make it much easier for you to put together your presentation!

An Illustrative Example
Florentine Pizza

Imagine you want to open a pizzeria near campus, and in order to secure financing, you need to prepare a pitch book presentation to prove your business model. Your first step in putting together a presentation is, of course, knowing your audience. So you should begin as always by answering some basic questions:

CLARIFY YOUR MESSAGE
Know your audience

Who is your audience?
Bankers, lawyers and other knowledge investors. If this were an actual presentation, we would research the names of the actual people involved. But for a class assignment it is enough to know that the people we will be presenting to are involved in finance).

Where are they?
A small boardroom. Big boardrooms are only necessary if there are a lot of potential stakeholders. As a small company, we don't need much space.

Why are they there?
This is their job. They are looking for promising investments.

What do they want?
To know that an investment in our company is a sound decision and will result in a good return on investment.

When do they want it?
The pitch has been scheduled. This meeting is just to deliver the information they want us to provide. They will make their ultimate decisions according to their own schedule.

How familiar are they with your topic?
They are very familiar with standard business practices, so we need to include all the "standard" relevant information (value propositions, business models, marketing strategies, competition analysis, management structure, fiscal reports, etc.). However, they may not be familiar with our particular business (the art of making pizza).

The Most Important Other Question

Pitch book presentations are informative presentations with many persuasive elements in them. Usually, potential clients go to investment banks and pitch their company as an investment. However sometimes, if the client is important enough, the investment bankers might go to the client's offices and pitch their services to them. The best way to know whether or not your pitch book presentation is primarily informative or persuasive is to ask the question:

> "If Florentine Pizza is such a good investment, **why isn't the investor already invested in it?**"

If you have made it to a pitch book meeting, the answer is that they are **on the verge of investing**. You would not have this meeting if you had not made it past the initial pitch. This presentation needs to be designed as an argument that they should invest (hence it will include some persuasive elements).

What will they LIKE ?

They will like the opportunity to make money. They might also like the opportunity to examine the quality of your product themselves. For maximum impact, we don't want to only appeal only to their intellect. Since we are selling pizza, we might want to use the opportunity to subtly influence their decision by appealing to the emotional sensations of smell and taste! We shouldn't hammer this angle too hard, but if we can manage to pull it off, we should bring in some fresh pizza to the pitch.

What will they NOT LIKE?

They will not like it if the business plan does not appear well thought out or is incomplete in any way. In fact, most of the information we will provide is designed to inoculate against any fears they have about the underlying business model and to prove to them that you have done due diligence on the competition and on the market as a whole.

What do you want them to FEEL?

Reassured that we have done due diligence. Enthusiastic about the opportunity we provide for them to get a return on their investment. Hungry for our pizza!

What do you want them to DO?

Invest.

What do you want them to THINK?

We want them to know our main points. We may need to provide value propositions, business models, marketing strategies, competition analysis, management structure, fiscal reports, and anything else that is assigned.

There are debates in business schools about the optimal order of the information in a pitch book. Our suggestion is to keep the order as simple as possible by sticking to a straightforward narrative structure. In other words, tell a clear, simple story about the problem your company solves and the way in which you go about solving it. We will describe a simple way to do this on the next page.

Getting Clearer: Zooming Out

After you have answered all the basic questions, it is always useful to zoom out and make sure your message is clear:

Who is your audience?

Bankers, lawyers and other knowledge investors.

What is their desire or problem?

They are looking for a business opportunity that will give them a good return on investment.

What is your solution?

A value proposition ("this is a good business opportunity") paired with a unique value proposition ("this is why we are the best people to do it").

Getting Clearest: Shortest Possible Description

In this case, the shortest possible description reads like a marketing line, which it really is:

"Florentine Pizza is poised to exploit a clear business opportunity."

Or, better yet:

"If you invest in us, you will make a lot of money because we are the right people in the right place at the right time."

STRUCTURE YOUR PRESENTATION
Your Audience Determines Your Content

A pitch book is a type of informative presentation in which the information you need to include is already well defined (the standard elements of business).

However, exactly what those elements are might differ from industry to industry and from business school to business school. Different business schools require different books and/or models for how to think about the required elements of a sound business plan.

The book most widely used in the Executive MBA program at our university is Guy Kawasaki's *The Art of the Start 2.0*. If you haven't read it, read it; it is a fantastic book. Kawasaki is one of the leading proponents of keeping presentations short and simple and presenting information as stories whenever possible. But more importantly, his model for what is expected in a start-up business plan is very straightforward and the things he describes as required for a pitch are applicable for designing a wide range of similar presentations.

To keep things simple, our example pitch follows that same model.

Figuring out what to say is easy.

A pitch book is the one type of presentation where all the chunks are defined in advance.

It is also the only type of presentation that doesn't start with a hook.

Pitch books start with title slides.

Organizing your slides is simple; just start by answering the questions you already know.

Who are you?
Who are we and why are we the people giving this pitch? We will start with a very simple title slide with our names and titles on it.

What is your hook?
How do we grab their attention? By laying out the problem/business opportunity and our value proposition (i.e. how we will solve the problem). To keep it simple, we will do this with two slides: one for the problem/opportunity, and one for the solution/value proposition.

How do you end with a bang?
Simple – easy breezy: reintegrate the opening hook (i.e. summarize the business opportunity) and describe our projections for future earnings and current status (i.e. That we are poised and ready to make lots of money).

What is your call to action?
"Invest now!" Or to soften the language a bit: "We look forward to working with you."

What is the LAST THING to leave with them?
Pitch book presentations are designed to be delivered on PowerPoint slides or other projected media. The last things we will leave with them are copies of our slides and any other relevant financial documents.

Then you will simply answer a few other questions about:
- your business' unique value
- your business model
- your marketing plan
- your competition analysis
- your management team

**That's it.
It really can be just that easy.**

If you follow this simple outline, you could give the entire pitch book in no more than 10 slides. Of course you could use more if you wanted to, but 10 slides is all you really need.

The best presentations are SHORT and simple. The fewer slides the better.

We realize that not everyone is comfortable using so few slides for such an important report, but it's important to realize that more is not always better. Clearer is better! If you need more slides to be clear about the information you need to relay, then by all means, use more slides. Just don't confuse quantity with quality. Your ultimate goal is to get the funding you need (or to demonstrate to your teacher that you understand how to go about doing that). If your teacher or lending institution requires a different format, simply follow their guidelines.

Visual Aids and Rehearsal

Because you know you need to use slides, you will need to design them. For this reason, the detailed example on the following pages is presented as sketches for slides rather than as a list.

Also, even though you will have these slides during the presentation, don't assume that they are the presentation. YOU are still presenting. Your body language and tone of voice are still important! The more important a good result is to you, the more you should rehearse.

Don't be a side show to your slide show!

Final Thoughts on Pitch Books

Pitch books are a very specific type of informative presentation in which the format of the content is already pre-determined. You goal is to be as clear and concise within that format as possible.

You will note that in the detailed example that follows, the slides do not include every word that will be said during the presentation. Even a presentation as detailed and data driven as a pitch book still does not require wordy, boring slides! If a picture is worth a thousand words then a video of people using your product, or a prototype of your product, or a slice of pizza is worth even more!

If you want to leave behind as much information as possible, consider typing out the words that accompany the images on each slide and putting those words in the NOTES section of your slide presentation software. Then you can either simply leave the file, or better yet - if you want to be fancy - you can print out hard copies of the slides with presenter notes and leave behind a bound copy of everything.

In fact, pitch book slides are almost always printed and left behind as a document. For this reason, you should avoid formatting your slide show with any fancy transitions, 3D effects, animations or anything else.

To facilitate the reading of the document in your absence you also might want to include additional slides that will be used as markers to help readers find information. These marker slides should not be read out loud during your presentation!

Common marker slides include:

- title slides
- table of contents
- list of diagrams or charts

Think of your overall presentation in three parts:

1. The presentation itself (the things you say, props you use, slides you show, and body language / vocal tone you employ when you are actually in the room)

2. Printed text within a "Notes" section that will explain each slide when you are not there

3. The formally printed version that you leave behind

Any additional marker slides you choose to include should be used only to help facilitate this third part. Don't read them out loud!

KEY TAKEAWAYS – PITCH BOOK PRESENTATIONS

■ Pitch books (or pitch decks) aren't really presentations so much as they are reports delivered on PowerPoint slides (or other presentation media).

■ As always, begin by considering your audience. The audience for a pitch book presentation wants more details and data than do audiences for most other types of presentations. Give them what they want.

■ One of the easiest parts of putting together a pitch book presentation is figuring out what information needs to go in it. Usually the format and required content is already standardized. Simply follow the blueprint or outline given to you by your particular audience.

■ Put together your pitch book just like you would any presentation: ask questions about your audience, define your purpose (feel, do, think), and answer questions about the other points you need to include.

■ Even though you need to convey a lot of concrete data, there is no need to write down every word you are going to say on the slides you show. Whenever possible, use pictures, graphs or other informatics to relay your data succinctly.

■ The worksheets in the design chapter will help you do this!

■ Think of your presentation in at least three parts: 1) the words you will say during the presentation; 2) the slides you will show; and 3) the words or bullet points you will include in the NOTES section of your presentation software. This will keep you from feeling you need to put every word you say on the slides you show.

■ The final thing you will leave behind is the pitch book itself.

■ For your convenience, the detailed example that follows is laid out in sticky note form. The next time you need to put together a pitch book presentation, just write your own sticky notes and place them over the ones in the example (if you want to include more than one slide per idea, simply sketch it out on more than one sticky note).

DESIGN A PITCH BOOK

Information to include:

TITLE OF YOUR PRESENTATION?

Who are you?

Give the name of our business and the executive staff.

Details or sketch of that slide:

Florentine Pizza

CEO and Head Chef: Roberto Calamai

CFO: Tomeka Enersen

Information to include:

WHAT IS YOUR BUSINESS OPPORTUNITY?

Problem your company will solve?

- No fresh pizzerias within five miles of campus
- Local chains sell boring pizza
- No traditional artisanal pizzerias that use fresh ingredients
- We have done market research a – there is a desire for better pizza options near campus.

Details or sketch of that slide:

OPPORTUNITY

Map of 5 mile radius of campus and words "245 of 250 students surveyed reported being HIGHLY INTERESTED in having an artisanal pizzeria within walking distance of campus."

DESIGN A PITCH BOOK

Information to include:

WHAT'S YOUR VALUE PROPOSAL?

Your solution to this problem?

We will open a pizzeria at this location close to the heart of campus. We already run a successful pizzeria on the other side of town. This is the profit margin at that other location.

Details or sketch of that slide:

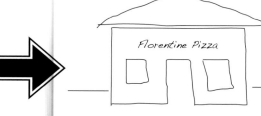

Picture of the front of other store, and the words "Profit Margin 20%"

Information to include:

YOUR UNIQUE VALUE?

What makes your company special?

Our recipe is based on traditional crusts and sauces from Florence, Italy.

Locally sourced fresh ingredients lead to lower food waste – increasing profits while making the pizza taste better than the competition's.

Details or sketch of that slide:

SPECIAL SAUCE

A picture of someone smiling eating pizza on the street in front of the Il Duomo di Firenze (a famous cathedral in Florence,) plus the words "Fresh local ingredients = 32% less food waste."

Most importantly, we will bring in fresh pizza to let everyone taste a slice!

DESIGN A PITCH BOOK

Information to include:

BUSINESS MODEL?

Potential customers?

There are 32,000 students at the university. Within this population 26% of males and 18% of females consume pizza on any given day. We will claim a portion of this pie.

Details or sketch of that slide:

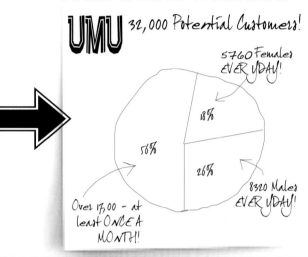

UMU 32,000 Potential Customers!

5760 Females EVERYDAY!

18%

56%

26%

Over 17,00 - at least ONCE A MONTH!

8320 Males EVERYDAY!

Information to include:

MARKETING PLAN?

How will you reach your potential customers?

The new location has heavy foot traffic. A city study shows that over 700 people walk by the proposed storefront every day. We will also advertise and place coupons in the local student papers. At our other location, reputation and word of mouth also generate up to 47% of repeat business.

Details or sketch of that slide:

MARKETING PLAN

Map of location, plus cover of city study and the words " >700 people per day".

Logos of the local school papers.

Screen grab of the Excel sheet results from our in-store study at the other location showing 47% report " reputation" and " word of mouth" for " reasons you chose to eat here."

DESIGN A PITCH BOOK

Information to include:

COMPETITIVE ANALYSIS?

Who's trying to reach those same customers?

Three other chain pizza stores within 5 miles of campus.

Plus many other food options.

Here is a complete list, including grocery stores and convenience stores (all the places that students go to get food of any kind).

Details or sketch of that slide:

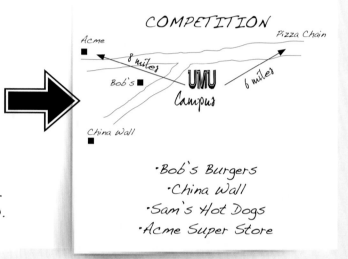

COMPETITION

- Bob's Burgers
- China Wall
- Sam's Hot Dogs
- Acme Super Store

Information to include:

MANAGEMENT TEAM?

What makes you the best people for this job?

Here are the people who will work at this location and their credentials for doing this job.

Most importantly – they've already proven that they can make money using this product in this competitive environment.

Details or sketch of that slide:

MANAGEMENT TEAM

Pictures of Roberto and Tomeka and two other chefs plus a short description of their work history.

DESIGN A PITCH BOOK

Information to include:

FINANCIAL PROJECTIONS?

When profitable?

Are you sure you will make money?

We have done a progressive analysis of estimated expenses and income based on figures from the other store plus comparative analysis with the other restaurants in the area. This is what we found and when we expect to recoup initial investment.

Details or sketch of that slide:

FINANCIAL PROJECTIONS AND KEY METRICS
Graphs showing projected expenses and profits with dates showing target milestones.

$45,000

Renovations

$25,000

$10,000

Jan Feb Mar Apr May Jun Jul Aug

Information to include:

CURRENT STATUS?

How far along are you in this plan?

We have signed a provisional lease for the space and are prepared to move in by the end of the month. Based on the length of time it took to set up the other location, we estimate it will take us two weeks to from initial move-in to grand opening.

Details or sketch of that slide:

• CURRENT STATUS
• ACCOMPLISHMENTS
• TIMELINE USE OF FUNDS
Graphs showing projected expenses with dates of target milestones with costs at each point.

Profitability!

Renovate Store

Opening

Jan Feb Mar Apr May Jun Jul Aug

CHAPTER 23
HOW TO GIVE OTHER TYPES OF PRESENTATIONS

"You can speak well if your tongue can deliver the message of your heart."
- John Ford, movie director

Presentation Type
One of many ways of describing the structure of a presentation as designed for a specific purpose.

Okay, so we've covered examples of informative and persuasive presentations, status reports, elevator pitches and much, much more. How many different types of presentations are there?

If you look through other books or websites on public speaking, you will see a bewildering array of other presentation types listed. For example you might also see:

Briefings	Comedic	Debates
Decision-making	Demonstrative	Entertaining
Goodwill	Image-building	Impromptu
Motivational	Multipurpose	Sales
Special occasion	Storytelling	Toastmaster

However it's important to realize that most of these aren't really different "types" of presentations so much as they are just different "purposes" for presentations.

Every one of those different presentations has the same basic structural needs:

- They all attempt to do something specific for a specific audience
- They all need a clear purpose
- They all need a clear beginning, a middle, and end
- They would all be better if they were kept short and simple

In case it's not yet perfectly clear for everyone how the exercises in this book can help you plan, practice, rehearse, and deliver ANY presentation, this chapter is designed to show how you might use the ideas in the book to put together a presentation of any type or style. We are not advocating a particular template for all presentations. All we are saying is that all presentations can be easily put together by first asking some simple questions about your audience and then designing a presentation that has the maximum impact for that particular group of people. This is true no matter what type of presentation you have to give. For instance, let's imagine you need to put together a presentation that clearly wouldn't use slides, props, or other visual aids and is usually thought of more as a speech than as presentation.

TEMPLATE - HOW TO GIVE OTHER TYPES OF PRESENTATION

BACKGROUND NOTES: Stuff you will keep in mind but not necessarily say out loud:

TITLE (May or may not be needed:_____

PURPOSE

Audience should FEEL:_____

    Audience should DO:_____

    Audience should THINK:_____

IN ONE SENTENCE:_____

PRESENTATION: Stuff you will say out loud and/or otherwise include in your presentation:

    BEGINNING / INTRODUCTION

      Hook:_____

      Desire / Problem:_____

      Solution:_____

      Name / Credibility:_____

    MIDDLE / BODY: For the most impact try to structure your presentation as a series of stories with transitions.

      Point 1:_____

        Hook or evidence:_____

      Point 2:_____

        Hook or evidence:_____

      Point 3:_____

        Hook or evidence:_____

      Points 4 & 5: (only if necessary)_____

        Hook or evidence:_____

    END / CONCLUSION

      End with a bang:_____

      Call to action:_____

      Question and answer:_____

      Last thing:_____

An Illustrative Example
A wedding toast

A wedding toast is a great example of why knowing the type of presentation you need to give isn't really all that helpful. After all, a wedding toast needs to be a little bit of several types: it needs to be entertaining (and maybe even a little comedic), it needs to build goodwill, it might be at least partially impromptu (or at least seem like it), it needs to be motivational about the benefits of love, and it's certainly part of a special occasion. A wedding toast is the perfect example of a multipurpose presentation!

So how exactly should you go about putting one together? You know the answer of course: start with your audience!

What follows is a real example of the process of putting together a toast that was really given at a recent wedding (the names of the people involved have been changed to protect the innocent). The goal of including it here is not to give you an example of a good toast, but rather simply to demonstrate that the steps in this book can help you put together ANY presentation.

Presentation subject: The "best man" toast at Brian and Kim's wedding.

CLARIFY YOUR MESSAGE
Know your audience

Who is the audience?
The bride and groom and everyone invited to the wedding.

Where are they?
At the reception immediately after the wedding service.

Why are they there?
To celebrate Brian and Kim's wedding.

What do they want?
An entertaining but moving toast to the newlyweds.

When do they want it?
At the beginning of the evening soon after dinner.

How familiar are they with your topic?
Very. They were all invited to the wedding.

What will they LIKE?
I was with Brian right after he first saw Kim. The audience will like the story of how they met. What everyone will like most is if I can draw attention to their love without making the toast too sappy.

What will they NOT LIKE?
I know a lot of things about him (and her) that might set the wrong tone or spoil the event. There is a lot riding on this toast. It will be remembered either as one of the high points or low points of the reception and everyone will know that as soon as I start to speak. Because best man toasts are sometimes bad, some people might even hold their breath at the beginning of the toast - afraid that I might say something too vulgar or silly.

What do I want them to FEEL?
I want both Brian and Kim to feel special and loved. I want the rest of the audience to feel warm and like they have learned something secret and beautiful about the couple. I want to stay one step ahead of the audience at all times, so that no one knows in what direction my talk will go. I want the person who has to give a toast after me to feel ashamed that their toast is not was good as mine. The toast has to be long enough that it feels substantial, but not so long that it begins to place the focus on me rather than on the bride and groom.

What do I want them to DO?
I want everyone to raise their glasses and toast the couple. I want to make at least one person in the room cry. I want many more people to dab their eyes and say "that was beautiful." I want to make everyone laugh. I want people to remember this toast as one of the highlights of the reception.

What do I want them to THINK ?
I have to tell at least one story about Brian. But

since it's her wedding too, I need to make sure to include a chunk of information about how wonderful Kim is as well. I also need to make sure to include space in my pre-planned remarks in case something memorable happens during the ceremony. The toast must be as short as possible yet still include all those parts.

Your Audience Determines Your Content

Once all of these questions are answered, a rough outline almost writes itself. Because this is a personal toast rather than a business presentation, the most important elements need to be stories rather than lists of facts. In fact, it will be easiest - and best - to think of the entire outline as a series of stories with transitions between them.

Getting Clearer: Zooming Out

Just to make sure I don't screw this up, I zoom out quickly to make sure I am focused as well as can be:

Who is your audience?
People who love Brian and Kim.

What is their desire or problem?
To celebrate their love.

What is your solution?
Tell a series of short stories that illuminate their love for one another.

In One Sentence

Even if there is a mix-up and my time is suddenly cut short, I need to be able to lead a toast no matter what. The shortest possible toast is:

"Ladies and gentlemen, please help me in welcoming the two best people I know to their new life: to Brian and Kim Wake – we love you both!"

This also has the added benefit of being a good last line for any toast I write.

STRUCTURE YOUR PRESENTATION

With these answers in mind, a basic outline develops just by putting the things I already know in order and then answering some basic questions about the most dynamic way to present all those parts. As I work thought building an outline in my head, my thoughts look like this:

The Beginning

Hook

I could tell a story that grabs their attention. What story? I'll figure that out later.

Credibility

Everyone will already know that I am the best man since I will have been standing up with him during the ceremony so there is no need to establish any other credibility. Wait a minute . . . Since most best-man toasts begin with a description of how long the best man has known the groom, and since one of my purposes is to stay ahead of the audience and leave them guessing, and another of my purposes is to alleviate fears early on that I might say something in poor taste, I could use this as an opportunity to pull a little judo move here by pretending that I approached this toast very seriously. Then I could tell a joke and transition to the first story. Hmmm. That's genius! But what story and what joke? I'll worry about that later, just build a basic outline now . . .

The Middle

Main points

I need to keep this short, so I need to be keep my main points to a bare minimum.

- Tell a story about when Brian met Kim.
- Highlight good things about Kim.
- Save a slot for an impromptu part about something that happens during the ceremony. I'll need to keep an eye out during the ceremony to find something good.

But just in case I can't think of anything during the ceremony - I should also memorize a few lines that tie the story about Brian first meeting Kim to the idea of marriage itself. I'll write those lines later …

End with a Bang
Conclusion

I can put the credibility part here (how long I have known Brian) to keep the audience off balance and tie everything back to love.

The last thing

At the end of my speech I want everyone to be focused on Brian and Kim, plus I should probably use the words "congratulations" and "love." My one sentence toast should go here.

It is clear that STORIES are the key to this speech. What do I remember about creating stories? They all have a basic narrative structure - all of them have the same basic parts. I'll start by trying to figure out a story for the opening hook. Let's see what happens when we answer the questions on a few of those sticky notes:

Background Notes

Since I'm going to tie my credibility in with my opening hook, maybe it will be okay if I make myself the focus of the first story. Then I can make Brian the focus of my second story, make Kim the focus of my third story, and then make the ceremony itself the focus of the last story before my conclusion.

What is the SETTING?
   The wedding reception.

Who is the MAIN CHARACTER?
   For the first story it's me. For the rest, it's them.

What is my DESIRE or PROBLEM?
   I want to be the best "best man" possible, but I have no idea what a best man is supposed to do at a wedding.

Why is this a CRISIS?
   Because I have to stand up and give a speech!
What is a possible SOLUTION?
   I could do some research to learn what best men are supposed to do.
If I do that, what will CHANGE?
   I have no idea. Maybe I should actually look it up and see what best men are supposed to do . . .

[I look up the "history of the best man" on the Internet, and find something funny].

Well what do you know? **That sticky note exercise worked.** I now have a great idea for how to do this. I will open with the story of my problem and the solution I found. The story almost writes itself - and after this, all the other stories are even easier to write.

Here are the words that are spoken, divided into labeled sections to demonstrate how simple and effective the organizing principles are (of course I don't say the labels out loud):

The Speech
Story 1: My problem and the history of the best man

"When Brian asked me to be the best man at his wedding, I had no idea what that meant. I've never been the best at anything before. But I decided that if he really needed me, I was going to be the best 'best man' possible. So I looked up the 'history of the best man' on the Internet, about where the idea came from and what the job is. And it turns out, it comes from a very long time ago when very unenlightened men used to go on raiding parties to try to capture a bride from another tribe or clan. If you were a creepy man who wanted a bride, you would gather up all your creepy friends to creep into the night to do this kind of work. And it turns out that the 'best' man to help you do this was someone who was the biggest, dumbest, ugliest - or sometimes just the most expendable - member of your group. [pause - first joke] So first of all, I'd just like to thank you, Brian, for thinking of me in this way."

[Pause for laughter.]

Transition to Story 2

"I stopped researching after that because I get the point - screw you too Brian – and also because this theory is wrong. [tiny mini pause] Brian didn't need anyone to help him capture Kim's heart. It was the other way around. She captured him the moment he saw her."

Story 2: How Brian met Kim

"I know this because the night after he first met her, Brian told me 'Last night I saw the most beautiful woman in the world, and I'm going to marry her one day.'

I said, 'That's amazing! What's her name?'

He said 'I don't know. I haven't gotten the nerve up to talk to her yet.'

[Pause for laugher again.]

I said: 'Well that does not bode well for the whole marriage thing.'

He said: 'Just wait. You'll see.'"

Transition to Story 3

"And as you can see, he was absolutely right. Kim is as beautiful as he said. And she is also deeply kind. After all, she married someone who looks like Brian."

[People are laughing, but I don't let the audience laugh too long - I don't want the focus to be on me and I want to keep ahead of them.]

Story 3: Focus on Kim

"I've known Brian longer than I've known Kim, but I feel like I've gotten to know her pretty well too. You see I've gotten to see her through Brian's eyes - through the wonderful things he says about her even when she's not around – and the way his eyes light up whenever he sees her. What some of you might not know is how much Kim has helped Brian become the man he always wanted to be."

Transition

[Deliberate tone change and mini-pause as if thinking, pretend to go off script a little, change tone of voice to demonstrate I'm speaking from the heart]

"Friends are supposed to be upset if their friend changes after they start dating someone. But I can tell you that I'm not upset at all. None of his friends are upset. Kim is caring and kind and nurturing. No one has ever seen him as happy as he has been since he met her."

[Look away from notes as if improvising.]

"There are some things I didn't write down, but I wanted to tell you because they say everything about how strong this love is:"

Story 4: Improvised story about the ceremony

"What many of you don't know is that right before the ceremony, the groomsmen and I played a practical joke on Brian. We pretended to get into a little argument on the bridge and 'accidentally' drop Kim's diamond ring onto the lake. [Aside] Everything's fine, it was a fake ring. But for those of you who were arriving, when you heard Brian shriek and saw him drop to his knees and clutch his chest, that's what that was. He wasn't panicked that he was about to get married. He was panicked that he wasn't going to be able to get married."

[Let tremor come out in voice to let the audience know that I am now trying not to cry.]

"In fact a few minutes later while we were standing up there watching Kim walk down the aisle, I peeked over to see how he was doing and cannot even describe the joy that was on his face. Brian had tears in his eyes - not because he was sad that the bachelor part of his life was over, but because of how happy he was that this new part of his life was just beginning . . ."

Backup plan for Story 4 with rehearsed words

"Because he finally got up enough nerve to ask the most beautiful woman he ever saw for her name, and because he was lucky enough to get her to take his name in return."

Conclusion: Reincorporate main hook

"Brian, you're my oldest, best friend and I love you. You were right about everything. I may be dumber, uglier, and more expendable than you, but you are the real best man here today."

The last thing

[Raise a glass of wine to toast] "Ladies and gentlemen, please help me in welcoming the two best people I know to their new life: To Brian and Kim Wake, we love you both. Congratulations!"

Mission Accomplished

[Everyone toasts. Everyone drinks. Brian's and Kim's mothers are both crying. Brian is trying not to cry. The next person to toast begins her remarks with "well that's a tough act to follow." Many people come up after the reception to say it was the best toast they ever heard. Mission accomplished!

Other Types of Presentations

It's important to note that this toast didn't just go well because of the words. It made people cry because it was well rehearsed and delivered in a heartfelt and authentic way. Note especially that some specific vocal and physical things were scored - or planned - in advance (like the mini-pauses for effect, or the choreographed putting aside of the notes).

These things, much more than the words, are what really conveyed the purpose of the entire speech (love and friendship, warmth and joy). These moments and these feelings were not left to chance. They were rehearsed out loud and standing in front of someone trusted to give honest feedback. **As with all presentations, it is the delivery that matters most. If the presentation is important, don't leave anything to chance.**

Again, this speech is not included here as an example of a great speech, but rather simply as a way of demonstrating that working through the exercises in this book can help you put together ANY type of presentation. In fact, knowing what type of presentation you need to give is much less important than simply focusing on your audience and figuring out what THEY need. The answers to the questions you ask will not only help you figure out WHAT to say, but will also help you figure out HOW to say it!

The specific format we've used in these presentations will work for most presentations, but it's also important to recognize that it is not the only way to structure what you say. If the organization you are presenting for has a standard format they want you to follow, use that. Though we've given you templates to meet most of your personal and professional needs, it's important for you to inquire about and follow the structure they give you.

The most important thing isn't the specific structure of your talk. **The most important thing is that you focus on your audience and give them what they need.**

KEY TAKEAWAYS - HOW TO GIVE OTHER TYPES OF PRESENTATIONS

■ Don't worry about the type of presentation you have to give. Focus on your audience and what they need.

■ The main difference between most presentation types is the PURPOSE of the presentation (what do you want your audience to, FEEL, DO and THINK - in that order?).

■ Working through some of the exercises in this book will not only help you figure out WHAT to say, it will also help you figure out HOW to say it.

■ How you say it is often far more important than what you say.

■ The more important your presentation is, the more important it is to rehearse!

■ Rehearse more than just the words you say. Also rehearse where and how to stand, what you do with your hands, how you use your breath and voice, and how to recover from some of the mistakes you might make.

■ Anytime you want help doing any of this, simply refer back to those chapters in this book.

■ Regardless of the specific structure of your presentations, remember this simple three-step process:

- **Prepare**
- **Practice what your prepare**
- **Present what you practiced**

■ And, finally **KEEP IT SHORT AND SIMPLE!**

CHAPTER 24
HOW TO TITLE YOUR TALK

"Your title is the first thing audience members read in their programs … it also determines how many of them will show up." – Judy Carter, author, <u>The Message of You</u>

Title

A name that describes the content of your talk and builds audience interest.

Depending on the occasion, you may want or need to title your presentation/training session/talk. So why did we place this chapter near the end of the book?

Because until you answer some questions about your audience and how best to structure a presentation for them, you don't have enough information to come up with an accurate description. **Deciding on a title happens only after you've planned, organized, written, and designed your presentation.** Sure, once in a while you'll need to submit a proposal long before you plan your presentation. When that happens, you can still use these guidelines to help you come up with an appropriate title.

The most important thing for you to remember is that a **good title can generate buzz and build interest** while a bad title can turn them away even before you get a chance to present. Use as the following points to help you create a title that is short, simple, clear, and strong.

Some guidelines for designing a good title:

■ **Short is better.**
Short titles stick with us. For instance "**Words That Sell**" is better than "**Finding the Optimum Language to Increase Sales Potential.**"

■ **Make sure it describes your content.**
Your title should blend seamlessly with what you say. The most interesting title in the world is useless if it doesn't accurately describe your subject.

■ **Use the word "you."**
A presentation isn't about information. It's about what that information means to your audience. Titles such as "**The Message of You**," and "**You Inc.**" make that connection clear.

■ **Always consider alliteration.**
"**Scintillating Slides that Stick**" and "**How to Top Ten Tips**" stay with you because they're catchy. Attention-getting devices like alliteration aren't always appropriate, but sometimes they can work wonders.

■ **Rhyme sometimes.**
Like alliteration (and assonance and consonance), rhyme

is a handy way to grab attention quickly. Rhymes can be partial or full. **"How to Fight Stage Fright,"** and **"Three Ways to Hook'em and Book'em"** are examples.

■ **Make it immediate.**

The more useful your information is to your audience NOW, the better. **"End Your Presentation with a Win"** is a good title, but **"Walk Away with a Win Today"** is better because it emphasizes the immediacy of the outcome.

■ **Everyone wants to know "how to."**

People always want to know how to do something. They're eager to learn, so give them what they want. **"How to Give a Great Presentation"** and **"How to Practice and Present"** are examples.

■ **Anything with numbers.**

Numbers are good because they help your audience visualize the content in chunks. Any title with numbers such as **"Five Ways to Wow Your Audience"** and **"The Three Secrets to Success"** are good examples.

■ **Evoke a feeling.**

Titles that evoke a strong feeling pique our interest. **"Facilitating With Ease** and **"Dynamic Delivery"** create interest because they highlight the emotion.

■ **Use active verbs.**

Audiences like to know that your presentation will give them something they can USE. Titles with active verbs point out that your presentation will help them DO something. **"Master the Basics"** and **"Perfect Your Presentation"** are good examples.

The bottom line is that your **title (like your presentation) is there to serve the audience.**

Make your title about your audience and what they will get out of it. Figure out what they want and how to give it to them in a way that is – if not interesting or memorable – at least accurate and useful.

PART 2 SECTION 2
REAL WORLD CHALLENGES

TEST YOURSELF
WHAT DO YOU ALREADY KNOW?

Before you read Part 2, circle T (true) or F (false) to test how much you already know.

1.   T / F   During a group presentation, presenters should stand just off to the side of the speaker so they can move easily to the center when it's their turn to speak.

2.   T / F   The goal of the first step in brainstorming is to collect as many ideas as possible.

3.   T / F   When asked to describe yourself, it's a good idea to list your best qualities such as high energy, good listener, imaginative, etc.

4.   T / F   When you read a written speech, it's less important to make it sound conversational.

5.   T / F   People are influenced more by feelings than facts.

6.   T / F   Your resume is more important than your interview.

7.   T / F   When you introduce a speaker or presenter, the most important thing for you to do is to excite the audience about their accomplishments.

8.   T / F   A Q&A should never be the very last part of your presentation.

9.   T / F   When you're being interviewed by video chat, always look directly into the computer screen when you are talking to make sure you are framed well.

10.   T / F   The first step in preparing for an interview begins by learning as much as possible about the organization/company.

Answers. 1. F   2. T   3. T   4. F   5. T   6. Usually but it depends on the job   7. F   8. T   9. F   10. T

HOW TO USE
PART 2 Section 2

Section 2 includes presentations that are somewhat different from the more traditional ones outlined earlier. These are life skills as much as they are presentation types. Like Part 1, each set of skills or type of presentation has its own chapter.

Each chapter describes in detail how to create that type of presentation, along with related stories and anecdotes. A checklist highlighting the contents is listed on the last page. When you plan your next presentation, go point by point to make sure you include all of the major components.

Within the chapter, we'll walk you through the thought process behind the topic and show you step by step how to use these skills to build a presentation of your own.

Because the purpose behind each type of presentation is different, you'll notice that each skill set requires a slightly different thought process. Though they differ slightly, you'll nevertheless see that every type of presentation requires you to think through the same things that we've been describing throughout this book.

SECTION 2 INCLUDES:

How to Present Yourself

How to Introduce Others

How to Interview (Phone, Skype, In-Person)

How to Conduct a Q&A Session

How to Conduct a Brainstorming Session

How to Give a Group Presentation

How to Deliver a Written Speech

CHAPTER 25
HOW TO PRESENT YOURSELF

"People don't want information. They are up to their eyeballs in information. They want faith – faith in you, your goals, your success, in the stories you tell."
Annette Simmons, business consultant, author, <u>The Story Factor</u>

Present yourself like your life depends on it. Because it does. What you do and where you work depend on it. Your friends and loved ones know you because of it. Even the house you buy or the apartment you rent depends on it. Sooner or later, someone is going to ask you:

"Can you tell me about yourself?"

"Who are you?"

"So, what do you do?"

When you answer those questions, you usually answer them by telling a story about yourself. And when you tell a story, you are in fact, giving a presentation.

You do this hundreds, maybe even thousands of times a year when you interview for a job, enroll in a class, go to a party, meet new people, go on a date, apply for a bank loan, visit your doctor, and so on.

Sometimes you'll need to introduce yourself before you give a standard "presentation" and it's best if you do that through a short story or anecdote. The truth is, **whether you know it or not, those stories are some of the most important presentations you'll ever make.**

When you can tell your story well, you build rapport and garner trust. You also create interest that makes people want to know more about you.

Once you master the art of storytelling, you can greatly enrich your presentations, speeches, interviews, and daily interaction with others.

You already learned a lot about crafting stories and how to use them in your presentations. However, when you talk about yourself, the way you present your own story is slightly different than what you've learned thus far.

Why Stories?

When you tell a story about yourself, your listeners get to know the real YOU. Instead of hearing a list of qualities, attributes, and information, they learn about your values and how they play a part in everything you do. Stories also describe your skills and expertise. They make you memorable by describing how you respond to real events.

As an example, let's look at an actual introduction told through a story that was presented in a public speaking class: an answer to the basic question: "Can you tell us about yourself?".

"I love puns. I do it so much that when my friends hang around me, some of them consider it to be punishment. What I love about it is that it's wordplay. I like to play. I like to bring play into everything I do.

When I pun, it makes me listen to people more carefully because I like to add humor into what they're saying or add liveliness to a conversation. Punning also forces me to be smart – because I have to listen carefully to words. Before I could even speak a single word, I remember hearing my parents punning. And then when I got older, we'd sit around and have pun-offs over dinner. I guess you could say that our food was rather homes-pun."

Her story is memorable. You can almost imagine what it would be like to sit at the dinner table with her family!

But if she had presented this information as a list, like a lot of people do, note how lifeless and boring it would sound:

"I like to pun. My whole family likes to pun and I learned to pun before I could say a complete sentence. We did it a lot at the dinner table."

Here's another answer to the question: "Can you tell us something about yourself?"

"One of the most significant things that helped shaped my life is the unexpected passing of my mother when I was a freshman. While it continues to be one of the biggest challenges in my life, I learned that I'm a very positive person. I was able to find even more confirmation of that during her funeral, which was a celebration of her life. Everyone was dancing, people were laughing and we realized that celebrating life and being positive was a huge part of who we are as a family even in a time of great loss. Laughter and optimism are really important to us. When one of my nephews found out that my mother had passed, he said 'Wow, I'm really gonna miss her laughter' - and he was only

6 years old. That's was what she was known for. So I try to really experience life. I'm constantly trying to find the next good thing, to expand myself and others around me."

Obviously, family, optimism, and laughter are very important to this storyteller. You can almost SEE the family dancing and laughing while coping with their loss. When the nephew begins to speak, the story comes to life even more! And the last line of her story is the most compelling sentence of all. In it, you hear that she's trying to better herself and others around her.

Can you imagine how boring and uneventful the story would be if she only gave us the **INFORMATION** instead of the story :

"I come from a family where laughter and optimism are important. My mother's passing helped shape who I am today."

The Difference Between INFORMATION and a STORY

When you talk about yourself through stories during a job interview, for example, the listener will know what values you'll bring to the workplace if they decide to employ you. Presenting yourself through stories is a great way to begin.

Here's a real dialogue for a medium-sized nonprofit company in the Washington, D.C. area (the job is real). This is the transcript of the interview between Tonya and Andrea Fitzgerald, director of human resources:

A: Thanks for coming in today. We really liked your application and want to get to know you better.

T: I'm really excited to be here.

A: We looked over your resume and feel like we know your timeline pretty well. Can you tell us something we don't know about you from your resume?

Here are two sample answers to Andrea's question. The first one is what Tonya could have said. The second one is what she did say.

T: **(Non-story answer)** I'm a self-starter, reliable and friendly. I'm well-organized and people say that I have a lot of initiative.

T: **(Story answer)** When I was a sophomore, my roommate spilled a cup of chai tea all over my laptop. I ran it to the Apple store and showed them the weird backlight stain on it on and they said "Sorry to tell you this, but the cost of repairing it is more than the cost of a new one."

I had no choice, so I put it on my credit card and walked out with $1,000 of debt for a new computer. I did it as an investment in my education.

At the time, I had a work-study job in the School of Music processing applications and one of my jobs was to email weekly announcements to students - we were supposed to have our own computers.

Anyway, we had a lot of students from Asia who spoke English as a second language and I decided to try to pay off my credit card by tutoring them. When I first started, I only had two students but by the end of the year, I ended up tutoring 12 people a week and was able to give up my work-study job by the time I was a senior.

A: That's impressive! How did you get so many students? Or should I say "clients?"

T: It really wasn't that big of a deal. Anytime a student wanted me to tutor them, I booked a room in the library and told them where to meet me. Then I just kept track of the hours we worked and sent them a bill every two weeks. By the time I graduated, I had a long waiting list of students - and now I also know how to say a few things in Chinese, Japanese, Vietnamese, and Korean!

What did we learn about Tonya? Even if she had applied for a job serving coffee at Starbucks, her story would have made a strong impression. They would know that:

- She has initiative
- She's a self-starter
- She's inventive (her booking and billing system)
- She's multi-talented (majored in business, understands music and language)
- She's reliable and organized (worked in the admissions office)
- She takes interest in and cares about others

Other Stories

Sara Blakely is the creator of the multimillion dollar intimate apparel company Spanx. In one of her stories, she tells how her brand came into existence.

One day, Sara wanted to wear sandals with a pair of pants. In an effort to benefit from the slimming effect, she cut the feet out of a pair of control-top pantyhose and wore them underneath her pants. She liked the way it made her look slimmer and shapelier and with that one innovation, she created a multi-million-dollar brand of shaping briefs and legwear.

Anderson Cooper is an esteemed journalist and respected CNN broadcaster. His story, told in the book *Getting There* by Gillian Zoe Segal, is about how he got started as a journalist.

When Cooper began, no one would hire him. So, what did he do? He created a fake press pass, borrowed a home video camera, flew to Thailand, and self-declared himself a foreign correspondent. His story about it illuminates his experiences and values.

Unlike Sara, you may not be worth millions of dollars (yet), and unlike Anderson, you probably don't deliver the nightly news, but each of you has stories that are equally engaging. **Dig deep in your stories file and uncover the things that are engaging and inspiring about yourself.** Ask your close friends and family to help you add to your list and soon you will have more stories than you'll ever need.

Stories Can Be Short

When you present yourself, your stories can be short. Very short. Imagine this dialogue at a social event.

A: "So, what do you do?"

B: "I teach people how to invent things that they didn't even know they need."

The listener's ears perk up and they lean in.

A: "Excuse me? Can you tell me more?"

B: "I teach mechanical engineering to college students. Right now we're working on a new refrigerator that will order groceries as you use them. It's part of a wave of innovation called the Internet of things."

That first sentence ("invent things they didn't even know they need") is a short story in and of itself. It achieved the purpose of piquing the listener's interest so that they asked for more. The second part of the exchange goes deeper, but it's part of the same story file in the speaker's repertoire.

You can create both a short and longer version for every story in your file.

As we said earlier, you tell stories all the time. With a little practice, you can present yourself through multiple stories that you can use whenever you interview, present, and speak.

It doesn't take the skills of a rocket scientist (or a mechanical engineer) to master the art of presenting yourself. It does, however, require you learn how to craft a compelling story, present yourself and others with polish, and deliver it with confidence and poise. And the three short and simple ways to do that are:

1) **Practice**
2) **Practice**
3) **More practice**

The following checklist will help you make sure that your skills are as strong as they can be for now.

CHAPTER CHECKLIST - HOW TO PRESENT YOURSELF

☐ Have you created a list of stories that illustrate your values and skills?

☐ Are your values clear without speaking them out loud?

☐ Will the listener understand the relevance of your story?

☐ Did you write out the story or at least a few key words and phrases?

☐ Does your story have elements of conflict, suspense, surprise, fun, or something unexpected?

☐ Does it use descriptive words and short pieces of dialogue?

☐ Do you have two versions: a short and longer version?

☐ Did you practice out loud?

☐ Is it conversational?

☐ Did you practice telling it to a friend or group of friends?

CHAPTER 26
HOW TO INTRODUCE OTHERS

"Every audience is different and your introduction matters… Getting them to want to hear what you have to say increases the likelihood that they will absorb the message."
– Darren LaCroix, 2001 Toastmasters World Champion of Public Speaking

Knowing how to introduce a presenter, speaker, guest, or friend is an important skill in your professional and personal life. Almost every day there is a business or social event at which you have to introduce someone.

Why It's Important

When you're asked to introduce someone, it's usually because you have a position of responsibility or you have a personal connection to that speaker. Either way, your goal is to build interest and get your audience excited about the speaker/presenter.

It's equally important to create a good impression when you introduce a good friend to your boss, your best friend to a potential date, and a new friend to your parents. Here's how you do it.

Start with Your Audience and What THEY Want

As with all presentations, the most important first step is to give some thought to your audience – the people to whom you are giving the introduction. For example, imagine you were asked to introduce a speaker at a writer's conference. What do writer's want? At this particular conference, they were hoping to be able to learn some tips about how to get published. So what should your introduction focus on? Of course you know the answer: the things the audience cares about.

The following is the transcript of an actual introduction given for author Dr. Joan Christopher at a writer's conference. Pay attention to how closely the structure (beginning, middle, and end) adheres to everything you already know how to do well.

The Three Parts

Like all presentations, there are three parts to an introduction. Each part builds to the next one so it's essential that it include all three.

Part 1: The opening hook and the name

The first part always begins with a hook. You need to pull the audience's attention away from what they're doing. Figure out a way to hook your audience and make sure it's relevant to your guest. As with all hooks, there are many ways to do this. Here is the first part of Dr. Christopher's introduction:

[A slide of Dr. Christopher's book cover *The Destruction of Pompeii* appears on the projector to the quiet sounds of dramatic music.]

"Ladies and gentlemen, what you see in front of you is *The Destruction of Pompeii*, winner of two national book-of-the-month awards - and it hasn't even hit the national market yet."

Written by a dear friend, the book has already broken the record for back-ordered historical fiction novels.

[Music fades out]

Immediately after the opening hook, note how the name of the speaker was mentioned and how a few notable and relevant achievements were shared. Depending upon the event or occasion, it's also common to let the audience know why the speaker was invited to present. The next part hints at the reason:

"I am delighted to introduce you to my friend, Dr. Joan Christopher. Joan graduated with honors from Bates College with a degree in creative writing before getting her M.A. in Renaissance poetry and her Ph.D. in Roman literature. Her doctoral dissertation was on the writings of ancient Roman women poets and she is the author of 11 published books. In 2003, she was awarded a Fulbright to teach at the University of Bologna."

Part 2: The body

The second part of the introduction always includes a story that relates to that specific audience and peaks their interest.

"Even above and beyond those achievements, I'd like to tell you why she's here today: Dr. Christopher literally saved Concord Press from going under. The publishing house was in trouble until her book ‚*Caesar's Women*, parked itself on the *New York Times* Best Seller List for a then-record 37 weeks.

Over the past 10 years, she's traveled all over the country in her red Volkswagen Beetle at her own expense to promote Concord Press' mission to make tomorrow's

writers known today. Because of her, Concord Press is now recognized as the nation's best publisher of historical fiction. In fact, they publish the work of over a dozen award-winning historical writers all under the age of 30. Some of them were found at conferences like this one."

When you create the body of your intro – the story – you may need to ask the person being introduced for some help if you don't know them. If you know the person well, make sure you use the the tips for presenting yourself that we described in an earlier chapter. Actually, a lot of professional speakers and presenters write their own intros so it'll make your job easier.

Part 3: End with a bang - the final hook

The last part of the introduction, especially for professional events and meetings should always **HOOK** the audience into the presentation by telling them benefits they'll gain by listening to them. This introduction did it succinctly:

"I'm excited to say that Joan, as she prefers to be called, is here to tell you the five best ways to get your work noticed by not only Concord Press but by other publishers as well.

Please put your hands together to welcome Dr. Joan Christopher, author, savior, and dancer extraordinaire."

The hook at the end of the introduction pulls the audience in by telling them what benefits they'll get by staying and listening. This is the most important part because it reinforces the audience's reason to listen.

Analyze the Introduction

What do you think was most memorable about the introduction? Her degrees, the name of her book, or her dissertation topic? Of course not. This audience of writers wanted to know exactly what they could do to get their books published - "The five best ways to get your book noticed."

The first paragraph is a "traditional" introduction. You've heard ones like it thousands of times before. But if you were to hear the first paragraph only, would that be enough to piqué your interest? Maybe if you are an avid reader of Roman historical fiction. But most of us aren't. Read the first paragraph - by itself - out loud to hear how uninspiring it sounds.

It's the second paragraph - the story - that makes us want to know more. Even if you're not a fan of historical fiction, doesn't this story kind of make you want to get to know her more? And then, if the occasion calls for it, you could piqué the interest of your audience even more by adding still another personal story to her introduction. The tip of it was hinted at in the introduction with "dancer extraordinaire," but if you wanted, you could easily expand on to would give Dr. Christopher greater depth. For instance:

"In her private time, she and her husband Tom practice ballroom dance and they just won the annual Boston Ballroom Dance Competition for the age bracket 35-50."

The addition of something completely unexpected (her dance prowess) would create even more interest in Dr. Christopher. With the addition of this little story, there's a good chance that her achievements as a novelist will now sound more interesting to everyone simply because they seem to contrast with what we expected her to be… People with PhD's in Roman literature don't dance, do they … ?"

When this little tidbit is put in anywhere, you can almost hear the inner thoughts of the audience: "I want to hear what she's going to say because she's led such an interesting and diverse life."

The final paragraph – the hook – also gives them reason to stay. That's why they came in the first place. Remember, what we said in Part 1 of this book? **Everyone in the audience listens to the same channel: WIIFM. They're listening for the answers to three questions. So, what? Who cares? And, what's in it for me?**

Don't Give Away the Secrets

Tell your audience what they're going to hear but don't give away the secrets. In other words, tell them that they're going to hear the "five best ways to get their work noticed by a publisher," but don't go into the details. If you do, there will be no reason for them to stay and, more importantly, they want to hear it from the guest presenter/speaker, not you. World champion public speaker Craig Valentine says it best: "Tease 'em but don't tell them."

Here's an example of an introduction for an event that piques the audience's interest without giving away the secrets:

> June Shannon spent her last 25 years coaching speakers on how to immediately hook their audience and get them to sit on the edge of their seats. Over the next few minutes, she's going to give you three techniques that are guaranteed to work for you the very next time you present.

More Examples

Here are a couple of examples of how you can do the same this for a more casual introduction"

- ■ "Charnell, I'm happy that you finally get to meet James. I've mentioned him to you so many times that you're probably tired of me talking about him. He's such a great guy and you already know how many people love the music that he writes."

- ■ "Ms. Valentine, I'd like to introduce you to my friend Julius. When Julius delivered his paper on the greenhouse effect at the high school environmental conference, he received first place for his research. Vice President Joe Biden (who served as the head judge) personally thanked him for his contribution and said he has a bright future in environmental studies."

Even these simple introductions will pique the audience's curiosity.

YOUR TURN
Infomercial introductions

Let's practice sharpening your skill at introducing another person by doing the following exercise. We learned this from World champions of public speaking Darren LaCroix and Ed Tate.

Pair up with a classmate. Tell one or two of your stories from the list that you created earlier in this Act. As the listener, take a few notes paying close attention to the **VALUES** and/or **BENEFITS** that you hear (things that you think **OTHERS would get out of knowing that person**).

Craft a compelling introduction about your partner. Stand up and present an "infomercial" describing the wonderfulness of your partner and the values and benefits your audience will learn from them.

For example, you might say:

Have you ever been stuck in traffic, but really, REALLY needed to get where you were going? Maybe you were late for an important meeting, or even just really needed to go to the bathroom? Well let me introduce you to Mr. Rubin Jennings. He once drove down the shoulder of the freeway for nearly 20 miles to get a friend in need to the hospital. Rubin can show you how to break the rules without breaking the law too much, how to do what is right regardless of what others think, and how to keep calm when others around you are panicking. I only met him five minutes ago and I'm already seeing the world in a different way. Ladies and gentlemen, may I introduce Mr. Rubin Jennings!

CHAPTER CHECKLIST - HOW TO INTRODUCE OTHERS

☐ Ask the presenter/speaker if they have an introduction they would like you to read.

☐ Start with a hook.

☐ If necessary, briefly explain why you're introducing the presenter/speaker.

☐ If necessary, tell the audience why the presenter/speaker has been invited.

☐ Highlight their notable training, achievements, and awards.

☐ Craft a compelling story that reveals their values.

☐ If necessary, interview the presenter/speaker to find a relevant story.

☐ Hook the audience and give them a reason to listen.

☐ Practice it out loud.

☐ Tell it to friends or coworkers and get feedback.

CHAPTER 27
HOW TO INTERVIEW

*"How effectively you pitch your product and differentiate it from others
will determine whether or not you get the job offer."*
Martin Yate, author, <u>Knock 'Em Dead: How to Turn Job Interviews into Job Offers</u>

A job interview is actually a long persuasive presentation. It's something that you'll do many, many times throughout your life. Even if you have job stability, you may still need to interview for certain promotions or if you want to transfer to another department within your company.

Employers typically begin the process of screening applicants by reading the cover letter, application, resume and related information. If they appear interested, they'll most likely call your references to see if you're qualified for the job and assuming that everything checks out, they'll interview you. If you've already done most of the exercises in this book, you already have most of the skills needed to successfully interview in person.

We strongly suggest you go back and re-read the chapters on **"How to Give a Persuasive Presentation"** and **"How to Present Yourself."** They'll remind how and why people make decisions.

The What vs. the How

This chapter could arguably be called Interviewing 601. Not Interviewing 101. This is not your basic nuts and bolts fly-over. In this chapter we'll dig in deep and take you through the whole process. But before we present the details, it's essential

for you to know that what you say and do during an interview is only a small piece of the puzzle. Unless you're interviewing for a position where you work by yourself in a cubicle tucked away in the corner, how you interview will largely determine whether you get the job or not.

What They're Looking For

When potential employers interview you, one of the main things they're checking to see is if you have the type of personality that fits seamlessly into their culture. Your resume and references get you in the door but how well you do on your interview largely determines whether or not you get a job offer.

It's beyond the scope of this book to discuss your personality but it's important for you to know that your overall likability, authenticity, politeness, patience, respectfulness, and your ability to work with others is going to be observed from the moment you arrive until the second you exit your interview.

What You Need to Do

As with all other types of presentations, your focus should be on your audience and not on you. Your preparation and research before the interview (as well as the interview itself) should be about you convincing them that you fit into their workplace. Do not make the mistake of making the interview about you. We have seen many people "bomb" their interview because they talked incessantly about how wonderful they were. Presenting yourself with an "I did this, I can do that, look what I did, and let me show you" attitude will usually get you a one-way ticket home.

Since your focus should be on them, make sure you create a sense of goodwill and ease during your interview.

If you (the interviewee) can make them (the interviewer) feel excited and happy to be around you, then you've just scored a home run.

Focus on your audience even during the interview itself. Of course you want them to know that you can do the job. But, you also need to get them excited, happy, and relieved that they've found the right person (you) who can make them even better. The same advice is as true for interviewing as it is for any presentation: **KNOW YOUR AUDIENCE and MAKE IT ABOUT THEM.**

Know Your Audience
Preparation is everything

It goes almost without saying that you need to study the potential employer's homepage, read what others say, study published materials (books, newsletters, press releases, etc.) and ask friends if they know anyone who can provide you with information about their organization. Pay close attention to their mission statement, current projects, products, services, important names, etc. Get to know the organization inside and out.

Types of Interviews

Employers interview by phone, video chat, and in person. Depending upon the company, job requirements or position responsibilities, organizations may also interview you over the phone and if you pass that test, you'll video chat with them, and finally if they're really interested, you'll be brought in to interview in person.

There are also variations in the types of live interviews you will encounter. On the formal side, you might be invited for a solo chat with the CEO, or you might be invited to give a presentation before a large group; and on the informal side you might find yourself interviewing while walking between locations, or at a dinner with potential coworkers. The most important piece of advice is to remember that you are presenting and selling yourself from the moment they first see you until the moment you leave (and even then, be careful what you post on social media).

Phone and video chat

For phone interviews and video chats, make a list of important names and other information and post it somewhere within easy eyesight. A good strategy is to tape it to the wall in front of you so you can refer to it as needed. When you video chat, make sure you can see this information easily without having to turn your head away from your computer's camera.

Here are some other tips that are applicable to both phone and video interviewing:

■ In addition to the list of names and company details, **write out a list of good answers to some questions you think you might be asked.** Put your answers in the form of bullet points (or talking points). Don't write too much – no more than three points per answer. Use these cheat sheets to help you keep your answers focused and succinct during the interview.

■ **Eliminate all noise distraction, especially when talking over the phone or through video chat.** Since they can't see you, ambient sound of any kind will be distracting to them.

Even if you are interviewing over the phone, dress as if you were going to a live interview. You'll feel and sound more professional. Practice in these clothes as a dress rehearsal before you do the real thing.

■ **Speak with confidence and clarity.** Work on eliminating fillers such as "um," "like," or "you know" and other verbal mannerisms. Using your cheat sheets will also help you avoid having to think and speak at the same time (one of the main reasons for those vocal fillers).

■ Make sure your body language projects confidence and authenticity. Believe it or not, your body language translates into vocal tone whether they can see you or not. If you have personal mannerisms that are distracting, practice strategies to minimize them prior your interview.

■ If possible, it is a good idea to do phone interviews while standing and using a hand-free device. The ability to move around and use your hands when you talk will translate into more energy and focus in your voice (but don't carry this too far: pacing quickly around the room while you talk can make you sound manic. Your goal is to sound present, calm, and capable. Let your body language reflect that).

Use the following lighting and framing tips when you interview over video chat.

■ **Make sure your face is well-lit.** Your major light source should be in front of your computer and soft enough to light your face but not so harsh that you appear washed out. It's also a good idea to have a little bit of support light on your left and right to balance out the front light.

■ **Give some thought to your background** so it's not distracting and it enhances the image you want to create.

■ **Practice talking into the camera** rather than looking at their image on your screen. This will allow you to have "eye contact" with your viewer rather than showing them an image of yourself looking at your screen.

■ **Make sure your online handle is appropriate.** For instance if your Skype address is "wildcrazysam," it will be hard to come across as professional no matter what you say.

Live interview

If you go out to eat, it's wise to order food that's easy to chew since you'll be doing most of the talking. If you spend most of your time cutting and chewing, you won't be able to answer their questions because you'll be busy eating. Avoid eating messy foods such as pasta and meatballs because you don't want to wear your meal on your clothes for the rest of the day.

Begin and end your interview in a cheerful and positive manner. Smile. Practice your opening greeting and closing farewell, paying close attention to your words, tone of voice and body language. You want create a good first and final impression.

If possible, carry any necessary materials (pocketbook, note-

Bad Interview Setup

Good Interview Setup

book, portfolio, etc.) in your left hand. That way you won't need to take a moment to put them down before your shake hands with someone (as all left-handed people know, most people shake with their right hands.) If you present a portfolio of any kind, be sure to choreograph how you remove and replace your work, how to hold it up so everyone can see, and how to pass it around.

So Many Tough Questions

Many early-career job seekers get nervous when they interview because they're afraid that they won't know how to answer tough questions. They think employers want to make it hard for them.

But it's actually quite the opposite; they want you to do well. They want you to be MS. RIGHT because they want to fill the position with the best person they can find - and they want to do it fast so they can get back to work. Among the two most costly HR activities are the time and money it takes to hire someone and the cost associated with making a bad hire. So in the long run, they're searching for the right person and they really want you to be that person.

Types of Questions

The way you answer questions will let them know if you have the requisite skills to do the job, if they can trust you, and if they want to get to know you at all. Most people who have been coached to interview well say that they enjoy interviewing. Having an extensive and well-prepared story file will help you stay relaxed throughout (see the chapter on **"How to Present Yourself"**).

In most instances, the person interviewing you will start out by asking simple icebreaker questions before proceeding to more situational questions. This is where the preparation you did for the phone interview will come in handy. Ideally, you should already have the answers to certain questions on the tip of your tongue. As the interview progresses, they will ask you more in-depth and probing questions. This is where your preparation becomes especially important.

How Do You Prepare?

Write down a list of questions that they might ask, as well as your responses. Ask friends and acquaintances to contribute to the list. Remember to write for the spoken word.

Practice your responses out loud and keep them clear and concise. Some questions can be answered with a story (short or long) or, depending on the situation, with a short, simple, and direct non-story answer. Knowing your audience is everything and you'll need to be sensitive at all times to the circumstances so you can respond to all questions appropriately.

Note: be aware of time constraints and deliver the appropriate response. Sometimes, an employer will say "My last meeting ran over and I only have 10 minutes." Then you'll need to keep your answers short. Again, it's a good idea to have no more than three main points prepared for each potential question. You want to do this not to limit what you might say, but to force yourself to think about the most important points you want to make sure to cover.

Icebreaker questions

Icebreaker questions almost always begin each and every interview. Here are some of the most common questions. We wrote sample good and bad answers so you can see how to reply.

Q: How did you learn about the job opening?

A: (Good answer) A teacher of mine in college, Dr. Grace Jones, some of you might remember her because she interned here when she was in graduate school mentioned this job opening to me because she liked my senior capstone project on social media. And since social media has played a major part in growing your reputation, she thought I would be a good fit.

A: (Bad answer) Dr. Grace Jones told me that I'm qualified to do this job.

The good answer provides the interviewer with a wealth of information in the form of a story. Your teacher thinks highly of you, you were recommended for the job, your interest matches their need, and you already know a lot about them.

Even if you read about the job in a newspaper, there's always a way to phrase your response so that it reveals who you are, your level of experience, and more.

Here are more opening icebreaker questions. See if you can figure out what information is contained in each good answer.

Q: Why do you want this job?

A: (Bad answer) I'm very creative and I want to work for a company that recognizes that.

A: (Good answer) I'm looking for a job that will allow me to use all of my creative skills. I'm a graphic designer and I paint and illustrate. Here are a couple of greeting cards that I did for Blue Mountain as a freelance job.

Q: Why are you leaving your current job?

A: (Bad answer) I'm ready to go on to something more challenging and want a better opportunity to use my writing skills.

A: (Good answer) My responsibility now is to proofread instruction manuals for new products. I'm also a teaching assistant in my illustration class. I enjoy these opportunities and am looking for ways to challenge myself even more.

Q: What do you know about this company?

A: (Bad answer) I know your brands include Charmin, Pampers, Luvs, and Tide.

A: (Good answer) Quite a bit. I developed an interest in Procter & Gamble back when I was in high school and since then have kept up with your products. My mother only uses Dawn dishwashing soap and my husband and I only use Charmin because we love the products.

Q: What are your long-term goals?

A: (Bad answer) Eventually, I'd like to be an HR specialist.
A: (Good answer) I would first like to develop my en-try-level skills in this HR position and then after a few years, I hope to work with people who specialize in conflict resolution. As a concierge at the Marriott in downtown D.C. ,I experienced lots of good and bad customer interactions and watched my boss handle them with grace. That is the area within HR that interests me the most.

The good answers to the above questions provide them with information that demonstrates your readiness and potential to do the job. The bad answers are not actually that bad; they just don't reveal anything about you. The bad answers are just information. They don't provide a reason to hire you.

Unspoken questions

During your interview there may be unspoken questions that potential employers would never ask outright. In fact, by law, some of these questions can't be asked. But the truth is, depending upon the job, the answers to some unspoken questions might be the essence of what they need to know in order to hire you. We're not talking about unethical questions about your gender, race, sexuality, whether or not you have children, etc. (although in the worst cases these do still come up in interviews). What we're talking about are less offensive but still tricky questions about your personality.

When you are asked a question, listen to hear if they might actually be asking about any of the following underlying questions. If you think they might be, try to tailor your answer to address what they are really asking.

Here's a sample list of common unspoken questions.

- Is your personality a good match with the people you will work with?
- Are you values consistent with that of the organization?
- Do you get along with others?
- Are you likable? Dependable? Organized?
- Are you disciplined? Do you meet deadlines?
- Are you a good communicator?

■ How well do you receive feedback?

■ Are you a team player? Can you work alone? Can you lead when necessary?

■ Are you a positive person with high energy and enthusiasm?

All of these are best answered through stories about how you interact with the world. Refer back to the chapter on **"How to Present Yourself"** and see if any of the stories from your story file will present your answers to these underlying questions in a good light. If not, now would be a good time to develop more stories that address each of these commonly asked unspoken questions.

Situational questions

Most of the questions you'll be asked will be designed to reveal something about your technical skill, talent, experience, maturity, management, leadership and/or overall people skills. Depending upon the job, this part of the interview usually carries a lot of weight.

Here is a list of the most common situational questions that you'll be asked. HOW you answer them can often make the difference between a job offer and a rejection. In a moment, we'll show you the best strategy for answering.

■ Can you tell us about yourself?

■ Why should we hire you?

■ Can you describe how you work?

■ How would your close friends and coworkers describe you?

■ What motivates you?

■ Can you tell us about your training?

■ Who or what has helped shape the way you work?

■ Can you describe your strengths?

■ Tell us about your weaknesses.

■ What was your toughest or most stressful work related assignment?

■ What is your greatest achievement?

■ Describe a work conflict and how it was resolved.

■ Tell us about a time when you made a mistake.

■ Describe a time when you disagreed with a decision from above.

■ Describe a time when you exercised leadership.

■ What's your management style?

■ What is your leadership style?

■ What will you do in your first 30 / 60 / 90 days on the job?

■ What do you do outside of work?

■ Tell us something about you that we don't know from your resume?

How to Answer These Questions

The best way to answer situational questions is by telling a story instead of giving them a list of qualities and attributes. If you need a refresher on how to answer with stories, we suggest you go back and reread the chapter on **"How to Present Yourself."**

Let's look at examples of interview question with a story answer and a non-story answer. The length of your own answer depends entirely on the given circumstances of the interview.

Q: **What was your toughest or most stressful work assignment?**

A: (Non-story answer.) "When my father was laid off I had to work long hours for a very demanding boss. I needed money to finish my senior year of college. I worked long hours at night by myself. I'm not afraid to get my hands dirty."

A: (Story answer) "Last June, my father was laid off from his job at the Portsmouth naval shipyard. I can still remember him walking in the door and saying, 'I'm sorry, I wanted to help you pay for college but I was laid off today.' Then he broke down and cried. You have to understand, my father is the strongest person in the world. I told him that I would figure it out somehow. I'm not sure I really believed it at the time, but I love my father and I knew he was hurting.

Within a week I got a second job at night at Target tidying shelves and putting things back in their right place after shoppers made a mess. You know what it's like to find a box of thawed-out fish fillets under a pile of linens? Anyway, about three days after I started, my boss Mr. Schmidt said "Kevin, you've gotta tidy up at least six departments per night or I'm gonna let you go." Six is a lot because the store was huge, but I went in early just to get the job done because that's what my father would have done. Mr. Schmidt didn't even know I worked the extra hours because I didn't punch in until after I'd already worked a couple of hours. Later on, I found out that no one else had ever done more than four a night."

Can you see how much richer and more convincing the story version is? The non-story answer contains all the same facts, but does not reveal anything at all about the depth of Kevin's character or the strength of his work ethic. For this reason, situational questions almost always need to be answered in story format.

Information is not enough. Without a story, there is no life to your facts. With a story, there is a picture the listener can see and passion the listener can feel.

A list of attributes or qualities doesn't reveal anything about you and – worse – it can sound like you're boasting about yourself. When you tell stories, you demonstrate that your attributes lead to good results. That's what ALL employers want. Stories about results make the most impact.

Kevin's story revealed many values that employers look for when hiring. Here's the list of some of them:

- He loves and cares about his father.
- He has integrity and humility.
- He has a sense of humor.
- He is willing to work long hours.
- He is willing to rise to a challenge – even one stacked against him.
- He has grit and determination.
- He showed initiative.
- He can solve problems.

Every employer in the world is looking for these traits. But if Kevin had listed them it would seem like he was boasting. In fact saying "I have integrity and humility" makes it sound like you have neither. Demonstrating these in story form is the only way to get that message across!

Earlier, we suggested that you bring the story to life by using descriptive words and short pieces of dialogue to create a clear picture of the events.

Let's show you what the first part of the Target story would sound like if we leave out all phrasing, descriptive words, and short bits of dialogue. See if you can notice a difference:

"Last June, my father was laid off from his job and told me that he couldn't help me pay for college. I told him that I would figure it out somehow.

So within a week I got a second job Target. Three days after I started, my boss told me that I had to work faster and get more done or he'd let me go. I went in early just to get the job done so I could make him happy.

He didn't even know I worked the extra hours cause I didn't punch in until after I started. Later on, I found out that no one had ever worked as fast as me."

An interview is a persuasive presentation. The power of emotion goes a very long way towards moving them (the interviewer) into action (hiring you). This emotion is conveyed primarily through the story and HOW you tell it. Descriptive words and dialogue will help you convey the feeling behind the facts. And your body language and tone of voice is even more important.

What Happens If You Don't Know the Answer?

Few organizations expect people applying for entry-level jobs to know everything there is to know about the job, position, or company. If you have done all the preparation we've suggested, you will make a strong enough impression by demonstrating the value you'll bring to their organization – so don't worry too much if you don't know the answer; they'll still think highly of you.

Still, not knowing the answer to a question can be stressful. Here are some tips for how to respond if you don't know the answer to a question:

- **Don't make stuff up.** That'll raise a big red flag in their minds.

- **If you don't have experience** with the particular thing they are asking about, you can say something like "I don't have experience with XYZ but I'm a fast learner and I'm willing to do whatever it takes to get up to speed."

- **Ask if you can rephrase the question into a different question that you feel comfortable answering.** For instance you can say: "I'm not sure I can answer that question in the way you're looking for, but I am familiar with [something like the same question]; can I answer from that point of view?"

- **Tell them how you could come up with the answer.** For instance, you can say something like: "I've not used that particular software but I know how to use [one you are familiar with]. I can upload [the new software] onto my computer and get myself up to speed within a day or two."

When you build rapport with the interviewer, a truthful "I don't know" will allow them to see your willingness to be vulnerable and transparent, which is highly valued in the workplace. The only thing you can't do is seem unprepared. As we mentioned earlier in this chapter, it's rare that a single interaction is going to make or break your interview. Their overall impression of you is what counts the most.

How to Ask Questions

During your interview, it's good to ask insightful questions that reveal your interest and knowledge of their organization. Give thought to what you ask, when you ask, and how you ask questions.

These points are worth making again: Practice and rehearse your questions and answers until you sound authentic and confident. Make sure you practice out loud. Yes, you've read that before – but only because it's important.

Here are examples of good questions to ask.

- "Your mission statement is that 'every guest who chooses your restaurant leaves happy.' Are there any special behaviorisms that you would like me to know as a host? When I worked in concessions at Disney, we had a full day of training on how to greet and interact with people."

- "I understand that interns for this law firm are sometimes invited to sit in on cases that go to trial. How would I find out about those opportunities and would it be appropriate for me to go?"

- "I think I know what my responsibilities will be if I am assigned to work in your lab. Are there other expectations that I should know that we haven't talked about yet?"

On the other hand, there are several types of questions that you should avoid asking. For instance:

- **Don't ask about anything that can be answered by looking at their website.** Doing so will immediately highlight that you haven't done your homework.

- **Don't ask questions related to salary unless they offer you the job and you are in the negotiating stage.** It might be appropriate to ask questions about benefits if that information is not on their website, but even that is better left for after an offer has been made.

■ **Don't ask any questions related to personal issues such as gender, age, race, ethnicity, color, religious affiliation, marital status, etc.** This is not a double standard. They can't ask you those questions either. If they do, it would demonstrate a lack of respect for or knowledge about the law and so you probably don't want to work there anyway.

The Day of the Interview

Make sure you arrive early and look around so you know exactly where you need to be. If you live in the same regional location, visit the company or organization in advance and walk around to get a feel for the place.

Check out where the restrooms are located as well as the coffee shop and any other places that you might want or need to visit. **Before your interview, find a place to sit down and review a few notes** about important things you want to ask or say and then relax. Let it all go. Don't stress yourself by thinking "I have to remember this and I have to remember that." Grab a cup of coffee or read. Do whatever it takes to relax. You can only focus intently for so long. Save your mental energy for the interview itself.

Know that the receptionist's first impressions of you will most likely be shared with the person or people who'll be interviewing you. Do not make the mistake of sharing your frustration about the slow elevator or locked bathroom. Your interview begins the minute you enter the building.

Remember to smile when you greet people. It's a cliché, but also true that you never get a second chance to make a good first impression.

Some people like to bring a toothbrush and toothpaste in case they have the chance to freshen up after a meal. Having said that, you'll need a private place to brush your teeth should you have the opportunity to do so.

How you exit is almost as important as how you enter. Leave them with a genuine smile and warm handshake and thank them for their time.

After Your Interview

Immediately after your interview, take a few minutes to do the following:

■ **Review and debrief.** Write down significant things that were said or questions that were asked so that you can remember them in case those things come up again.

■ **Make a list of things that went well.** Sometimes we don't pay enough attention when things go well. Making a list of the things you did well will make it easier to replicate on future interviews.

■ **Make a list of what you want to improve upon for the next interview.** Don't worry about minor details. Focus only on key things that will improve future interviews.

■ **Send a handwritten thank-you note.** Handwritten notes demonstrate thoughtfulness and an investment of time. Avoid sending a thank you via email because it seems impersonal and looks like you expect a reply. Don't write too much. A simple "I enjoyed meeting you" goes a long way. The more you write, the more time it will take them to read. Respect their time.

■ **Let it go.** Don't dwell on "what if I said this or what if I said that?" The overall impression you make is more important than any one particular response. Besides, at this point there's nothing more you can do to influence their decision.

CHAPTER CHECKLIST - HOW TO INTERVIEW

Know Your Audience

☐ Make a list of important names along with notes.

☐ Make a file of the company or organization's current activities/projects/products.

☐ Read everything on their website.

☐ Talk to anyone you know who now works or who has worked for them.

☐ Research everything possible on the Internet.

☐ If possible, go to their location to get a feel for the organization.

Phone Interview

☐ Have important information at hand during the phone interview.

☐ Tape info to the wall directly at your eye level.

☐ Have paper and pens around to take notes.

☐ Partner with someone and do a mock interview.

☐ Write down names of people when they identify themselves.

Video Chat Interview

☐ Arrange background space, adjust light, and eliminate noise distractions.

☐ Practice talking into the camera instead of at the screen.

☐ Partner with someone and do a mock interview.

Dress Rehearsal

☐ Go through from start to end without stopping.

☐ Practice how to begin and end the interview in a cheerful and upbeat manner.

☐ If you have a portfolio to show them, practice how you handle it.

In-Person Interview

☐ Make a list of questions they might ask.

☐ Make a list of stories to use when answering questions.

☐ Write down important stories.

☐ Practice them out loud.

☐ Write down a list of questions you have.

☐ Practice them out loud.

The Day Of

☐ Arrive early.

☐ Review all important ideas/stories/people you want to include.

☐ Relax.

If You Go to Lunch or Dinner

☐ Do not order messy food that you'll end up wearing throughout the day.

☐ Order food that's easy to chew because you'll be doing all the talking.

After the Interview

☐ Send a handwritten thankyou note when appropriate.

☐ Try not to think about the interview. **Good luck with that one!**

CHAPTER 28
HOW TO DELIVER A WRITTEN SPEECH

"It's not all books that are as dull as their readers."
- Henry David Thoreau, author, <u>Walden</u> and <u>Civil Disobedience</u>

Some situations require you to write and deliver a speech. For instance, your boss may have been called away on short notice and she asks you to present her report to the executive committee. Or written speeches may just happen to be the way your company operates.

Legal functions, business meetings, keynote addresses, and commencement ceremonies are a few more examples where written speeches are often required. You might need to deliver a written speech when your message is particularly important or when a video of your talk or transcript of your words will be distributed. Anytime you need to make sure you communicate precise and exact words, you'll need to deliver a written speech.

One of the keys to delivering a written speech is making sure that you don't sound like you are reading.

The Need for Practice

Political figures and TV correspondents have teleprompters placed on the camera lens or on screens at eye level to make it easy for them to speak every word precisely as written while looking directly at their audience. But even with those technical aids, they still need to practice in order to sound natural. And so do you.

Here are the guidelines for how to deliver a written speech so it doesn't sound like you're reading. Pick and choose what works best for you and feel free to create your own way of formatting and notating your speech text. Everyone likes their speech laid out a little differently. The bottom line is this – make sure your source text is easy on your eye and easy for you to follow.

Reading Doesn't Give You Permission to be Boring

Believe it or not, it's possible to read a speech and still be lively, interesting and entertaining. As you practice, keep in mind that you're not trying to hide the fact that you're reading. The guidelines below are meant to keep your message clear even though everyone knows you're reading.

Even though every word of your speech is written, you still need to practice a lot to make it sound natural and conversational. So how do you do that? How do you present a written speech without gluing your eyes to the text? How do you maintain eye contact with your audience while glancing at your script? And how do you format your text so that it's easy to read while speaking in public?

Guidelines

We're going to use President Barack Obama's 2016 commencement address to Howard University students to illustrate how best to set up and rehearse your next written speech.

■ **Make sure your speech is written in a larger font size in order for you to read it easily.** Most print documents are formatted in 11 or 12 point font. Larger sizes (14 or 16) make it easier for you to find your place on the page.

■ **Format your text in either 1.5 line spacing or doublespace it so it's easy to read.** Here's the opening of the President Obama's speech written in single spacing:

> *To President Frederick, the board of trustees, faculty and staff, fellow recipients of honorary degrees, thank you for the honor of spending this day with you. And congratulations to the Class of 2016!*

Now look at the same text formatted in 1.5 line spacing. Which one is easier to read?

> *To President Frederick, the board of trustees, faculty and staff, fellow recipients of honorary degrees, thank you for the honor of spending this day with you. And congratulations to the Class of 2016!*

■ **Some people prefer to make narrow columns instead of wider ones that you normally use for printed documents.** Wider columns force your eye to move laterally from side to side and may be distracting for your audience while you deliver your speech. Note that the text above is indented and that the columns are narrower than the printed text you are now reading.

■ **Make sure your speech is written conversationally.** If you need a refresher on how to do this, go back and reread the section on **"Write It."**

Note the conversational style in the graduation speech. His words are warm and friendly. Even though a graduation ceremony is one of life's most formal events, he (or his speech writers) still chose casual words rather than formal ones.

> *Four years ago, back when you were just freshmen, I understand many of you came by my house the night I was reelected. So I decided to return the favor and come by yours.*

■ **Make sure you read your speech out loud** as you write and make sure it's easy to understand.

Take a look at the president's use of short sentences and conversational words.

> *I know you're all excited today.*
> *You might be a little tired as well.*
> *Some of you were up all night making sure your credits were in order.*
> *Some of you stayed up too late, ended up at HoChi at 2 a.m.*

■ **Format your speech in bite-sized phrases** so that it's easy to read when you speak. If you must include longer sentences, write them so they have logical places for you to pause. These pauses give you the opportunity to glance at your speech and return your eyes to the audience. They also make your delivery more impactful.

■ **Make a forward slash (/) between thoughts instead of your natural punctuation.** These notations remind you where to pause and so give you the opportunity to look briefly at your speech.

> *The generations of men and women who walked through this yard / helped reform our government / cure disease / grow a black middle class / advance civil rights / shape our culture. / The seeds of change for all Americans were sown here.*

Look at the same section of his speech without the forward slash notations and without formatting it in bite-sized phrases.

The generations of men and women who walked through this yard helped reform our government, cure disease, grow a black middle class, advance civil rights, shape our culture. The seeds of change for all Americans were sown here.

Note how hard it would be to glance up from the page and then go back to find your place in the block of text. Note too how much easier it will be to repeat short phrases rather than trying to get through long ones between glances at the page.

Now, you might be saying to yourself "But if I pause that often, it won't sound natural." Wrong. If you listen to any conversation, you'll notice that people pause frequently. That's one of the things that makes dialogue sound conversational. In fact, if you engage in conversation without pausing, it will most certainly sound like you're reading!

The same is true when you present. Pauses in your delivery give you the opportunity to build anticipation and allow your audience time to reflect on what they just heard. And more importantly, they allow you to glance briefly at your text.

Frequent pauses only sound unnatural if your chunks are all the same length. Note how the length of the lines between the pauses in President Obama's speech is sometimes greater and sometimes less but is never more than a few words. In fact the **RHYTHM of your delivery – and variations in it – is the key to delivering a great speech.**

Obama's oratorical style borrows from other great speakers before him, including Martin Luther King Jr. King's icon-

ic "I Have a Dream" speech is memorable not only for the words that were said, but also for the lyrical way in which the words were delivered. Look at King's speech with the pauses noted.

"I have a dream /
that one day /
this nation will rise up, /
live out the true meaning of its creed: /
" we hold these truths to be self evident /
that all men are created equal.' /
I have a dream …"

If you've ever heard a recording of the speech, you will remember the rising and falling cadence that accompanied these pauses. It was this rhythm – as much as the words – that made this a truly magnificent speech. Even if you never have to deliver a speech from the Lincoln Memorial, you'd still do well to pause often and vary the rhythm and cadence of your delivery.

■ **Underline, italicize, or boldface words that emphasize what you're saying.** These notations remind you where and what to emphasize as you make your way through the speech. Look again at King's speech with highlights on the words he emphasizes.

*"that one day on the <u>**red hills**</u> of Georgia /*

*the sons of <u>**former slaves**</u> and the sons of former <u>**slave owners**</u> /*

*will be able to <u>**sit down together**</u> at the table of brotherhood. I have a <u>**dream**</u> /*

*that one <u>**day**</u> … /"*

■ **Some speakers like to print their speech text only on the top half of each page.** When the bottom of your page is empty, you don't need to drop your eyes down too far when you look at your text.

Look at Obama's graduation speech again. Here are the closing lines of his address written out on the top half of two pages.

Now it's your turn. /
And the good news is you're ready. /
And when your journey seems too hard /
and when you run into a chorus of cynics /
who tell you that you're being foolish /
to keep believing or that you can't do something, or
*   that you should just give up /*
or you should just settle /

you might say to yourself a little phrase that I've
*   found handy these last eight years /*
Yes, we can /
Congratulations, Class of 2016!
Good luck! / God bless you. /
God bless the United States of America. /
I'm proud of you.

speaking each thought without worrying about saying it word for word. Practice pausing between thoughts and looking briefly down at your text. With each new thought, lift your eyes and look at your audience before continuing. The thoughts are more important than the words.

■ **When delivering longer speeches, it's best to have a podium** or speaking platform large enough for you to slide the page you just read to the side and out of your immediate eye contact. Your audience doesn't want to watch you shuffle about as you remove the top page and place it underneath your remaining text. Sliding the page is much less disruptive and allows you to keep more of your focus on the audience.

■ **Don't read every word.** You should know the content of your speech well enough to use your text as a reminder. Otherwise, it will sound like you're reading - badly. Practice

CHAPTER CHECKLIST - HOW TO DELIVER A WRITTEN SPEECH

☐ Write for the ear not for the eye. Read out loud as you write.

☐ Practice out loud so it sounds natural and conversational.

☐ Format the speech with a larger font size in order to make it easier to read.

☐ Space your text in 1.5 or double space it to make it easier to read.

☐ Boldface, italicize or underline words you want to emphasize.

☐ Place your text in narrower columns in order to avoid reading too much to the left and right.

☐ Format your speech in bite-sized phrases. Use forward slashes (/) to separate thoughts.

☐ Pay attention to rhythm as you write.

☐ Don't read every word. Learn the content well enough so that you can glance down frequently to remember what to say.

☐ Practice turning the pages or sliding the top one to the side to avoid distracting your audience.

CHAPTER 29
HOW TO CONDUCT A BRAINSTORMING SESSION

"The way to get good ideas is to get a lot of ideas and throw the bad ones away."
- Linus Pauling, Nobel Prize winner

Brainstorming is the process of coming up with as many ideas as possible. Though it is most often done in a group setting, it can also be done in pairs or even by yourself. You can brainstorm potential topics, the message you want to make, main ideas, openings and closings, calls to action, etc. It is a good way to begin creating any presentation.

Guidelines

■ **When you and your group are ready to brainstorm, select a location that minimizes distractions** in order to keep everyone's mind on the task at hand.

■ **Designate a person to facilitate.** It is often useful to have an outside eye to keep the process on track.

■ **Identify tell to the entire group the focus of the session** - the topic, the message, the closing, etc. Do not brainstorm more than one idea at a time. The more focused you can be the better. For instance, you might say, "Let's brainstorm the hook for our presentation" instead of a more general "Let's brainstorm ideas for our presentation." Brainstorming more than one idea will diffuse the effectiveness of your time.

■ **If you have a very large group, divide into smaller groups.** It's hard to keep everyone energized and focused when the group is too large. Groups of 4-6 people usually work best.

■ **There are no bad ideas.** Don't edit. Include every idea no matter what. For your first few passes, don't edit a single suggestion. Just write them all down. One of the main things that gets in the way of effective brainstorming is people editing their own or other people's ideas too early. Your main purpose is to list as many ideas as possible. Go for quantity and don't even think about whether or not the ideas are good or bad.

■ **Set a time limit.** Ten minutes is a useful measure. Brainstorming suggestions should be high energy, fast paced, and fun to avoid editing or discussion.

■ **Avoid using technology.** It also wastes time. There's no need for people to be surfing the Internet for ideas. Brainstorming is not about research (you should do that at another time). It is about tapping into the ideas of the people in the room. You also need to keep the group's energy upbeat and focused at all times.

■ **When writing down ideas, keep your notes short and simple.** Abbreviate if necessary. For instance if someone suggests a speech topic about the economic impact of an international bike race in your city, just write down "bike race $." Taking time to write things down can slow the process and kill the energy that is essential for successful brainstorming.

■ **Keep pushing.** The first few ideas are often mediocre. The most creative ideas usually emerge only after the obvious ones have already been pointed out.

■ **After time is up or you have exhausted the creative contributions of the group, you can begin the process of determining which ideas show the most potential.** Narrow your list one item at a time by answering the following questions:

• Are we excited about this idea?
• Do we have right people to execute this idea?
• Do we have the time to execute this idea?
• Do we have the money to pull this off?
• Do we have the equipment and facilities to pull this off?

■ **When you answer those questions, you'll know which ones work best for your group.** After you narrow the list to a few potential ideas, you can begin to discuss in detail the effectiveness of each one. Depending upon the idea, it's sometimes good to break into smaller groups to try out an idea. Then you can reassemble to "show and tell" what you find.

■ **The best idea wins.** Everyone needs to set aside their egos when brainstorming because the purpose of working collaboratively is to tap into the power of the whole group. Having said that, not every decision can or should be set to a vote. Brainstorming is the process of coming up with ideas. Leadership is the process of figuring out what to do with them.

CHAPTER CHECKLIST - HOW TO CONDUCT A BRAINSTORMING SESSION

☐ Select a location that minimizes distractions.

☐ Designate a facilitator.

☐ Brainstorm one idea at a time and set a time limit for each idea.

☐ Don't edit your initial ideas. Create as many ideas as possible. Keep pushing.

☐ Avoid using technology.

☐ Keep notes short and simple.

☐ Break large groups into smaller ones.

☐ Narrow your list after all ideas are on the table.

☐ Try out your ideas in small groups and then bring them back to the table.

☐ The best idea wins.

CHAPTER 30
HOW TO GIVE A GROUP PRESENTATION

"People who are practiced in collaboration will do better than those who insist on their individuality."
- Twyla Tharp, award winning choreographer and author

In a university setting, when people have to present in groups, often every member of the team is expected to speak. This makes it easier for the teacher to grade the exercise. However, this is the opposite of best professional practice.

In the real world, many projects are created and delivered by group effort. However unlike in training, in the professional world, one person typically speaks on behalf of the whole team. Sometimes this person is the most senior member of a group. Other times the presenter is the one most familiar with the subject matter. Ideally, the presenter is also the one with the most experience speaking in public.

In addition to the quality of his products, Apple founder Steve Jobs was noted for the "magic" of his presentations. He spent hours preparing, planning and practicing. He was a master presenter. People still study every word he said, every gesture, and every nuance of his presentations. But he didn't do it alone. There were dozens of people helping him every step of the way.

If his group followed the university standard of group speeches (where everyone stands together and waits their turn to speak), none of us would be talking about his presentations.

We'd talk about his computers but we wouldn't talk about his presentations.

Having just said that, there are times when it is a good idea for each member of the group to present. Use the following guidelines to help you through the process of staging your group presentation.

Guidelines

■ **Don't randomly select people to present each section.** When possible, match the content with the person. For instance, if there is a section that is lighter or more humorous in tone, pick the person whose personality is best suited to deliver that content. Everyone should serve in different capacities, depending on their strengths. This is how a sports team is assembled. Think of your presentation group as a team with each member contributing a different piece of chemistry.

Select the part that you're excited about or most able to present. For example, you'll need to captivate your audience with a hook at the start of your presentation. Determine who has the personality/ability to "hit a home run" with that section. Keep it interesting and effective by matching personality/ability with what you hope to accomplish through each section.

Designate a person to facilitate the question and answer session. This person will not answer all the questions (the group participant most qualified to answer a particular question should respond to any specialized questions), however, you will want to have a single person designated to respond first in the event that it's otherwise unclear who should answer. This will give other group members time to think and will make the group as a whole seem more cohesive and capable.

■ **Match the group's introductions to the event and content.** Sometimes, you will find that it will be best for the opening speaker to introduce all the presenters at the beginning; however, other times you might find it better to allow each speaker to introduce themselves as they begin their section. There will also be times when you will realize that no introductions are needed until the final question and answer session. Your content and purpose will help determine what approach is best.

■ **Ideally, the person speaking should be the only person on stage.** However, that's not always possible or practical. The second best option is that the only person standing should be the one delivering at that time. All others need to be seated. Of course, this isn't always possible or practical either. The third best – and bottom line – option is to make sure that the person speaking should be front and center and the other members of the group should be out of the way with their attention focused on the speaker.

■ **Give your full attention to the speaker.** When your colleague is speaking, focus on them. If you are looking at the audience, the audience will have a split focus between the person presenting and the other people looking out at them. If you are distracted and looking in another direction, the audience will lose focus too. When other members of the group focus on the speaker, their gaze directs the audience's eyes to focus on the speaker as well.

■ **Plan out the overall traffic pattern of where to stand and when done, where to sit.** The flow of "people traffic" needs to be simple and seamless as you transition from one speaker to another. Discuss who goes where and

---

YOUR TURN

Go through the entire presentation with just the beginning and ending of each chunk.

Here's how to do it:

Each person gets up from their seat and moves to where they will go when they present.

For this exercise, they should say just their first line.

Then, they should skip to their last line and when done, move to where they'll go after speaking. The next speaker in line takes it from there and does the same thing (first line, last line, move).

Go through the entire presentation several times like this until everyone knows their parts. Then and only then should you put together the whole thing with every person presenting their entire part.

Note: Spend some time making the transitions as smooth as possible and consider ways to change the visual stage picture. Movement keeps things interesting for the audience and helps keep their focus on the right person at the right time. Above all, make sure the transitions are unnoticeable to the audience. They shouldn't notice what is happening as people come and go because if they do, your message will get lost in the shuffle.

when first. Then, practice the transitions from one person to another one chunk at a time. There should be no "dead air" in the handoffs between presenters. The first words of the next presenter should follow immediately after the last words of the presenter in front of them. You do not need to take this to extremes, but the audience should never be waiting for a handoff to finish.

■ The next person who takes the stage should begin immediately. Do not introduce yourself again if you were introduced at the beginning. Never say "Thank you" or explain that your section is done after you finish. Each group member should know their cues so that transitions happen seamlessly.

■ If your group uses slides, designate one person as the slide changer to avoid unnecessary handoffs. You can also leave the remote unit at the podium or table or hand it off to the next speaker as they walk to their speaking area. Whatever you do, the hand off should or slide changing should be "invisible" to avoid distraction.

■ Discuss and plan your clothes accordingly. You want your team to look neat and unified. Perhaps it's as simple as determining that you will all be dressed in business casual attire. One step further would be to color coordinate with each other (again, don't take this to extremes). Be creative and professional without drawing attention to yourselves. Whatever you wear, it should look natural and appropriate for the event.

■ Practice on your own before you begin rehearsing with others. Come to the group rehearsal well-prepared with your own part so you don't waste anyone's time. Know your part and know it well.

■ Rehearse as a group the same way you would for a solo presentation: on your feet with full vocals and in costume. Again, start by chunking it - rehearsing one section at a time. When the sections are solid, add the transitions and run the whole presentation from beginning to end. Your transitions should be smooth. Do it as many times as you can until you feel comfortable. Don't forget to time yourselves!

Collaboration is paramount when presenting as a group.

For the collaboration to be successful you must communicate your ideas, be respectful of each other, and work together to achieve a common goal. At some point in your career you will have to present in a group, or at the very least, in a duo.

What If There Is No Clear Facilitator to Take the Lead?

When people are grouped together and no leader is designated, one will eventually emerge or very little will get accomplished. If no one naturally emerges as the leader, designate one. Think of the leader as the organizer and facilitator, not a dictator. Everyone works together, the leader organizes deadlines and schedules and facilitates work sessions.

In the theatre world, the most important rule of improvisation is to say "yes" to what your partners give you. This means that you and your group members need to stay open and receptive to each other's comments and suggestions, especially early in the process when you are figuring out how to work with each other. A positive attitude in rehearsal goes a long way toward making your final presentation great.

CHAPTER CHECKLIST – HOW TO GIVE A GROUP PRESENTATION

☐ For your presentation, determine whether or not it's necessary for all creative participants to deliver.

☐ If the answer is yes, match the content to the personality of the presenter.

☐ Designate a person to lead the Q&A session.

☐ Ideally, only the person presenting should be on stage; however, if this is not possible or practical, consider having people sit, or at least make sure that only the person speaking has focus.

☐ All creative participants should focus on the person presenting so they don't pull focus away from the audience.

☐ Make a decision in advance and practice how the slides will be changed and how any props will be handled.

☐ Decide where and when all presenters sit, stand, and move in advance.

☐ Rehearse each chunk starting with your opening line and ending with your last line only. Do these "ins and outs" until everyone knows where they are supposed to be at all times. Then when everyone's comfortable, you can rehearse each chunk in its entirety.

☐ Begin speaking as soon as you rise out of your seat. Do not wait until you arrive at your speaking location to begin.

☐ Plan how you're going to dress and then do a dress rehearsal to see if your clothing is appropriate for the presentation.

CHAPTER 31
HOW TO CONDUCT A QUESTION & ANSWER SESSION

"Not knowing the answer to a question is a common fear of many presenters . . .
One thing to bear in mind, is that no audience can expect you to know absolutely everything about your subject."
- Louise Palmer, author, <u>Presentation Skills: Portraying Confidence, Answering Tricky Questions & Structuring Content</u>

You don't have to have a Q&A session every time you make a presentation. But if you do decide to have one, make sure you prepare for it ahead of time. Write down a list of questions you think your audience will ask and practice answering them out loud to make sure your answers are clear and concise.

If you think it's important and appropriate to have one, you need to decide where you want to place the Q&A session. Use these guidelines when you prepare for it.

Guidelines

■ Leave a few minutes near but not at the end for your Q&A.
The closing remarks belong to you, not your audience. Executive speech coach Patricia Fripp says "Even if you receive excellent questions during a Q&A, you still must conclude your presentation by delivering a powerful closing."

Never leave the last words to your audience. Your message will be lost if you allow them to close your presentation.

When you place your Q&A near the end, let your audience know in advance that you have budgeted time to answer questions. If you don't, people will feel they need to interrupt you in the middle of your presentation to ask their questions. Think of it in terms of time management: if you answer questions in the middle of your presentation, you have no control over how long your presentation will run.

■ The purpose of your presentation and your audience needs determine if it is best to take questions at the end or in the middle of your presentation.
For instance ,if your purpose is to generate discussion, then having questions in the middle IS part of that discussion. Likewise, the purpose of a training session or an informative presentation is usually helped by allowing questions throughout. And of course when you're presenting to someone like your boss – whom you cannot ask to hold questions – you will have to take questions in the middle whether you really want to or not.

Taking questions in the middle also means that you need to be more flexible in the chunks you present. For instance, you may find that answering certain questions makes delivering parts of your presentation as planned unnecessary or redundant. Answering questions in the middle also means you might need to alter how much time you had planned to spend on certain parts. If you have designed and rehearsed your presentation in chunks and have a one-sentence description at your disposal, then these last minute changes will be no problem at all. No matter what though, still make sure to have a strong closing statement prepared so that you can leave your audience with what you want to.

When you are ready to go into your Q&A, make the transition clear. You might say something like "I have a few minutes to respond to any questions after which I'll end with some closing remarks." When you get to the end of your Q&A, you can transition back to your closing by saying "we have time for one more question." After that, conclude with your prepared closing.

Keep your Q&A session upbeat and high energy. Do not make the audience wait while you quietly ponder for the answer. Repeat the question out loud for your audience so that everyone knows what you were asked. Doing so provides you with the opportunity to reword a question in case it was vague or ambiguous (see the rewording chapter on **"How to Interview"** for good strategies for rewording questions you cannot answer).

Keep your Q&A session focused. Some people make the mistake of beginning their Q&A with the very broad question "Are there any questions?" Starting that way doesn't inspire your audience to reflect back upon what they just heard and often leads to an awkward silence. Much better is to direct your audience toward specific questions by recalling a few things from your talk by saying something like "In the last few minutes I gave you three reasons why … [the list]; Does anyone have a question about any of those?" You can repeat this with each of your sections as a way to help your audience remember the information you've covered.

Repeat the question out loud. Repeating the question ensures that everyone in the audience knows what you're talking about when you answer. Some people speak softly, especially when they're in a large crowd so their question may not be au-

dible to the entire group. Repeating the question helps everyone in the audience focus.

The most important thing for you to remember during your Q&A session is to listen carefully and respond accordingly. Not all questions are really questions. Some questions are statements in disguise. For instance, anyone who begins a question with "Have you considered [a thing they want you to consider]?" isn't really wondering if you considered it; they are telling you that they want you to consider it. Likewise, some people have their own agenda or like to show off how much they think they know. At other times, someone might not have been listening and will ask you questions about content that you already covered in your presentation.

Questions like these are best answered by focusing on the audience and giving them what they are really looking for: For instance, the person "asking" if you have considered a certain thing is really looking for reassurance that the thing that is important to them will not be adversely affected. People with agendas or who think they are very smart are often appeased with a simple "that's a very good question" and then acknowledging the validity of that viewpoint.

Focusing on your audience and trying to understand the underlying intent of their question is always the best policy. Some people honestly want to know more or need clarification to better understand your message. The best way to respond to those types of questions is to be as clear in your response as possible. Usually honest questions allow an honest dialogue between you and your audience.

There's at least one in every crowd: When dealing with a "look how smart I am" question, you might find there's no real question to answer, so thank them for their comment and move on to the next question. Likewise, if you happen to encounter a question challenging your authority, don't panic or get defensive. Remember that their "question" is more about them than about you. If you have

done all the preparation from Chapters 1 and 2 of this book, then it is very likely you have already prepared an answer to this type of challenge. At a minimum, you can acknowledge their concerns and then redirect the group back to the next question.

■ **It's okay if you don't know the answer to all questions.** The only real rule is that you cannot appear to be unprepared. If someone asks you a question that you are unable to answer, it's perfectly acceptable to say, "That is a good question and at this moment I don't have the answer for you, but I'll find out and get back to you ASAP."

Again, see the chapter on **"How to Interview"** for advice on how to rephrase a question you can't answer into one that you can answer. The key to doing this ethically is to ask the questioner for permission to rephrase and then ask them at the end if that answered their original question.

■ **As a final note, always end with a powerful closing.** You want to leave your audience with a strong impression. Even if you have designed a brilliant presentation and delivered it with confidence and clarity, if you lack polish during your Q&A, you can damage your overall credibility and destroy your message. **Plan your closing. Rehearse it. And then do what you have rehearsed.**

CHAPTER CHECKLIST – HOW TO CONDUCT A Q&A SESSION

☐ Write down a list of questions you think the audience will ask and practice answering them out loud.

☐ Decide in advance the most effective place to conduct the Q&A session.

☐ Leave a few minutes near the end but not at the end of the presentation for the Q&A session.

☐ Make the transition in and out of the Q&A clear to the audience.

☐ Repeat the question out loud for everyone to hear.

☐ Keep the Q &A upbeat and high energy.

☐ Do not allow one specific audience member to dominate the entire Q&A session.

☐ Recognize the types of questions that audience members ask and practice responding accordingly.

☐ Practice how to respond if you do not know the answer to a question.

☐ End with a powerful closing.

AFTERWORD

Congratulations! You now know how to plan and organize, write, design and deliver a great presentation.

But what about those times when you need to write and deliver a speech instead of a presentation? For instance, what if your boss asks you to give a thank-you speech in her absence to the employees for their hard work over the past year? Or if your son's school principal asks you to convince the parents at the next PTA meeting to donate money for new desks? Or the times you have to give a pep talk, or a eulogy, or accept an award?

Relax - good news - all speeches are presentations. You already know how to do everything you need to do. The only additional step you need to take is to write out your whole speech from hook to closing. In fact, if you have a time limit for delivering your speech, writing it out and timing it when you practice is the only way to know if you can deliver it in the allowed time.

So where do you go from here?

Keeping it short and simple isn't just an ideal to strive for. In today's fast-paced world, it's a necessity. Businesses will always try to do more with less. Few people can afford to take time trying to figure out what you're trying to say. You need to get to the point and do so in a way that has impact.

Practice every day

Every time you speak out loud, you're giving a kind of mini-presentation. Practice when you go to the grocery store or when you talk with friends or family members. Practice every time you have something to say.

Every time you speak, you develop and hone your speaking skills. Make sure you're developing good habits rather than bad ones. Try to improve a little more each time. Try out a new introduction. Excite your friends with an engaging hook. Say goodbye to a friend with a warm and loving "closing statement." You don't have to tell anyone what you're doing, but you should take every opportunity you can to master your skills.

When you present, you practice success. Now, go out give a great presentation. Or better yet, give lots of them. You have all the tools you need.